BOSTON:
A SOCIAL
HISTORY

BOSTON: A SOCIAL HISTORY

BRETT HOWARD

HAWTHORN BOOKS, INC.
Publishers / New York

To Jay Emerson Richards

Library of Congress Catalog Card Number: 74-18686

ISBN: 0-8015-0832-0

1 2 3 4 5 6 7 8 9 10

"Plus ça change, plus c'est la même chose."
Alphonse Karr

Contents

Preface

To write a book about the city Boston is somewhat incongruous, for in point of fact Boston is not in actuality a city. It is a sprawling conglomerate of wards, precincts, graphic neighborhoods—communal organisms composed of many radically different units of human life. Veritably it is the American melting pot, in which the ingredients failed to brew into a solid form. It is built upon layers of society, separate races—Protestant English, Catholic Irish, black Afro–American, European Italian, Russian and Polish Jew, Oriental Chinese, and import-export Puerto Rican.

Yet, despite the apparent social confusion and conflict of ideas of social and religious identity and responsibility, Boston is one of the great cities of the world.

The Boston to which the author was introduced as an impressionable young woman—falsely, or otherwise—was the harried city of the forties and fifties, in which many of the obsolete and rigid patterns of the social behavior of the nineteenth and early twentieth centuries were being put to the ultimate test. There still remained a handful of "proper" people who would cling until the end of time to a closeted skeleton of the past rather than create a living human being of contemporary mien. It was a city whose "watch and ward" censors in the thirties had banned Theodore Dreiser's *An American Tragedy* as obscene. Boston was not aware that, in so doing, it was declaring *itself* an American tragedy.

Like a cardboard house, the city was easily collapsible. Before it fell on our heads we departed—a Beacon Hill dropout!

After thirty years we returned—briefly, but filled with remembrances of the past, acutely conscious of the present, and concerned for the future. At first we were appalled! How could so much change, with so little apparent forethought, have occurred? Then we recalled that we had experienced a similar reaction upon visiting other cities. We have lived in an era of radical change. What we saw in some instances was bad; in others, good. For example, the modern architecture of Phillip Johnson in the annex of the Boston Public Library blending with the old architecture of Charles Bulfinch in a state of harmony and satisfaction—a perfect example of the linking of the old with the new in pure intellectual and aesthetic integrity.

Why, then, had the people failed to integrate? One answer seemed to be affiliated with the old Boston meaning of the word *turf*. To outsiders the word means an area of matted earth, but to the people of 340-year-old Boston the word is both sacred and profane in definition. It represents neighborhood land held exclusively by one ethnic group and cherished by its occupants as dearly as life itself. It is land that is holy against invasion; intrusion without invitation is rape. Turf is as old as Boston and is not really understood by those individuals who reside outside the pale of the Boston Common—the suburbanites.

From the moment of conception there were two Bostons—one pre-eminent in national identity, created out of the minds and ideals of the Adamses, the Boston Brahmins, the Boston clergy, the Boston abolitionists —the stern, the pure; the other composed of the congenitally poor, the illiterate, the unemployed, the labor racketeers, the Boston–Irish politicians. There always had been present the Boston reformer and the Boston unregenerate. The reformer's aspirations knew no limitations—his scope was universal; the unregenerate was confined to the Boston ghetto, his boundaries mentally and physically turfside.

This book of Boston, like any book, is essentially autobiographical, although it is classified as a form of historical reporting and observing. It is one individual's attempt to understand the phenomenon of Boston from a personal point of view. To the author the problem appears to lie in the original precept of purity as delineated by the Founding Fathers—a purity that seems to have been created by the artificial insemination of the intellect, an abstract purity lacking the elements of compassion and the old-fashioned love of a neighbor as oneself.

Since the beginning the word of God seems to have come forth from the lips of man into the idle wind—manifesting in deed strange achievements, endured not only in the area of Boston but throughout the nation.

Certainly at the moment of the writing of this book there is a particularly bitter irony in the contrast between two events that have occurred— one in Boston, the other in Montgomery, Alabama.

More than a century ago Boston was a sternly self-righteous center of abolition sentiment, while Montgomery, Alabama, was the home of the

Confederacy. After World War II, Bostonians played a major role in carrying the crusade for civil rights to the South, and Montgomery remained one of the obdurate centers of resistance. At the conclusion of this manuscript the federal government had decided that Montgomery was so peaceful that it could remove the guards from the home of U.S. District Judge Frank M. Johnson—guards who had stood since 1956, when two fiery crosses were burned on Johnson's lawn in protest against his liberal decisions on civil rights. But, while all was calm in Montgomery, Boston was in a state of shock, reeling from angry demonstrations against the busing of black children to schools in white neighborhoods.

In short, what good has it done for Boston to lend a helping hand to the poor and the dispossessed in other areas while trampling upon its own underprivileged?

Since this book was conceived in Boston but born in California in the shadow of Cesar Chavez migrant laborers (who have been supported morally and financially by Bostonians), we have thought perhaps it should be entitled "To Boston from Santa Monica—with love!"

Acknowledgments

In addition to the many librarians whose assistance has been invaluable, I am also deeply indebted to many personal friends who have supplied me with the use of family manuscripts and Boston memorabilia.

There remain a few special acknowledgments I would like to make: First, to my editor, Elizabeth Backman, who read my article on Boston in *Mankind Magazine* and persuaded Hawthorn Books to let me expand it into a full-length social history; second, to my loyal friend and sponsor, Robert Helmer, M.D.; third, to my three editor friends, Raymond Friday Locke, Jared Rutter, and Walter Schmidt, who have endured the gravid days; fourth, to a beautiful guy, Major Victor Cutrer, who gave me housing in his Santa Monica cottage during the early days of creation; fifth, to two pals, Francis Crowley and Bruce McIntosh, who never lost faith in me or in my ability. And last, but not least, kudos to Zane Rhodes, who scrutinized the finished manuscript with his Harvard eye and gave it his approval.

BOSTON:
A SOCIAL
HISTORY

1

The Floundering Fathers

Contrary to popular belief, the city of Boston was not founded by passengers of the *Mayflower*.

However the first person to set foot upon Plymouth Rock that cold December day in 1620 when the band of approximately 150 persons landed was a young woman, Mary Chilton by name, who was the first Pilgrim as well as the first white woman to come to Boston to live.[1]

The Pilgrims were a group of ardent religious zealots who, believing they were divinely ordained, were determined to bring the purity and convictions of their faith to the newly discovered land of America. They boasted that hardly any one of them had a single drop of old English blue blood in his or her veins. In contrast, the group of Puritans who settled Boston a decade later was definitely on the aristocratic side, financed with a sum equal to five million dollars, and composed mainly of uppercrust merchant adventurers. This group was organized as the Massachusetts Bay Company under the leadership of John Winthrop and John Cotton.

John Winthrop, who was to be chosen governor, had been born in Groton, Suffolk, England. He had studied at Cambridge and was, at the time of his departure, a practicing attorney with an affluent clientele. He had strong Puritan leanings and had come to believe in the political power of theocracy.

John Cotton was the young vicar of the rich St. Botolph's Church in Boston, Lincolnshire. He was also a graduate of Trinity College, Cambridge. Under fire for political beliefs that he promulgated from his pulpit, he was forced into hiding. When he joined Winthrop and sailed for America, many of his congregation followed. It was in his honor that the new colony site was named Boston.

The Puritans sailed on the *Arbella*[2] in 1630, arrived in Salem, and shortly thereafter founded the settlement on the Shawmut peninsula that was to become Boston. The discovery that the area was geographically well

The Pilgrims by Henry Oliver Walker. From *Bookman*, October 1908.

John Winthrop, shown in early seventeenth-century dress, by Henry Alexander Ogden.

John Cotton. Engraving by Kilburn.

protected was of vital importance to a people who were wary of the Indians and faced very real threats from the French, Dutch, Spanish, and even rival English colonizers. In 1663 John Josselyn, visiting Boston, noted "two hills of equal height on the frontier part" of the town that were "well fortified on the superfices with some artillery mounted, commanding any ship as she sails into the harbor within the still bay." Behind these stood "a high mountain that out-tops all, with its three little rising hills on the summit called Tramount, this is furnished with a beacon and great guns."

The weather, according to Captain John Smith in 1616, was worth a paean of praise. He raved over "the moderate temper of the air." Governor Winthrop assumed the role of meteorologist, noting in his journal the changing moods of Mother Nature. In April 1631, the governor made the following observation: "In the beginning of the month we had very much rain and warm weather. It is a general rule, that when the wind blows twelve hours in any part of the east, it brings rain or snow in great abundance." In time he was to concur with the Indians, who had informed the early settlers that every tenth year there was little or no winter. Fortunately for the colonists, the first winters of the new settlement were mild; but the third winter was bitter and harsh, and the bay froze over "so as horses and carts went over in many places where ships have sailed," according to the weathercaster, Winthrop.

In August, 1635, the colonists experienced the first hurricane. "Beginning before midnight," wrote Winthrop,

> it blew down many hundreds of trees . . . overthrew some houses, and drove ships from their anchors. . . . The four hundred-ton vessel, the *Great Hope,* was twice driven ashore. The tide which was high fell three feet in an hour then an hour later rose several feet again. From the first "Act of God" which was followed by earthquakes, some of violent proportions, the weather of Boston has been a topic of discussion, a reason for concern and precaution. . . . It's a sorry clime for living in, but a first rate one to die in.

In the Pilgrim and the Puritan was the physiognomy of the contemporary Anglican Bostonian. These first settlers were not democrats: "If the people be governors," asked John Cotton, "who, then shall be governed?" It is almost ironic, yet sacredly prophetic, that these colonists from the beginning seemed destined to witness the growth not of the aristocratic liberty of their former home but of the freedom of the middle and lower orders of which world history hitherto had furnished no complete example. The original settlers of Boston brought with them the best elements of law and order and Christian morality. They landed accompanied by their wives and children. The austerity of their religious principles gave them their name, *Puritans.*

The Puritans believed that God was the supreme ruler and that the executors of his divine will were ordained ministers. They carried the Calvinist distinction between the elect and the ordained into their theory of the church, in which membership consisted only of the regenerate minority who publicly confessed their experience of conversion. It is only consistent that the ministers of New England were the guiding political personalities and that, within another ten years after landing, there were thirty-five flourishing churches.

To the Puritan, man was by nature wholly sinful and could achieve good only by severe and unremitting discipline. Hard work was a religious duty; constant self-examination and order were mandatory. From the hour of arrival there seemed to be little link between the Puritan emigrants and their English ancestors. The Puritans continually exercised the right of sovereignty, named their magistrates, concluded peace or declared "wars," made police regulations, and enacted laws as if their allegiance was due only to God. Laws were written and enforced on issues of temporal morality and were upheld with Puritan vigor. These founders of Boston were inspired with theologic and philosophic conviction that exceeded the mere "desire for religious freedom." Their concept of their destiny made Boston, from the day of its founding, unique.

With God at the helm and an ever-increasing abundance of a popular commodity—money—the early days of Boston were spectacular. Boston harbor was an excellent port, and the population grew with incredible speed. But relations between Boston and nearby Plymouth had never been cordial. In 1645, the Pilgrims asked Governor Winthrop and his Bostonians to assist them against the invading French. This Winthrop agreed to do providing the Pilgrims would bear all the expense. But Plymouth was not a wealthy community, and the undertaking fell through—and the shrewd Bostonians promptly began a profitable trade with the French. In 1691, Boston absorbed Plymouth entirely under the Massachusetts Bay Colony charter.

The spirit of the new community, despite its religious rigidity, was fresh and invigorating. Because of the high educational level of the founders, the atmosphere was academic, if not intellectual, and as soon as the comforts of the body were assured, thoughts were directed toward the development of the mind. The Boston Public Latin School opened in 1635; Harvard College was founded in nearby Cambridge in 1636; a public library was started in 1653; and *Newsletter,* the first newspaper printed in the thirteen colonies, was founded in 1704. All of this was

The Old Town House in Boston. Seventeenth century. Sketch by Kilburn. From *Memorial History of Boston*, ed. by Justin Winsor (Boston: Osgood, 1880–1881).

accomplished nearly two hundred years before Boston was incorporated as a city in the year 1822.

To understand the city as an organ rather than an organism, one must be acquainted with the history of the crawling century of colonization that preceded Boston's metamorphosis. Change that occurred outside the area affected the lives of the persons dwelling within. Due to political unrest in England, permissiveness was allowed in the development of the colonies, and, unnoticed, a cleavage commenced. The mother country was too preoccupied to pay much attention to her offspring. And, in addition, the Atlantic Ocean presented a formidable barrier to communication.

For the original settlers, agriculture was the prime source of employment even though the season was short and the products with which they were working unfamiliar. The ingenuity with which the original settlers adapted the products of their new environment to profit was indicative of the bounty that lay ahead.

In the winter months the menfolk, relieved of their heavier farm chores, took muskets into the forest to shoot wild turkey, deer, or a marauding fox or wolf; or they fetched a line and hook and broke through the ice to fish. In time, the cod became sacred. When the men were confined to their homes, they turned to secondary trades. Some cobbled shoes; some fashioned trenchers and trays of good-smelling wood. Even if a man had no craft there were always plenty of odd jobs of carpentry, patching, and mending to do about the houses and the outerhouses.

The women performed the chores of housekeeping, childbearing, and maintaining a direct line of communication with God through constant contact with the ordained ministers.

Politics (law and order) were of utmost importance. The political format for the Massachusetts Bay Colony was administered by a general court consisting of a governor, a deputy governor, 18 assistants, and 118 freemen. Freemanship was restricted to church members until 1664. When this circumscription was lifted, it greatly increased the number of freemen. The colonial government contained traces of democracy, but the established social order made the practice of a democratic form of government impossible, since the individual was subject to God's will as interpreted by the ruling clergy. The first settlers maintained they were carrying out God's will and that any dissent was the work of the devil.

That dissent would occur among such an opinionated, dogmatic clique was obvious. It happened soon after the pecking order was established.

One of the original progenitors of dissent was a woman, Anne Hutchinson. She had left Lincolnshire in 1634 to emigrate with her husband and family and settle in Boston. Her brilliant mind and kindness won a following of enthusiastic admirers. Informal discussions held in her home gave scope to the Puritan intellect, but her frank espousal of the covenant of grace as opposed to the covenant of works (she tended to believe that faith alone was necessary to salvation) caused John Cotton and John Winthrop to view her with disfavor and denounce her as an antinomian heretic. She defied them, was tried by the general court, and in 1637 was sentenced to banishment for "traducing the ministers." She was destined to wander—first, to Rhode Island with Roger Williams, then to Pelham, New York, where she and her family were wiped out by a band of hostile Indians—a most misunderstood woman.

As trade grew, the physical design of Boston established a community pattern that was copied throughout New England. The houses, individually owned, were grouped around the green, a plot of land held in common by the community and hence known as the common. The dominant structure of the common was the meetinghouse, where town meetings were held. Here the pastor held forth in long Sabbath services. These town meetings have been highly touted as strongholds of American democracy, but actually they were formidably restricted; only male property owners who had reached their majority and were active church members could participate in the deliberations.

Because Protestantism required daily reading of the Bible and because the Puritans were determined to have an educated ministry, formal education got off to a good start in Boston. Although the schools were not free, they were open to all and generally are regarded as the foundation of popular education in America. The avid missionary efforts of one leading minister, John Eliot, saw learning extended even to the Indians. Although the Indians did not resent acquiring the knowledge of the English alphabet, they were becoming increasingly alarmed and discontented with the Puritan zest for land-grabbing and with their own growing dependence upon the colonists for living materials and foodstuffs.

The once friendly tribe of Chief Massasoit, the ruling sachem for whom the state was named, became militant under Massasoit's son, King Philip. Pious, Sunday-praying Puritans murdered several Indians and protested innocence. The Indians, unable to procure satisfaction, commenced retaliating and massacres of men, women, and children became commonplace. Raids instigated by the Indians were daily occurrences, and the

Ancient houses in Boston's North End. Seventeenth century. Illustration by F. T. Merill. From *A Book of New England Legends and Folklore in Prose and Poetry* by Samuel Adams Drake (Boston: Roberts, 1896).

Eliot, the Apostle of the Indians, preaching to his flock. From *A Child's History of the United States* by John Dawson Gilmany Shea (New York: McMenamy, 1872).

English settlers, unable to force the Indians into open battle, countered with similar raids. It was an expensive era for the Founding Fathers and the ever-fleeing Indians, both in men and in money. In 1676, Philip, his son, and his wife were executed and their bodies were drawn, atop a wagon, down the streets of Plymouth for the God-fearing to see. It was a strange performance for a community that claimed to get its orders from a supreme Christian Godhead. But the death of Philip discouraged his people, and they moved westward in search of new lands, frontiers far removed from the trespassing white man—or so they innocently thought. Enmity had replaced amity and the children of the God of love had succeeded in giving birth to generations filled with hatred and revenge.

The withdrawal of the Indians brought about the founding of the New England Confederation, the first organized attempt of the colonies to establish a unified constituency. The revolution in England that had unseated a king, placed a commoner, Oliver Cromwell, in power, and augmented the cause of advanced Protestantism under the Commonwealth had come to an end. Under Charles II and the Restoration, England began to look to her infant colonies for increased revenues to support the expensive court of the new and somewhat licentious regent.

When the original charter for the Massachusetts Bay Colony was revoked the results were disastrous for Bostonians. Although this act had been expected by the Bostonians, in view of the fact they had consistently violated the terms of their charter and had repeatedly evaded or ignored royal orders by operating an illegal mint, establishing religious rather than property qualifications for suffrage, and discriminating against Anglicans, the shock was severe. The Massachusetts Bay Colony became incorporated into the Dominion of New England under the appointed governorship of Sir Edmund Andros. The "Bible Commonwealth" was dissolved.

The colonists sent the Reverend Increase Mather to England to bargain for their rights and to protest the rule of Andros. Mather journeyed to England, but his visit was a disappointing compromise. He managed to get a new charter incorporating Maine, Plymouth, and Boston as the Royal colony of Massachusetts, with Sir William Phips of Maine appointed governor. The new charter abolished church membership as a test for voting, but the Congregational Church remained the established religion.

Certainly if God had guided the settlers and was dictating their governing laws, his fellow traveler, the devil, was not far behind.

In 1692, in an area of Salem known as Danvers (now the site of the Danvers State Hospital for mental patients), the devil made his presence felt in the parsonage of the Reverend Samuel Parris in the forms of two small children, aged nine and eleven. One was the daughter of the Reverend Mr. Parris and the other was her cousin, Abigail Williams.

The time was ripe for the devil to barter for souls. The colonists were facing a winter of discontent, for they feared that the near independence they had enjoyed under the original charter had been revoked by the new royal charter. Secretly, people wondered if God had turned his countenance against his children, whom he had found unworthy of his magnanimity. He, who had once chosen them and led them to their Promised Land appeared displeased with his choice. Soul-searching for remission was constant, and the searching transgressed into peering into the souls and worldly affairs of neighbors who might have committed the sin against God.

With the loss of the charter, fear of insecurity penetrated the minds of the New Englanders. They worried about the loss of their lands, which they had struggled to make productive, the wealth that they had begun to accumulate. They saw themselves returned to a state of feudalism, and they foresaw the punishment that would be meted to them now that Cromwell had lost his power. Whispers of doomsday were on the lips of the pious, who spent their Bible-reading leisure hours perusing and interpreting the enigmatic Book of Revelations. "Repent," they cried, "the Kingdom of God is at hand!"

The colony was rudderless, and their ship of state was floundering. The ministers enforced rules of extra-hard labor to please God and to make amends for their sloth, but the labor was no longer coming forth joyfully, with inspired inner strength; it was arduous. The workers were abashed.

It is conceivable that history would never have heard of little Betty Parris and Abigail Williams. Their names might have been known only to collectors of early American graveyard epitaphs, half concealed on moss-covered tombstones, had it not been for one Tituba, a half-Carib, half-Negro slave imported from Barbados who worked for the Parris household.

Tituba was confined to household chores, while Mrs. Parris tended to the many errands of mercy that good women performed. In the absence of her mistress, Tituba took the children into her own snuggery by the open fireplace. She began to amuse them with tricks and spells, fragments of voodoo she remembered from Barbados. The children were fascinated and fell under her influence. Although in their upright Puritan hearts they knew they were tampering with the forbidden, they could not break the mystical affinity between themselves and the devil's agent.

Adjoining the parsonage lived three teen-aged girls who had secretly begun to indulge in "little sorceries," as such mischief was described by the Reverend Cotton Mather. These naughties consisted of the reading of palms and the telling of fortunes by means of sieve, scissors, and candle. Such conduct was obviously forbidden, since "God who reveals all things in His own good time does not permit His providence to be tempted." To attempt to see the future by magical means was to traffic with the devil.

Gradually, these sexually frustrated, emotionally disturbed older girls, fed intellectually on the pabulum of Michael Wigglesworth's best-selling *Day of Doom,* became apostles of Tituba, and passed by word of mouth their newfound wisdom to other girls throughout the Massachusetts Bay Colony. The seige of witchcraft was balanced on the thin end of the wedge.

There was no exorcist to expel the evil spirit living within the bodies of the troubled girls, but the temptation to perform such a feat spiked the Puritan flame of no less a personage than the Reverend Cotton Mather. He found a likely witch in the person of a girl who fell into convulsions while he was preaching the words of his God to his eager-eared congregation. From the girl, Mather obtained a firsthand description of the devil: "A short and black man . . . a witch no taller than an ordinary walking staff; he was not a Negro, but of tawny or Indian color, he wore a high-crowned hat with straight hair; and he had a cloven foot." The eyes of this creature flamed unbearably, having a strange resemblance to the glass ball of the lantern Mather took with him through the dim streets of Boston on his nocturnal rambles.

The scourge of the devil raged throughout Massachusetts. In 1688 Mrs. Glover was executed in Boston, and the witchcraft panic, aflame with the arsonic but bigoted words of the brilliant Mather reached massive proportions. In 1692, fifteen persons in Salem were hanged as witches.

No one was wholly innocent in this tragedy; it was chargeable to a kind of collective guilt on the part of the early settlers for falling away from the high consecration of the Pilgrim Fathers. A schism had occurred. Husbands "broke charity" with wives, wives with husbands, mother with child, child with mother. Even worse was the tattling of neighbor upon neighbor.

The Reverend Cotton Mather. Engraving by H. B. Halls Sons, New York.

In so small a community as the settlement of Boston, relationships are organic. There must be, in a crisis, a community of sympathy and understanding; otherwise, there exists an atmosphere of disease. A debilitating sickness had infiltrated Boston and the adjoining villages, and it was reaching epidemic proportions. But Boston had been birthed under a caul of enlightenment, and somehow the community managed to rise from its sickbed of delusion and heal itself without outside aid. Gradually the citizenry acquired the spiritual health with which to restore its sanity, re-

The Trial of George Jacobs for Witchcraft by Tompkins Harrison Matteson. George Jacobs was convicted and hanged on Gallows Hill, August 19, 1692, along with the Reverend George Burrough and three others. Historians are inclined to believe that Burroughs was hounded to the scaffold by the Reverend Samuel Parris, a successor of Burroughs as pastor in Salem Village. Courtesy of the Essex Institute, Salem, Massachusetts.

nounce its errors, rectify its wrongs (with monetary payments and moral forgiveness), and rejoin, in order to survive.

That the plague fostered by the devil had upset Boston was apparent, but the hour of a more serious disaster was approaching—the break with England.

Boston, despite the devil's intrusion, was prosperous. The citizens treasured their class distinctions—a man had to be worth a thousand dollars for his wife to wear a silk scarf—but they also believed in economic regulations, which had the effect of forbidding the rise of high society dynasties. Society now began to settle upon Beacon Hill, overlooking the sea. "The forme of this Towne is like a heart," wrote Edward

Johnson twenty years after moving to Boston. Houses that were small mansions were being erected, "The buildings beautiful and large, some fairly set forth with Brick, Tile, Stone and Slate and orderly placed with comply streets, whose continuall inlargement presages some sumptious City." They were built with the building techniques and prevailing forms of the home country, giving rise to a form of architecture that would become known as "colonial," in which the classicism of English architecture was reflected.

The original houses were based on the small-scale activities of farming, fishing, lumbering, and commerce, which were the sources of wealth. The first designers tried to build as they had at home—many-gabled, half-timber houses of late-Gothic inspiration—but the rough weather rapidly forced the covering of the half-lumber houses, the lowering of the slopes, and the simplification of plans. Religious influence and self-inflicted austerity and poverty prompted unalloyed detail.

The cobbled streets of Boston were tapered and crooked. Most people traveled by foot. In the houses on the hill lived the wealthy establishment of Boston: John Hancock, importer; Paul Revere, silversmith; Robert Keayne, English tailor who became Boston's first great society merchant; Thomas Boylston, the richest man in colonial Massachusetts, who left his name on Boston's chief uptown commercial thoroughfare; James Otis, lawyer—and many others, who laid the cornerstone for the city's wealth.

Their spiritual home was the Old North Church; their political rallying center the Old South Meeting House; their edifice of law, the State House; their social gathering place, the Boston Common; their shopping center, a public marketplace donated by Peter Faneuil, who in 1740 offered "to erect a noble and complete structure . . . for the sole use and benefit and advantage of the town." The hall over the market stalls became one of the most famous rooms in the history of the world.[3]

In the spring the hobblebush and the holly were in bloom with tiny flowers and berries, and during the late summer months the New England aster with its deep purple rays brightened the prim gardens. The elm, the hemlock, and the spruce stretched toward the sky, and their lean, lithe limbs were almost imitative of the stalwart men who walked in their shade. The air was chill and penetrating, but stimulating to driving ambition and hardihood.

The smug matrons saw that the interiors were immaculate and unfrivolous in decor. Festivity was not a familiar word; the Puritan calendar provided no alleviation from the tedious hours of winter. Husking bees,

Faneuil Hall in Boston, 1838. Engraving by W. H. Bartlett and H. Griffiths.

quilting parties, the bustle of the harvest followed by the annual solemn Thanksgiving, were the highlights of the social season. Pagan rituals celebrating Christmas and Mardi Gras, presaging spring, were obliterated. For the young the atmosphere was bleak and cold—so cold, in fact, that courtship was conducted in the notorious bundling bed—a contraption wherein the sweethearts, separated by a wooden plank, pursued their courtship fully clothed—in bed—in order to conserve heat. Yet it was a lusty society, for the pioneering wives were pregnant nearly as often as the milk cows in the pasture. And the hardships of childbirth were tolerated as part of the role woman had brought upon herself by her misconduct in the Garden of Eden.

Because the British government favored a policy of mercantilism, many colonials felt their commercial activities were fairly unlimited. The Navigation Acts, intended to regulate commerce in the British interest, were not easily enforced on the long American coast; and smuggling, though officially a crime, was generally regarded in Boston as an honorable profession. In 1763, George Grenville in England endeavored to undertake a new colonial tax policy to make the colonies pay for their defense and return revenue to England. In 1764, a tax levied on sugar and molasses caused consternation among the Boston manufacturers and importers of rum and the merchants who sold rum. The specter of stringent enforcement of the law was unexpected and ominous. In 1765, the Stamp Act roused the inhabitants of Boston into violent outcry. James Otis became the leader of the radical wing of colonial opposition, and in nearby Quincy, Samuel Adams, a brewer, immortalized the words of Otis in his printed pamphlets.

"No taxation without representation!" became the hue and cry. In 1768, the ship *Liberty,* belonging to John Hancock, was seized by the British authorities, exercising the laws of the crown in Boston. It was declared "the property of a smuggler" and was confiscated and destroyed. With the sinking of the hulk, waves of riot and revolution rose from the deep and dark blue ocean and washed the Boston harbor.

From 1765 to 1770 Boston was the molten center of smoldering hatreds and dissident beliefs. The old truism "no one loves a revenue collector" was solidifying Bostonians into disordered mobs.

Just when the Founding Fathers decided to use mobs to achieve their political ends is not accurately placed in time, but it represents a conscious conclusion that American words could not alone, or even combined with words of English friends, reach the ears of those with the power to change the revenue policy. "Force was introduced into the Revolutionary movement in a form long familiar but not newly empowered by orderly shared principles and beliefs. It would never thereafter be absent." (Bernard Beilyn)

The moment the Boston mob was permitted to roar its angry way into the Stamp Act controversy, the effect was frightening. Actually, the result was exactly what those who fostered the mob intended. Their objectives were simple: to repeal the Stamp Act by putting fear into the lives of those who were to administer and enforce the law. The radicals sought a political goal by physical means, and they achieved it as they were to achieve other such goals in the immediate future. But in so doing at such an early stage of the dispute they ensured that the future course of the disagreement could never be resolved without force.

It has been argued in defense of the Boston mobs that they did not cause wholesale or even retail slaughter but acted decently and even decorously. The essential characteristic of the prerevolutionary mobs in Boston, as of mobs anywhere, anytime, was the impression of unpredictability. He whom the mob threatened never knew how far the mob would go. The victim knew he faced a crew of bullies, rough, loud, even drunk. Sometimes the victim was confronted with such demands as to resign from office or to swear not to import British goods. The confrontation presented these alternatives: Do what the mob demands, or the mob will destroy your property—or, perhaps, you.

Amazingly, the violence in the streets of Boston from 1765 to 1770 was enacted by rioters who seemed uncontrolled and uncontrollable, when they were, in fact, almost under military discipline. According to Tory Peter Oliver, one of the leaders of the mob, Mackintosh,

> paraded the Town with a Mob of 2000 Men in Two Files, and passed by the Stadthouse when the General Assembly were sitting to display His Power if a Whisper was heard among his Followers, the holding up of his Finger hushed it in a Moment; & when he had fully displayed his Authority, he matched his Men to the first Rendezvous, & ordered them to retire peacefully to their several Homes; & was punctually obeyed.

The mob's ardor apparently could be turned on or off to suit the policies of its directors. It was a shaped political instrument consciously used as such.

The presence of British troops, sent to enforce the unpopular Townshend Acts that taxed numerous imports, was a military bête noir to the rebellious Bostonians. Finally, on the night of March 5, 1770, the British troops, badgered by a long period of harassment, fired into a rioting crowd killing five men—three on the spot, two dying of wounds later.

The leaders of the fracas, with blackened faces (only one leader, Crispus Attucks, was black), wearing outlandish costumes, could not be identified in life; but the three dead men, with faces washed and clothes removed, were identifiable, proving that death in itself is a mockery. The funeral for the victims of the Boston Massacre was the first occasion for a great patriot demonstration.

This period of dissension was taut, the nerves of the populace highstrung, and even though the Townshend Acts were repealed the damage was evident. The abrogation had merely removed the cancer from the surface; but the sanguinary killer had been implanted in the principles involved. Many of the colonists were thinking compliantly in one direction—separation from the mother country.

The Puritan concept of God's will being supreme counterpointed the possibility that man might eventually be the master of his soul. The words of the great Puritan poet John Milton were being analyzed by many of the best minds in Boston:

> Methinks I see in my mind a noble and puissant nation rousing herself like a strong man after sleep, and shaking her invincible locks: methinks I see her as an eagle mewing her mighty youth, and kindling her undazzled eyes at the full midday beam.

"A noble and puissant nation"—the thought was rarely spoken aloud even among the most intense. The current plan was to persuade the British government to give way to the demands of the colonists. Yet one cannot read the words of the men who met in the State House and Faneuil Court and not be aware that they must have been cognizant of the fact that eventually there would be a complete break with the mother country.

It cannot have been an easy decision to make once they had accepted this. It demanded of the leaders seemingly impossible tasks. First, the cutting of the umbilical cord with the mother country was a traumatic prospect for all of the colonists. Each insurgent must have felt like Orestes plotting the murder of Clytemnestra. Second, the organization of any form of a physical militia was almost impossible, for there existed in Boston no proper form of a colonial police force, no skeleton upon which to construct a body army with which to uphold their resolution.

The abominable task was made feasible with the ascension of George III to the throne of England.

George III was a stubborn man of limited intellectual powers. His suspicions were paranoiac to the extreme, and he regarded the actions of the colonists as insolent and disrespectful. Despite the pleadings of William Pitt (whom he discharged despite the statesman's popularity), George continued to pursue his program of taxation. It was his imposing of a tax upon tea to sustain the near-bankrupt East India Tea Company that awakened Bostonian feelings of resentment, which had been lying dormant for two years following the Boston Massacre.

The tax on tea struck at gut level with every Bostonian to whom the brew was a quaff of life.

In December 1773, three ships arrived in Boston Harbor. They remained unloaded, but Governor Thomas Hutchinson refused to let the ships depart without first paying their duties. Samuel Adams, Paul Revere, and other Boston "radicals" convened secretly. On the night of December

16 the first citizens, disguised as Indians carrying tomahawks and screeching war whoops boarded the ship and tossed the tea into the Boston harbor.

When the news of this misbehavior reached the ears of the king, he determined to punish the population of Boston, to administer his will by force if not by reason or justice. He authorized legislation known as the Intolerable Acts that gave the now recognized revolutionary leaders their raison d'être for the founding of the First Continental Congress. Even if it did not accomplish anything notable, this did make the founding of a colonial militia possible.

On August 19, 1775, General Thomas Gage, in the midst of the unrest created by the enforcing of the Intolerable Acts, sought to avoid armed rebellion by sending a column of royal infantry under Major John Pitcain from Boston to capture colonial military stores at Concord.

Words like leaves lifted by a casual wind of breath reached the open ears of Paul Revere, chatting with William Dawes and Samuel Prescott. "The best laid plans of General Gage . . ."

The story of the midnight ride of Paul Revere has been immortalized by Henry Wadsworth Longfellow, so the words fall glibly from every schoolchild's tongue. The signal from the tower of the Old North Church, "One if by land, two if by sea," was the password to the countryside, warning that the British were coming to seize secret arsenals. When the British column reached Lexington, a group of newly organized militia, called minutemen, greeted the British soldiers. After an exchange of shots, in which several Americans were killed, the colonists withdrew and the British continued on to Concord. It was here that the first battle of the American Revolution was fought. With two hundred casualties the British made a hurried retreat to Boston, and the exultant but wearied minutemen pondered their fate. It was quite different from any their forefathers had envisioned.

Boston was under seige. The rifts that occurred in human relationships were many, and one of the most dramatic examples is the case of Benjamin Franklin (Boston-born, but Philadelphia-claimed) and his son, William. Benjamin Franklin, who had made his residence for many years in Paris and London, had anticipated living out his life in one of these cities until the Revolution commenced. He chose to return to America to take his stand with the colonists. William became a loyalist leader and quarreled bitterly with his father. Even after the war ended neither son nor father ever spoke to one another again. Their situation was not an uncommon one.

General Gage made no attempt, until he was assured of reinforcements, to break the siege of Boston. When he was guaranteed that he would be reinforced, he decided to seize the heights of Dorchester and Charlestown. Through espionage the Bostonians learned of the plan, and William Prescott was sent to occupy Bunker Hill. Acting on his own initiative, Prescott and his men moved on to Breed's Hill, and on June 17, 1775, a battle ensued that is recorded as the Battle of Bunker Hill.

The British won when the colonists ran out of gunpowder, but their victory was minimal because the gallant defense heightened morale and increased colonial resistance not only in Boston but in other colonies, which chose to come to their aid. "Their shoulders held the sky suspended; what God abandoned, these defended." (A. E. Housman)

In the meanwhile the Continental Congress, at the insistence of Samuel Adams, had selected George Washington as commander in chief of the Continental Armed Forces. The American Revolution had begun in earnest.

Yet, despite the official dictum, a large part of the population of Boston remained more or less neutral, swaying first to one side and then to the other, or else remaining inert during the struggle, thus creating a sort of civil war. Local government and administration had fallen apart at the seams, and the mending had to be done with the crooked needle and burnt thread of inadequacy. Much of the game plan of Boston, under seige, was influenced not by the words of the original radicals but by the writings of an English-born Quaker, Thomas Paine, whose pamphlet "Common Sense" was smuggled through the underground and widely read. It urged to a tired and weary people the cause of patriotism, and the admonition that "government, even in its best state is but a necessary evil; in its worst state, an intolerable one" did not go unheeded.

Consequently, when the British finally evacuated Boston in 1776, most of the population were in accord with the signing of the Declaration of Independence. It should be noted that this famous ambiguous document, which was drafted by a Virginian, Thomas Jefferson, was first signed by John Hancock of Boston. So large, so proud, so unquavering was that original signature that the name John Hancock has become synonymous with the word *signature*.

Many people believe that the finest hours of Boston and the original Bostonians were those of the prerevolutionary and revolutionary days. Yet, with few exceptions, within ten years after the Revolution the names of the most important of the cast of characters were buried, resurrected only

Hancock House, Boston. Engraving by Samuel Walker.

by students of history and lovers of nostalgia. Hutchinsons, Gores, Royalls, Dudleys, Pinchons—even Revere and Hancock—and many other names to be conjured with lapsed from the social and political archives.

What happened? Some, undoubtedly died out from natural causes. Many abdicated to Halifax or England, following the British evacuation of Boston, and never returned. And a third group failed to survive because they lived too well, too soon. Boston since its founding has been a city in which the loss of financial stability is a major clue to the oblivion of a Boston family. For example, take the case of John Hancock, who spent more than a half-million dollars inherited from his merchant uncle, Tom, in less than a decade after the Revolution. Hancock, who had been martyr and hero for the Revolution, afterward became the self-proclaimed king of Boston society. He lived on a grand scale. Even his buttons were made of solid gold. He snubbed George Washington, who, he felt, had played a poor role as Father of His Country. When Hancock died in 1793 he left no will, and eventually everything, including the famed Hancock House, which was torn down in 1863 for taxes, was lost to posterity.

The truth is that, although Boston is one of the oldest cities in America, it is most typically a nineteenth-century city. Despite its early American history, it was in the nineteenth century that Boston matured as a city based upon a rigid family structure pivoted upon material wealth. Money was the chief essential. "Money is power. Every good man and woman should strive for power. Tens and thousands of men get rich honestly. But they are often accused by an envious, lazy crowd of unsuccessful persons of being dishonest and oppressive. I say . . . Get rich! Get rich!"

These words from a Boston minister, the Reverend Russell H. Conwell, in a lecture entitled "Acres of Diamonds," are a far cry from the notions of the Puritan fathers who fined Robert Keayne, the first millionaire merchant, for "making too much profit" and made him publicly lament his "covetous and corrupt heart."

2
The Bean and the Cod

In the port of Boston Harbor stands the Boston Light, the oldest lighthouse in America. Following the victorious hours of the Revolution its lambent beam cast the single ray of brightness, for the days were dark, and the nights penetrated with a gloom echoing the sound of the foghorn.

The people of Boston were bewildered, coping with a serious economic depression that succeeded on the heels of the retreating British. Exits and entrances were being made in the Boston political arena, and the cast of players was constantly changing. The Tories and the British expected the new state to sink in its own morass, catapulted by an unwieldy heterogeneous crew. Opinions as to governing laws and governing people were at variance, and two opposing ways of life—agrarian and industrial— presented themselves. Farmers were deserting nearby territories for Boston, and many original Boston Puritans, frightened by the specter of big city growth, retreated into less complex communities. It was a day of transition.

In 1786, a general discontent pervaded the countryside surrounding Boston. Here the small farmers, organized by one Daniel Shays, a revolutionary hero, rose up in armed insurrection. Sentiment against the ever-growing city, the well-to-do Boston merchants and lawyers, ran high amongst the oppressed farmers and laborers. They felt taxes were too high, legal costs exorbitant, and salaries of public officials out of proportion. The insurrectionists, having been well tutored in mob rule, prevented the sitting of the courts, and in 1787 Governor James Bowdoin appointed General Ben Lincoln to lead 4,400 men against the rebels, who were routed and dispersed. The rebellion ousted Bowdoin from office and resulted in some legislative controls, but above all else it influenced Massachusetts's ratification of the new federal Constitution.

The authors of this Constitution were equipped with the old Calvinistic sense of human evil and damnation. They were men of affairs—merchants, lawyers, planter-businessmen, speculators, investors. Having seen human nature on display in the marketplace, the courtroom, the legislative chamber, and every secret path and alleyway where wealth and power are courted, they felt they knew it in all its frailty. To them a human being was an atom of self-interest. They did not believe in man but in the power of a good political constitution to control him.

Perhaps this seems an abstract notion to ascribe to practical men, but it follows the language that the Fathers themselves used. For example, in his letter to George Washington after the quelling of Shays' Rebellion, General Knox wrote, "Americans were men—actual men possessing all the turbulent passions belonging to that animal."

Throughout their discussions during the writing of the Constitution, the distrust of man was first and foremost a distrust of the common man and democratic rule. Although the Bostonians of the late eighteenth century had not fled like their Tory cousins, there still flowed a continuous lineage of upper-class contempt that was not too far removed from the

Paul Revere by Gilbert Stuart, Boston, 1813. Courtesy of the Museum of Fine Arts, Boston. Cheek photograph.

cry of prerevolutionary Peggy Hutchinson, who wrote one day: "The dirty mob was all about me as I drove into town!" The rulers who were to father the approaching nineteenth century found themselves set off from the masses by a hundred viable, tangible, and audible distinctions of dress, speech, manners, and education. The proper new governing class was concerned with creating a government that could not only regulate commerce and pay for its debts but could also prevent currency inflation, stay laws, and check uprisings such as Shays' Rebellion. The old king was dead; long live the new!

The Boston Light must have been a monitoring guide to the Boston citizenry. On the shores off the somber sea came mysterious calls beckoning men to leave the land and seek their fortunes. Even in prerevolutionary days shipbuilding had existed in Boston, and by the end of the Revolution the beacon light beckoned to fortunes that lay waiting for plunder, especially in the West Indies and farther around the Horn to the Orient.

In 1797, in Hart's shipyard, the *Constitution* was built and launched, her bolts and spikes made by Paul Revere of drawn copper (drawing being a new hardening process). After a few embarrassing failures, while crowds of excited Bostonians gathered to watch her launching and the *Constitution* staunchly refused to budge from the ways, she was finally set afloat on Columbus Day, 1797. Money to buy the site for the Charlestown Navy Yard was not appropriated until March 1, 1801, but it was 1803 before the *Constitution* set off for Tripoli. She sailed to foreign shores bedecked with plates coppered by Paul Revere. "The carpenters gave nine cheers which were answered by the seamen and calkers, because they had in fourteen days completed coppering the ship with copper made in the United States." In the pumice isles of the Mediterranean she earned her soubriquet "Old Ironsides," but she might better have been dubbed "Old Coppersides."

In 1822, when Boston's ships had made its name famous in the ports of the world it was officially baptized as a city. The birth of the nineteenth century brought new prosperity. Shipping wiped out the postrevolutionary depression and set the community on a course of financial success that would last until the dying days of that century. During that era the merchant prince would rule and create a city that would become known both as "The Hub" and "The Athens of America."

The story of the acquisition of wealth and the distribution of it is essentially the real story of Boston, which overnight altered from a farm-surrounded commercial city to an industrial metropolis. In addition to shipping, mills and factories built on New England rivers produced shoes and textiles for world markets. Other businesses—fishing (especially whaling), food-processing, wool, manufacturing of machines, printing, banking, marine insurance—were flourishing in the nineteenth-century port, which had become overnight a major financial center.

The single interruption to the progress of Boston was "Mr. Madison's War," as one merchant prince referred to the War of 1812. European wars in the beginning of the nineteenth century stimulated the carrying trade, but then led to interference with American shipping—which was, largely, Bostonian. From the fifteenth to the nineteenth century, England, Spain, and Portugal attempted successfully to exclude commercial vessels from ports of the open sea. The strongest advocate of the traditional freedom of the seas was the new United States. In 1807, Jefferson's Embargo Act was passed. To Bostonians it was an act of anathema, and in 1812, when war with Great Britain came anyway, Nathaniel Appleton wrote: "This horrible madness has been perpetrated! We stand gaping at each other, hardly realizing that it can be true—then bursting into execrations of the madmen who have sacrificed us." He spoke for most of Boston.

For some time after the declaration of war, business proceeded as usual. The British granted licenses for American ships to sail—the price of a license being $1,000 to $2,000. Ships were able to enter American ports, and if it could be proven that goods had come aboard before the declaration of war they were allowed to proceed, tie up, and post bond until proof of their claim could be established, when the bond was refunded. Naturally there were delays, spoilage of goods, and many irritants to increase the "temper of the British people," who were becoming more and more incensed at naval victories on the part of a navy that they felt had no rights on the high seas. By the end of May 1813, the British men-of-war *Shannon* and *Temedos* were guarding Boston Harbor.

The *Chesapeake,* sister ship of the *Constitution,* came into the Charlestown Navy Yard to be refitted and recruit a crew. Her newly appointed captain was James Lawrence. He was ordered to proceed northward to intercept British supply ships coming to Canada. On his way out he encountered the British frigate *Shannon,* and they immediately engaged in gunfire. The ships were out of sight of Boston but the sound of cannons was heard, and people along Hanover Street rushed up to the captain's walks or to housetops for a wider view of the combat. All they could see was the grey smoke rising like a menacing fog from a steel blue sea. Had they been closer, they would have heard the cry of Captain

Lawrence as he was being carried from the deck, mortally wounded, "Don't give up the ship!" Longboats were launched. Men rowed them out to the Atlantic only to row them back slowly and sorrowfully. The *Chesapeake* had been captured.

It was another dark hour for Boston, followed by the knowledge that the British had captured Washington and burned to the ground the original White House—"a fine building of free-stone," in the words of one Boston visitor.

By June 27, 1814, a general sense of alarm prevailed. Boston suddenly began to wonder if fifteen heavy cannon on Governor's Island and ten on Charlestown Point Battery would really protect the town. Paul Revere, then aged seventy-nine, assumed the helm. A conference was held about the "sinking of the hulks" in Boston Harbor. Hulks of old ships were made ready, and it was arranged that ten companies of artillery would come to Boston from neighboring towns, at the first alarm, to assist Boston militia. A "temporary gun house" was built on the Boston Common. By the end of August there was "voluntary digging." Fort Strong was built in East Boston, a battery set up in Dorchester Heights, and other defenses built in Cambridge and Roxbury. A notebook entitled "Mechanics of the Town" listed those ready to "cooperate by manual labor in the measure for the Defense of the Town and Naval Arsenal."

The British, who advanced as expected upon New York, were defeated at Plattsburg. On the morning of February 12, 1815, an express arrived from New York with a confirmation of the treaty of peace "already ratified by His Brittanic Majesty," signed in Ghent, December 24, 1814!

The guns in Boston roared salute after salute. Bells were ringing. On Pearl Street, the dignified Eliza Cabot pounded on Ellen Quincy's door. "Do you know why the bells are ringing?" she asked. "Why for fire, I suppose," countered the startled senator's wife. "No, it's *peace . . . peace!*" screamed Miss Cabot as she streaked through the street without her bonnet!

The cultural heritage of the nineteenth-century Boston merchant prince was that of seventeenth-century English republicanism, with its opposition to arbitrary rule and its faith in popular sovereignty. If the merchant princes had misgivings about the advance of democracy, they also feared turning to the extreme right. Jeremy Belknap, a New England clergyman, wrote: "Let it stand on principle that government originates from the people; but let the people be taught that they are not able to govern themselves." Their conception of man reflected conflicting interests. They thought man was a creature of rapacious self-interest, yet they wanted him to be free to engage in umpired strife, to use property to obtain property. They thought self-interest was the most dangerous and unbrookable quality of man, yet they underwrote it in trying to control it. They succeeded in both respects; under the competitive capitalism of the nineteenth century, Boston developed into an arena for grasping and contending self-interests, while the newly ordained federal government continued to serve as a proper medium within which they could promote the policy of free enterprise.

That "all men were created equal" was accepted as legal, not a political or psychological proposition. To the nineteenth-century Bostonian, the "natural rights" philosophy of his new government did not mean that uneducated farmers, grimy-handed ship caulkers, or men incapable of owning property were in any sense his equal. It merely meant that his

Opening of the New Merchant's Exchange on Waltham Street. Scene in the Reading Room. Sketched by E. R. Morse. From *Leslie's Monthly Magazine*, February 1874.

revolutionary ancestors had felt that any British colonial had the same right to self-government as a Briton at home, and that the average American was the legal peer of the average Briton. This schizophrenic conception of government is evident in the words of John Adams, who warned: "Remember Democracy never lasts long. It soon wastes, exhausts, murders itself. There has never been a Democracy that did not commit suicide." Government, thought the Boston merchant prince, is based upon the ownership of property, and the government of Boston was based upon the philosophies and behavior of those Bostonians who owned property and whose greatest achievement was the possession of money.

Since 1846 people have been prating that Bostonian society is based upon money. "It is no degradation then, to the Boston aristocracy that it rests upon money. Money is something substantial. Everybody knows that and feels it. Birth is a mere idea which grows every day, more and more intangible." ("Our First Men, a Calendar of Wealth, Fashion and Gentility.")

But, to the Bostonian mind, it was money made, honorably, at the right time!

The right time was the day when "they that go down to the sea in ships, that do business in great waters, These see the works of the Lord, and His wonders in the deep." (Psalm 107:23) As one Boston wit observed, "Every real Boston family has a sea captain in its background." Although this fact is not necessarily true, there is an element of romance attached to the seafaring captains of nineteenth-century Boston. And romantic fiction is a powerful ingredient in the making of a social stew.

The king of the merchant princes was unquestionably Colonel Thomas Handasyd Perkins, who came from Salem. (It is interesting to note that while we associate the title "Colonel" with Kentucky, the title was also quite prevalent in Boston. Most of the early sea captains managed to secure the title colonel during their lifetimes.) If ever there was a sea witch she harkened to Long Tom, as he was called, and lured him to sea before he had obtained manhood. By this date young Tom already had a shipping business reaching from Rio to Canton. When the new government of the United States was being formed, Perkins was offered the post of secretary of the navy by George Washington. He refused, since he owned a larger fleet of ships than did the government. It was more important to him to remain in Boston and tend to his own property.

Not only did Long Tom launch the Perkins family fortune but also, by merging and creating Russell and Company, he was responsible to a large degree in the establishing of all of Boston's merchant families—Cabots, Lodges, Forbes, Cunninghams, Appletons, Bacons, Russells, Coolidges, Parkmans, Shaws, Codmans, Boylstons and Hunnewells.

Perkins instigated the formula for success as a merchant prince that was founded upon the school of hard knocks, later popularized in Horatio Alger books and even today regarded as a prime factor in the making of a leader in legitimate American business—"Come up the hard way, young man!" In Perkins's school, one either went to sea and learned to become a sea captain or one entered the counting room and learned to be a supercargo, a position that had nothing to do with the physical running of the ship but entailed sailing on a vessel and assuming complete charge of the commercial concerns of the voyage. There was little patronage in the early days, and few merchant princes got in "through the cabin windows."

Nicholas Boylston, a rich Boston merchant, is shown wearing swank lounge robe and cap of the late eighteenth century. Portrait by John Singleton Copley, 1776. Courtesy of the Harvard University Portrait Collection.

The origin of the trade between the Boston merchant princes and the seaports of China lay in the conquest of China by the Manchus in 1644. The establishment of the Ch'ing Dynasty opened China to overseas trade. Marco Polo brought back stories of vast riches of the Orient, and the Western mind became intrigued with the East—a world of unlimited wealth, Hindu philosophies, frankincense, and myrrh. To a young imagination, confined in the straitlaced girdle of Puritan thought, what could be more tempting than a visit to an exotic world, such as Xanadu.

In the Boston shipyards a long and narrow sailing ship was constructed with the largest beam yet conceived aft center. Its bow cleaved to the waves, and the ship, a veritable cloud of sails, carried, besides top gallant and royal sails, sky sails and moonrakers. It had incredible speed, and because of the long stretch from Boston to China it became known as the China clipper. It dominated ocean commerce until the development of the steamship. The clipper ship was brought to perfection by Donald McKay of Boston, who built the *Flying Cloud, Glory of the Seas,* and *Lightning.*

If Perkins was the headmaster of the merchant prince school, the brothers Forbes were certainly the prize students. Arriving in China at the age of seventeen, John Murray Forbes, a supercargo, won the respect of the great Chinese merchant, Houqua, a man whose wealth exceeded twenty-five million dollars in 1830. Before Forbes was old enough to grow a full-length beard, he was conducting all of the elder Houqua's correspondence while clerking and loading ships on his own. His pay was 10 percent of the profits. At twenty, bald and ancient in appearance, John Murray Forbes had acquired his first million.

Like the good Bostonian he was, Forbes came back and married a Boston girl. But he soon returned to China, where he stayed for three years because he felt that the acquisition of a spouse required that he "make more than a good income." When he finally retired to Boston, the days of the merchant princes were on the wane, and he turned his shrewd eyes (always cast on a geographical exit) toward the railroads. In 1826, with his partner, Colonel Perkins, he constructed what is generally considered one of the first railroads built in America—a horsepowered line from Quincy to Boston, whose sole mission was to transport stone from Quincy quarries to erect the monument at the scene of the Battle of Bunker Hill.

In a most permanent fashion, the nineteenth-century architect Charles Bulfinch, designer of the State House and many other Boston buildings and mansions, created India Wharf's solid-looking block of stores with counting rooms overhead. The ghosts of old-time merchants, dressed in stocks and long coats, seemed to float against a background of brocades and silks and the aromas of teas and spices.

The embodiment of this form of physical aristocracy was Black Ben Forbes, an old commodore, who was tall and slender and whose coal-black hair had turned into a premature white mane shading suntanned mahogany skin. He so identified with the sea that he built a house with portholes in place of windows, and in the celler he constructed a completely closed-in room reached only by following a long passageway through an opening in the brick—a room so well concealed that it was only discovered by members of the Forbes family three-quarters of a century after the old sea captain had died.

While the fortunes of many of the nineteenth-century families of Boston were founded on money procured through a certain piracy of the seas and by bartering in the triangular traffic of the early days (the carrying of rum to Africa, slaves from Africa to the West Indies, and rum and slaves from the West Indies to Boston), another group made their fortunes by investing their moneys and interests in real estate businesses close at hand. Led by Harrison Gray Otis, a trio of merchants, upon learning that Beacon Hill would be the site of the State House, procured rights to the fifteen acres of land known as Copley's Beacon Hill. The heir was none other than John Singleton Copley, the famous portrait painter who had left Boston to study in England. He was appalled at the manner in which his inheritance was procured from him and accused Otis and his agent, Samuel Cabot, of chicanery, if not out-and-out stealing. The land value was greater than Copley was ever to earn in his entire lifetime of painting, and it is sheer irony that the Beacon Hill homes of the "better people of Boston" owned Copley canvases, commissioned, in all probability, with moneys obtained from the fraudulent development of Copley lands.

But morality mattered little in the early days of the merchant princes. Money acquired from the sea was solid gold bullion, and money obtained at home was its counterpart, sterling silver. For their wealth, the Jacksons made nails; the Ames, shovels; the Ayers, patent medicines; and the Lawrences, textiles.

For a composite daguerreotype of the Boston man of the nineteenth century we delve into the diaries of Nathan and William Appleton. William penned his manuscript for a period of more than fifty years and intended it to be read only by his immediate family and his descendants.

Eventually it became household reading on Beacon Hill and set an example for the private publication of their memoirs by men of wealth, establishing their rights to financial success and social prestige. These tomes, found on library shelves and cherished by the immediate family, lauded the virtues of hard work and Yankee cunning. Tall tales still echo throughout the halls of Beacon Hill homes, tales reputedly emitted from the mouths of the stern-visaged, Puritan-minded, fortune-founding ancestors. Tales of shrewdness and cupidity interlocked with the eternal romantic legend of the brave sea captain, whose adventures live on in memory like tales of the knights of old in Arthurian armor. Legends and fact meet point counterpoint in oft-repeated stories, such as the one concerning the British sea captain, who pointed to the Stars and Stripes and observed it wasn't a flag "that has braved for one thousand years the battle of the

Boston from City Point near Sea Street. 1833. Etching and aquatint, hand-colored. Courtesy of the Museum of Fine Arts, Boston, M. and M. Karolik Collection.

sea!" He was answered by a Boston sea captain who wryly commented, "No—it ain't, but it licked one that did!"

These sayings were handed from father to son in Homeric tradition. "Business before friends" is attributed to Amos Lawrence, who also admitted that he selected his wife because she had "such a reciprocity of feelings, sentiments and principles" to those he possessed. "Cold water, inside and out," is another euphemism, reputedly the words of Peter Chardon Brooks, Boston's first multimillionaire, who made his fortune in marine insurance and who attested to the value of ice-cold baths and abstinence from hard liquor. His advice to young men wishing to succeed in business was a cryptic "Let him mind his business!"

The genealogy of the Appletons of Beacon Hill reads like a recitation of the "begat" books of the Bible, and the lives of the members of the

Samuel Appleton. From *The Illustrated American Biography*, 3 vols. (New York: Milton Emerson, 1853–1855).

family have an Old Testament aura about them. The first immigrant Appleton was Samuel, born in Suffolk County, England, in 1586. Next in direct line was a son, also named Samuel, born in 1625. The first Samuel negotiated in England with the Winthrop Company to invest money in New England. His grant was 468 acres. He and his family sailed out of Ipswich, England, and in 1637 settled in New Ipswich. Through the years the Samuel Appletons begat Isaacs and the Isaacs begat Samuels and their history is in every woof, warp, and weft of early American tradition.

In November, 1794, one Samuel recognized the potentials of Boston. After what he saw on a trip to that locale he determined to desert the uneventful life of a small town and the loneliness of the Maine woods, and at twenty-eight years of age he ventured to Boston to

seek my fortune. . . . I wished to hire a shop for the retail trade but found it very difficult to procure one in a good situation. After a few days of a fruitless search William J. White offered to sell me his lease of a small shop of about 20 feet by 18. Five hundred dollars was the rent, on condition I would buy his stock at a cost which he figured at about $2,500. He was honest enough to say that he didn't think the goods worth two-thirds the amount because they were not imported but bought in Boston.

Cornhill was the most popular place to shop. It curved from the corner of School Street to intersect with State Street, which led directly to Long Wharf and continued to Dock Square and Market Square. On the corner of State Street and Cornhill was the Old State House, and on the square was Faneuil Hall. There were market stalls on the square where country people came to trade—and there was also the smell of the sea in the air, the tar on the ropes and the rigging. The Old North and Old South churches and King's Chapel were all nearby, and the sound of church bells pealing the hours of the day and calling the faithful to worship on Sunday made Samuel Appleton cognizant of the fact that Boston was a very unique locale.

In a short time, Samuel realized that in order to make real money he would have to buy goods at auction to sell "for cash or short-term credit, for a small profit." He set his sites on London, but he had to have someone operate the Boston store. Who else but his younger brother, Nathan? He could be trusted completely and was now fifteen years old.

In 1809, when this fifteen-year-old boy had advanced to the age of twenty-nine, he wrote to Samuel in London, "At this season of the year, this part of town is truly delectable." This part of town was Beacon Hill, Boston, and the house from which Nathan Appleton wrote was one of a pair of twin houses at Number 54 Beacon Street. It was to be the scene of Appleton hospitality, anxieties, and successes for the greater part of the nineteenth century. Already Beacon Hill was established as an exclusive residential area, and Nathan Appleton was quite proud of his newly acquired residence. The houses had been built in 1806; it is possible that they were designed by one of Boston's early architects, Asher Benjamin, whose own home was at 58 Beacon before it was demolished by fire. The two Appleton houses with their white columns, wrought-iron galleries, and classical details in the interior are consistent with Benjamin's work.

Directly across the street from Nathan's house was the Boston Common. From the balcony he could see the waters of the Charles River washing against the wood pilings of Charles Street. There was no Public Garden of roses and stately poplar trees when Nathan Appleton wrote of his "delectable" view; there were instead rope walks—long, low, barnlike buildings, where ropes for Boston's sailing ships were spun by hand.

Nathan married Maria Theresa Gold of Pittsfield. So impressed was he with the dark beauty of his twenty-year-old bride that he commissioned Gilbert Stuart to paint her portrait. Perhaps Gilbert was as good a businessman as an artist and he persuaded Appleton to have two portraits painted instead of one; or perhaps Maria Theresa was as proud of her husband's looks as he was of hers. At any rate, two Stuart portraits have survived. Maria was dark and, like the lady of the sonnets, the sun did not glow in her midnight eyes. In her portrait, her hair is parted in the center and brought forward in ringlets, touching the outer edges of her brows. It was combed back at the crown and fell in cascades of curls at the nape of her neck. Her gown is high-waisted and cut low to expose her full bosom.

When Maria was being painted, she was accompanied by a school friend. Maria wrote about Stuart, "He is a vain man and a great egoist, so that we had an opportunity of paying him many fine compliments without offending his delicacy. We availed ourselves of this opportunity and put him in a wonderful good humor."

The Stuart portrait of Nathan Appleton shows a remarkably handsome man, blue-eyed, with light reddish hair curling like a coxcomb over the top of his head, with a straying curl or two falling mischievously over his forehead. He had sideburns, a sensitive mouth, and ruddy cheeks—appleblossom pink. Stuart endows Appleton with the aristocratic Roman nose identified with Yankee traders of British descent; but according to Appleton's passport, his nose was "middling."

The house in which Maria and Nathan were married was the Thomas Gold house in Pittsfield, originally a farmhouse, with a huge chimney and a keeping room where Maria's mother loved to sit, even after her husband added a parlor with a white-paneled fireplace wall, wainscot, and French landscape wallpaper. Eventually, improved finances and changing tastes brought about extensive alterations—a portico in the Greek style, more rooms for an expanding family, a beautiful staircase with carved balusters, and a landing where a wall clock stood. It is this clock which Henry Wadsworth Longfellow, who had married Maria and Nathan's daughter Fanny, immortalized in one of his best-loved poems, "The Clock on the Stairs":

> Somewhat back from the village street
> Stands the old fashioned country seat.
> Across this antique portico
> Tall poplar trees their shadows throw.

> In that mansion used to be
> Free-hearted hospitality.
> Here great fires up the chimney roared
> The stranger feasted at his board . . .

The Embargo Act saw reverses for many Boston merchants, but the Appletons survived the "Jeffersonian gloom" and even prospered. The house on Beacon Street was to become the embodiment of the new era of Boston wealth. Nathan wrote to his brother Samuel in London his request for special furnishings:

> We want a pair of Grecian lamps—rather elegant than showy and some handsome chimney ornaments—novel and elegant—a pair of stylish bell ropes for the drawing rooms—something tasty, prevailing colors orange and light green with some wood color or pearl color— but you know the paper and judge for yourself.

In the postscript Nathan wished "some English cheese—but what is cheese without Porter—freight is cheap now."

William, son of the Nathan Appletons, entered business in 1807 with N. Giddings. "We kept at the corner of India and Central Streets, the only store occupied in the street. Our business was the buying and selling of West India goods and crockery ware." This business partnership lasted until 1809. "Then considering myself worth about four thousand dollars, I bought the ship, *Triumphant,* at Salem for Five Thousand dollars." William was twenty-three years old, and his pride of possession was only equaled by his obsession for wealth—a combination that was countered by anxieties that were manifest throughout his lifetime in chronic dyspepsia, a condition which today would undoubtedly be diagnosed as psychosomatic in origin.

The young man placed his ship under Portuguese colors and sent her off to Liverpool while he himself crossed the ocean in another vessel. When he reached Liverpool, William learned his ship had been captured by a French privateer! For two weeks he was inconsolable, not only over the loss of his entire fortune but over the first ship he had owned. Then he received a letter informing him that the *Triumphant* had been retaken and brought to Plymouth, England, where he went to take charge of his property. The *Triumphant* was a triumph for William and an omen that he was not only a natural-born trader, but born lucky. However, like most chronic worriers, none of the signs of good fortune that hovered over William alleviated his pressures.

Beacon Street, 1947. Photograph by Arthur Griffin. From *Boston Book* by Esther Forbes (Boston: Houghton, Mifflin, 1947).

William Appleton stayed in England until July 10, 1810, when he loaded about ten thousand pounds of goods "for account of myself, Parker, Appleton and Company. These goods and another importation," which he sold at the close of 1811, were worth ten thousand dollars.

At the time England was struggling to maintain her supremacy at sea against Napoleon's expanding power, so William loaded two ships with naval stores for England. In the House of Commons he heard debates concerning England's insistence upon her right to search American vessels. Feeling certain that this would mean the end of embargoes, William went out and bought goods. He had thirty thousand English pounds worth of cargo either on the high seas or loading when the War of 1812 was declared. "When I closed out my importations I thought myself worth Sixty Thousand dollars and I did not attend to any business of importance during the war."

His ships had come in, their cargoes selling at tremendous markups. But William Appleton had, undoubtedly, suffered what today would be called a nervous or emotional breakdown. He returned to bide out his time with Nathan and Maria in their Beacon Street home.

It was here that the frail, small, intense-looking young man with a prominent, fine Roman nose, lay brooding about his fortunes. To cheer up his spirits young ladies were invited to call upon him. One cheerful girl, Mary Ann Cutler, full of good health and abounding with spirit, came down from her stepfather, Jonathan Amory's, house on Park Street to tend to poor William. Within a very short time, William was able to rise from his bed and escort Mary Ann up the hill to home. William Appleton's comment upon his marriage to Mary Ann follows: "I engaged in a matrimonial speculation, the whole result of which is not ascertained. In January 1815, I was married."

During the spring of 1815, William went back into business—the building of ships, and a new venture. "A new insurance company is incorporating—to be underwriting what the New England bank is banking," wrote Nathan of William's new project. William, meanwhile, "was attacked by dyspepsy, so called." The doctors gave him emetics and purges until he soon weighed only 116 pounds. He was quite sensitive about his fragile physique, especially in view of the fact that local tittle-tattle observed that William's dyspepsy took over every time one of his ships was late upon arriving in port.

His wife was expecting their first child when the doctor, baffled by William's state of health, sent him on a journey to Charleston, South Carolina, to recover. William wrote love letters to Mary Ann:

> The time shall not be long, dear Angel, that we are separated and then we shall enjoy life more (if possible) then before we were torn from each other. If any persons were ever more happy than we have been, no one will ever be than we, when I again reach the arm of my much beloved Mary Ann. In my sleep I imagine myself with my wife and boy and when I awake I feel much disappointed to find we are many thousand miles from each other.

He cherished his letter from Mary Ann, reading "more than twenty times" one in which she described how her small son enjoyed sucking a fig which came from Smyrna. "I cannot help thinking how that dear little rascal would look, sucking a fig, but I don't believe he is as pretty as when sucking —— [William's dashes] you know what!"

It had been Maria's frail health that had originally sent Nathan to England. In Manchester, Maria took a cold "while riding in the rain," and during that time her husband visited the great textile mills. To combine business with pleasure or a search for health—a prime precept for

Boston's merchant princes—the Nathan Appletons traveled from Manchester to London to Edinburgh. It was in this city that Nathan encountered Mr. and Mrs. Francis Cabot Lowell (formerly Hannah Jackson), also of Boston. While the two women chatted idly of home and women problems, the two men talked of textile mills. Both men were angry and frustrated by the various embargoes that had plagued their businesses. Why should a young country like America be almost totally dependent on foreign manufactured goods? There was cotton in the South and waterpower as well as ingenuity in New England.

The two men spent many hours in the cotton mills watching their operation. Since Lowell made no drawings and took no notes, the guarded secret of the machinery was considered safe. Appleton was concerned with price, rate of production, quality of products—and profit margin.

When Francis C. Lowell returned from Europe in 1812, he found low-cost land available, plus a defunct power mill for sale in Waltham, a small farming community on the Charles River, nine miles from Boston. With Nathan Appleton, he built the first textile mill, with all the processes from raw cotton to finished cloth constructed under one roof. Their system plus improved machines formed the foundation upon which American textile mills were built at the beginning of the Machine Age.

However, money for the project was not easily come by at first. Lowell's Cabot uncles refused to have anything to do with it because they had

Portrait of the Reverend Charles Lowell, D.D. Engraving by J.W. Orr, N.Y. From *Illustrated American Biography,* ed, by D. I. Nelke (Chicago: The Publishing Company, c. 1895–1900).

been badly burnt with an early attempt at manufacturing cloth in an American mill. They were more than satisfied with the returns they procured from importing cotton cloth from China. Their refusal to participate stymied early financing.

But Patrick Tracy Jackson, a sea captain who had been an apprentice when he was fifteen, supercargo on a merchant ship before he was twenty, then captain's clerk, and finally captain, was interested in the project. After three voyages he retired and set himself up as a merchant in East and West Indian goods. His sister, Hannah, was married to Francis Lowell, and Jackson was the husband of a Cabot. Since the proposed mill was now a family matter, Jackson undertook to assume management. It was Jackson who got Appleton to subscribe for $10,000, and although his commitment was one of the lowest, Appleton was chosen one of the directors of the Boston Manufacturing Company. The company hired a mechanical genius, Paul Moody, who was able to execute the knowledge Lowell had retained in his head and produce wheels of cast iron and spindles whittled out of wood.

There was one problem, however. The product of this new machine didn't sell! It was at this point that Nathan Appleton was called in.

"At the time," wrote Lowell, "when the Waltham Company began to produce cloth there was but one place in Boston where domestic goods were sold. That was a shop in Cornhill kept by Mr. Isaac Bowers or rather Mrs. Bowers." Mr. Appleton went to see Mrs. Bowers, who said, "Everybody praised the goods and had no objection to the price. They just wouldn't buy American-made cotton sheets even though it was thirty-seven inches wide instead of a yard like the goods from India, which it was supposed to imitate."

Nathan Appleton suggested that a "parcel of goods" from the mill be sent to B. C. Ward and Company, a new firm in which he was a partner. Lowell set a price of twenty-five cents a yard.

I found a purchaser, in Mr. Forsaith, an auctioneer, who sold them at auction, at once, for something over thirty cents. We continued to sell them at auction with little variance of the price. I found an interesting and agreeable occupation in paying attention to the sales and made up the first account with a charge of one percent commission. This was purely a nominal charge for time spent in a pleasant occupation—and not an adequate commission but satisfactory under the circumstances. The rate of commission was continued and finally we became the established rate, under the great increase of manufacture. Thus what was at the commencement rather unreasonably low, became, when the amount of the annual sale concentrated in single houses amounted to millions of dollars, a desirable and profitable business.

While Nathan was prospering, William was fighting for his health. Business was bad in Boston. Five firms failed, all of them owing the Appletons money. "September 30, 1816, Monday. A pleasant morning; rose early and went to my Store to make arrangements for sailing in the ship, *Roxanna,* for the Mediterranean." The William Appletons remained in Europe for two years, during which time William saw little that met his approval. He seemed constantly in search of the hardworking, self-respecting middle-class Bostonian, of which he was one. Of the average day in the life of a Sicilian prince in Palermo where he and Mary Ann had a villa, he wrote scornfully:

> They repair to the playhouse at nine o'clock, they have supper in their boxes or in adjacent rooms prepared for the purpose, called conversation rooms, where they gamble till two or three when they retire. They rise about ten, take very little breakfast, then ride a short time, dine at two, take a siesta at four, and again resort to the Marina where they ride till nearly dark. Thus ends twenty-four hours.

Upon his return William bought Nathan's house at 54 Beacon Street. He summed up his advantages:

> During my absence, I expended some Ten Thousand dollars, which sum I made in shipments from Sicily to the United States and in goods from England to Charleston.

Back in Boston he went into business

> with Messers Paige and Chase which continued six years. I made by that concern about thirty thousand dollars and carried on considerable business on my own account, my health feeble, yet able to attend to business.

Of his wife, at this time he wrote:

> My good Wife is happy and deservedly so; she is all that any reasonable man could wish, ever finding friends and so fortunate as not to have any enemies, I have been better satisfied with her the last year in troubles and anxieties than in prosperity; she has strong

powers of mind not brought into action on commone occasions; take her all in all her husband and friends have cause to be proud of her.

This tribute must give us pause to examine the women of Boston who after all did possess the hand that rocked the cradle. If there is a city in America that can boast of the hardihood of its womenfolk, that city is Boston. The women who helped construct the "Athens of America" were strangely Spartan. The Boston lady's resoluteness of character, commencing with the prerevolutionary and Revolutionary days never wavered, regardless of which side of the issue she defended. She was staunch and stalwart. The grandmother of James Russell Lowell, for example, was a Loyalist, and although she continued to live in Boston she never recognized Independence Day; until her death, on this festive occasion she wore mourning, fasted all day, and "lamented our late unhappy differences with His Most Gracious Majesty."

Portrait of George Cabot, U.S. Senator, 1791–1796. Engraving by J. C. Buttre Co., from a portrait in the possession of Colonel Henry Lee, Boston, Massachusetts.

In the nineteenth century—the golden days of Boston families—the Boston woman enacted a sturdy role, both as merchant's mother and sea captain's wife. Married early, the girls often went to sea side by side with their ship captain husbands, and their acts of bravery and heroics were epitomized in the words and actions of one nineteen-year-old bride who, upon witnessing her husband's ship floundering on a shoal in the China Sea, donned his pants and coat, clipped her hair to boyish length and, satisfied with her performance, asked her husband: "There don't I look like a boy?" By impersonating a young man, she felt she could help lower the sails.

In the nineteenth-century Boston woman we find the genus of the women's liberationist. In an era when ladies were subject to the vapors and acted out the poetry of Christina Rossetti and Elizabeth Barrett Browning, the archetype of the nineteenth-century Boston woman was Margaret Fuller, who commented: "It is a vulgar error that love, *a* love, is to a woman her whole existence. She is also born for Truth and Love is their universal energy."

The behavior of the women did not seem to ruffle the dander of the nineteenth-century Boston merchant prince. The "reform" and Puritanical bent of the women rather pleased the men, and the more the men attended to their businesses, the more their energetic wives attended to the business of others. It is possible that the nineteenth-century Boston woman was distressed by a Puritan conscience, which demanded that she exonerate her husband's obsession with obtaining wealth by her personal involvement with "good works." Marriages were made within family circles, where the merchant prince married a member of his class (a merchant princess)—a girl endowed with Jane Austen's "sense and sensibility." This requisite virtue often produced a nerve-racked, tormented, anguished soul.

The chief protagonist of Bostonian women undoubtedly was Margaret Fuller, whose security in her own mental prowess was exemplified in her words: "I know all the people worth knowing in America, and I find no intellect comparable to my own." And, indeed, she was accurate. Her friends consisted of young scholarly students at Harvard rather than merchant princes, and she kept pace with them without effort. After years of living in Rome and exposing herself to the leading intellectuals of the day, including George Sand, among others, she returned to Boston and attempted to make a living for herself by conducting "conversations," discussion groups for other Boston women who aspired to rise above the

Margaret Fuller, from the portrait by Chappel. Courtesy of the Picture Collection, The Branch Libraries, The New York Public Library.

nineteenth-century relations between the sexes in which the woman belonged to the man instead of forming a whole with him. Margaret Fuller urged:

> I wish women to live, first, for God's sake. Then she will not make an imperfect man her God, and thus sink into idolatry. Then she will not take what is not fit for her from a sense of weakness and poverty. Then if she finds what she needs in Man embodied, she will know how to love, and be worthy of being loved.

Although Margaret Fuller is perhaps best known as the pioneer of votes for women, her contribution to society was much greater. She recognized that women's rights were only a subordinate part of the most comprehensive program of nineteenth-century liberation. It was she and her friends who inspired Boston women to support Brook Farm. Also, it was she who gave women the first ultramodern landmark in emancipation—the establishment of the first nursery school in America.

At the final illness of his wife, William Appleton was to write of marriage in Boston's nineteenth century:

It is sad, very sad. I have almost from the commencement of our married life contemplated from my Age and broken Constitution that when we separated I should be the first called—(and it may be so)—and from the time I was making my first will in 1816 She was first considered; I then gave her half the property I might have, and in all the changes since I have ever thought of her comfort and independence when I was gone and provided accordingly. This is the first serious illness she has had during our married life of forty-five years within a few days. We during that period have had many, many blessings. We have lived happily (I think) as the World goes, but I would not be understood to say we always thought alike and that difference of opinion was always expressed in as mild and considerate terms as it should have been. There was never a want of love, confidence, or respect. She always leaned on me. I always loved her dearly and never doubted her affection for a moment. Were I to say there was never a Word passed that was not in harmony, my children, should this come to their eyes, would not give me this credit for sincerity that I wish from them.

Portrait of Elizabeth Frelinghuysen Davis, later Mrs. George Cabot Lodge, mother of Senator Henry Cabot Lodge. Courtesy of the Picture Collection, The Branch Libraries, The New York Public Library.

Two portraits of Isabella Stewart Gardner. Left, pastel by James McNeill Whistler, 1886. Right, oil by Winthrop Sargent, 1888. © *ARTnews Annual*, 1946–1947.

It was William Appleton's son-in-law, T. Jefferson Coolidge, who observed: "I doubt if she could have formed any opinion without knowing his."

This "yes, dear—no, dear" role did not survive much beyond the nineteenth century, when not only did the wife-reformer appear upon the horizon, but the type of marriages consummated became, while still first family marriages, marriages of firebrand origin, in which the militant lady-reformer fighting the merchant prince father image married the rebellious son fighting the same image.

Xantippe might have been the Greek model for the emerging Boston woman, for talk was her weapon. If Socrates wearied of Xantippe's tongue, the latter day merchant prince may have been exhausted with the verbiage that came from his Fuller-indoctrinated female counterpart: "I have urged on Woman independence of Man, not that I do not think the sexes are mutually needed by one another but because in Woman this has led to excessive devotion." What emerged was the complete Boston woman, such as Julia Ward Howe, New York-born author of "The Battle Hymn of the Republic"; Amy Lowell; and the Carys, the Cabots, Sturgises, Shaws, Parkmans, Sears, Lymans, Lodges, Saltonstalls—to list but a few.

Yet, ironically, the woman who had the greatest single impact upon cultural and social nineteenth-century Boston was not this Boston "breed of cat" but a native New Yorker, Isabella Stewart Gardner, who married John Lowell Gardner and became known to Boston and the world alike as Mrs. Jack.

Like Margaret Fuller, hypnotic was the word to describe this woman. She was short of stature and plain to the point of homeliness, yet she attracted artists by the score, and most of them painted her for the sheer pleasure of doing so. When she commissioned John Singer Sargent to paint her portrait she showed her contempt for superficial Boston propriety by posing in a low-cut dress with a rope of pearls around her waist and a black shawl drawn tightly around her hips. Exhibited for the first time at the gentlemanly St. Botolph's Club in the winter of 1888–1889, the picture caused so much comment that her husband had it removed and declared it would never again be exhibited in his lifetime. And, daring as Mrs. Jack was, her portrait was not shown as long as Jack Gardner was alive. Today it is part of the famous collection in Fenway Court, the palace that Mrs. Jack built for herself, in which she hung the art collection she imported from Europe to glorify Boston.

So in the nineteenth century Boston—the city and the men and women who created the city—grew to form a social structure of such a special identity that it could be quipped:

> And this is good ole Boston
> The home of the bean and the cod,
> Where the Cabots talk to the Lowells
> And the Lowells talk only to God.[1]

3

A Money Tree Grows
in Brookline

The forces that created the modern city of Boston originated outside the city's limits; consequently, everything was unexpected and unanticipated. Before the nineteenth century came to an end, Boston housed a pack of people seeking personal gain, "Where everyman is for himself; And no man for all." (Robert Crowley)

Boston had since its founding been accustomed to receiving homeless men who sought its shelter. It had also provided a marketplace for the products of the neighboring countryside. After the transformation of agriculture and industry during the eighteenth century, new needs were thrust upon the city.

Early Boston markets resembled country fairs, with buyers and sellers trading directly with one another. Later, actual contacts became more haphazard as stratagems, monopolies, and political controls were devised in the marketing of the great staples—wine, wool, tea, tobacco, sugar, and spices. The new techniques of buying, selling, and manufacturing created a production far beyond local consumption and involved heavy capital investments, considerable risks, and difficult administrative problems. Two problems faced nineteenth-century Boston: the lack of facilities for shipping, storing, and processing commodities from producer to consumer and the lack of banks with the facilities for accounting and credit that would make the movement of goods feasible.

This new city identity created the Hub, with profound consequences for the internal life of the city and its inhabitants.

Originally, an entire new pattern of alloting space appeared. Churches, meeting places, and monumental structures occupied most of eighteenth-century Boston. The streets were short; there was no reason for them to be longer—for men had little need to travel, since the household was both residence and place of business. Districts were differentiated by occupa-

May Sheep Fair, Boston. Taken from a painting by George Northoues, an actor and scene painter at the Boston Theatre in the early part of the nineteenth century.

tion, class, or religious differences, but the basic unit was a self-contained family unit that had an especially designed place in the corporate life of Boston—even into the middle of the nineteenth century. At that time a reconstruction began, the city was recast, and many of its ties to the past were obliterated. Hills were razed, marshes and lakes were filled in, and shorelines were extended to make way for the limitless grid.

At the beginning of the nineteenth century every travel conveyance was related to the personal or family carriage—even the stagecoaches that charged fares. The first breakthrough was the common carrier, first horse-drawn, then motor-propelled. In time, the wheels rolled above and below the ground, over and under the river. Mass travel had arrived.

With the founding of nearby Lowell as a mill town, transportation became a major factor. In 1825, a Boston to Lowell railroad was proposed. Popular sentiment against such a project was voiced in the *Boston Courier*, "as every person of common sense knows that it would be useless as a railroad to the moon." But rails and engine were transported from England and the same ability that had been used in copying the textile machines was employed—the engines were copied, an American engineer hired, and "after that, Lowell locomotives did as well as English," wrote Charles Francis Adams in his *Memorial History of Boston.*

In 1833 Andrew Jackson visited Boston and Lowell. His chief impression of the famous mills seems to have been the twenty-five hundred mill girls marched two abreast in his honor, forming a parade two miles long. They had on white dresses, blue sashes, and carried parasols. Jackson's pronouncement was, "Very pretty women, by the Eternal!"

When Charles Dickens visited Boston and Lowell in 1842, his impressions were varied. He had no kind words for the Boston and Lowell railroad: "The cars are shabby omnibuses but larger; holding thirty, forty, fifty people. The seats instead of stretching end to end, are placed crosswise. In the center of the carriage is usually a stove fed with charcoal or anthracite coal, which is for the most part red-hot." The train stopped at lonely waystations, where Mr. Dickens saw no one getting on or off, and then it "roared like a mad dragon through the main street of some populous town, waking the echoes, scaring the horses and dashing on pell-mell, neck or nothing, down the middle of the road."

Of the girls working in the mills, Dickens wrote:

> These girls are all well-dressed; and that phrase necessarily includes extreme cleanliness. They had serviceable bonnets, good warm cloaks and shawls; and were not above glogs and pattens. Moreover, there were places in the mills in which they could deposit these things without injury; and there were conveniences for washing. They were healthy in appearance, many of them remarkably so, and had the manners and deportment of young women . . . not degraded brutes of burden. . . .
>
> The rooms in which they worked were as well ordered as themselves. In the windows of some, there were green plants which were trained to shade the eye.

The Boston builders of Lowell and the mills were pleased with Mr. Dickens's comments, and they were pleased with the price of cotton yard goods manufactured in America. In 1816, Waltham sheeting sold for thirty cents a yard. In 1819, it went down to twenty-one cents, and by 1826 to thirteen cents a yard, with a fine profit for the producer. But wages remained static and working conditions became more crowded as consumer demand increased. In time the relationships between management and labor began to cool into hostile, impersonal association before the end of the century.

Boston was no melting pot. Its Anglo-Saxon culture was old and hard. It was still—at the turn of the century—basically a seafaring city, and as such it was a port where a few French and German immigrants had settled and even become a part of Boston proper without being assimilated into the Anglo-Saxon proper Bostonian world. In the mid-nineteenth century a catastrophe occurred in Europe that was to affect the city of Boston perhaps more seriously than any single outside influence, with repercussions that have survived right to this very moment.

In 1845, when Boston was enjoying the peak of its city identity as a young cultural and social center, a potato famine fell like a black shroud over Ireland, closely followed by epidemics of typhus, cholera, and relapsing fever. A blight attacked the Irish potato, the main source of food and money for the Irish farmer, and the farmers stood by, helpless, watching their major source of income and food rot before their eyes. Ill-prepared British civil servants, brave clergymen, charitable landlords, and such groups as the Society of Friends could do little to mitigate a catastrophe that was really rooted in ancient poverty and misrule. Under the scourge of famine, disease, and rack-rent landlords, at least one million Irish fled in desperation to North America, while at least another million died between 1846 and 1849. The tragedy was whole and complete.

Disease dogged the fleeing Irish; the hasty medical examinations on the quay allowed the sick to slip aboard with the healthy and sent fever raging through the packed holes. On their passage to the New World, the Irish suffered a subhuman existence equaling in horror the dread middle passage of the African slave trade. Actually the African Negro slave probably fared better in transit, for he was regarded as valuable property while the Irish were looked upon as worthless chaff. The circumstances of the first Irish mass emigration to America cannot be drawn too starkly. Unlike the adventurers, traders, religious dissenters, and land-seeking yeomen who preceded them, the Irish were an uprooted peasantry from the poorest poorhouse in Europe. They were illiterate because the English had foisted illiteracy upon them. The Irish debarked in America with only the strength of their backs—and only a few had this, for most were ridden with the diseases of filth and poverty.

Numerous Irish immigrants arrived and settled around Boston, with many landing on a small strip of island lying across the Boston Harbor, which was named for its founder, a notorious ne'er-do-well, Samuel Maverick, who in prerevolutionary days had mounted four large cannons to ward off Indians and posted a welcome sign to visitors. Riotous excesses in his public house, plus the hospitality he extended to felons who had escaped the clutches of the law, offended Boston's puritan decorum. But Maverick was the first of the island's line of resourceful politicians. He claimed the elders' wrath, kept his wine-selling license, and even won the island for himself and his heirs. A skirmish during the Revolution won the island fame, but it remained farmland until 1883. In that year, the Cunard Line fixed Boston as the western terminus of its Liverpool run, and a syndicate of Boston land speculators organized as the East Boston Company began laying out streets and lots. Lack of wharf space on old Boston waterfront attracted shipping and shipbuilders to the island. With work available for the strongbodied, many of the Irish immigrants ended their journey where they disembarked.

By 1849, the island had grown to more than nine thousand inhabitants, mostly newly transplanted Irish. The Irish were accused—and not unjustly—of being a drunken lot. They had a reason to seek oblivion in whiskey. Cheated by conniving countrymen, sweated by native employers

Brookline, Massachusetts, from the road, five miles from Boston. From *Gleason's Pictorial Drawing-Room Companion,* July 11, 1854.

Ten million eager immigrants entered the United States between 1860 and 1890. From *The American Past: A History of the United States from Concord to Hiroshima, 1775–1947* by Roger Butterfield (New York: Simon & Schuster, 1947, 1950).

who paid a dollar for fourteen hours' work a day, the Irish were stupefied and constantly bewildered. Wherever the Irish settled they resembled a huddled cove of human beings living without the common necessities that separated man from beast. Boston, which had prided itself on being a clean, healthy city and had not had a major epidemic of smallpox since 1792, suddenly found itself with slums where the pox flourished, along with cholera, typhus, and tuberculosis.

The city was frightened by this horde of Irishmen loosed in its midst. Before the arrival of the Irish, Boston had been a community composed largely of tradesmen, artisans, and merchants. Now it harbored a seemingly inexhaustible supply of men and women who accepted wages and working conditions that local labor scorned. In 1850, of the city's boasted 136,831 citizens, 30,000 were newly settled Irish immigrants, who brought with them a religion that was antipathetic to the religious convictions of the original English settlers.

And so in the nineteenth century there came into existence a Boston with two distinct cultures, with no more contact than if three thousand miles of ocean had separated them, rather than an impregnable wall of ideas. The clash of the newcomers and the incumbents was bitter. Drawn to their own kind by homesickness and shared affliction, the Irish became a clannish foreign element, of whom established Bostonians spoke with mounting alarm.

However, the fact that their city was growing with their wealth did not go unnoticed. Many of the intellectuals were not negative to the physical changes and to the effect of the newcomers upon their way of life. They built parks and playgrounds in addition to their elaborate homes and handsome churches, beautified the Charles River Basin, established a Symphony Orchestra, promoted education, founded a great museum of fine arts, and engaged in numerous charitable enterprises to rectify the ills that city expansion and concentrated wealth had induced.

Habits had changed—radically. No longer was dancing forbidden; in fact, it was almost more essential for every young woman's education than the liberal arts. And, by the turn of the century, every proper Boston gentleman knew how to execute the cotillion, the polka, the quadrille, and the waltz.

So popular did the dance become that the city became the home of the social ball and was called the "Caper City." The father of the All-Age Ball, peculiar to Boston, was not a Bostonian but an Italian count, Lorenzo Papanti. Under the sponsorship of Mrs. Harrison Gray Otis, he established the first dancing academy, housed in palatial quarters on Tremont Street. From 1837 until 1899 four generations of Boston's best people were initiated into the art of the Boston ball beautiful.

In 1845, the famous Boston Assemblies were organized. The assemblies were rigidly formal, with no invitation being issued to anyone outside the First Family circle. The prevailing tone was dignity. A gentleman could never attend without full dress, including gloves, a fine linen handkerchief to be placed between his hand and the back of his dancing partner—and shoe polish with which to shine his dancing pumps in the men's room during intermission. The ladies were resplendent in their traditional black velvet gowns, their heads crowned with diamond tiaras and their necks strangling in ropes of pearls. The only oddity about the balls was the scarcity of youth. Only one or two of the season's debutantes would be invited, and a few very carefully screened stags from Harvard. By the end of the nineteenth century the assemblies had become a Boston business, supervised by S. Hooper Hooper, who gloried in his venture right up to the eve of World War I, when the balls languished.

In the nineteenth century, with walking still socially correct and almost a daily ritual for Boston men and women, Commonwealth Avenue was the scene of a fashion parade—especially on Sunday, when church attendance was a command performance—and a stroll through the Commons mandatory.

As Boston grew physically and the wealth of the families increased, new homes studded the avenues of Boston's finest residential area. After the War of 1812 there was no simplicity to Boston's architecture, nor to the interior decor of its homes, hotels, and public buildings. The new houses (the Alexander Parris-David Sears mansion, which is now the Somerset Club, is an example of this new architecture) had French windows with lacy iron grilles for protection, such as those in New Orleans. In addition, many had second-story balconies that extended the width of the house and were excellent examples of the fine art of wrought-iron decor. The distinctive curves of the floor plans were far removed from the box-square rooms of earlier days when humble craftsmen executed the primitive drawings. Parquet floors abounded, as did marble mantels and carved mahogany doors. Spiral staircases were in style, usually winding up to a small dome of glass, which replaced the cubicle known as the "widow's walk." Front entrances were in black and white marbles, and in some homes imports of pink Carrara marble from Tuscany adorned the threshold. The plaster ceilings were molded in classic designs, and elaborate crystal chandeliers, glittering like crown jewels, quivered overhead. Wallpapers by Dufour of Paris decorated many vestibules, and white, pied, striated marble statuaries embellished the corridors of the mansions. Clearly, the influence of travel abroad was seen everywhere. One visitor described Boston as Edinburgh revisited, another of London, and a third observed that there was no need for any American to visit Rome since Mrs. Jack Gardner had transported the better part to Boston.

The theater, too, was no longer frowned upon for attendance or participation; however, the programs offered were not very stimulating to intellectual taste, although they were highly favored by the socially prominent. The actress of the day was Fanny Kemble, daughter of Charles Kemble, the celebrated Shakespearean actor. Fanny was her father's leading lady and, as a reigning star, she captivated Pierce Butler, a Philadelphia millionaire who owned a vast estate outside of that city as well as a plantation in Georgia.

To have Fanny Kemble Butler as a dinner guest was a Boston social coup. The guest list would be comprised of: A-Appleton, A-Bigelow, A-Cabot, A-Grant, A-Peabody, A-Lawrence, A-Sears, A-Endicott, A-Brooks, A-Perkins, A-Thayer, A-Otis, A-Amory, A-Lowell, A-Lodge, A-Saltonstall, A-Lyman—the A-ffluent Society. Fanny, in her favorite plum-colored

Scene in the Public Garden. Boston, 1874. From *Picturesque America*, ed. by
William Cullen Bryant (New York: Appleton, 1872–1874).

velvet, would be radiant as she and the guests dined on a menu consisting
of cold oysters, sherry wine; brown and white soup, oyster pâtés, hock
wine; boiled and baked fish; boiled turkey, roast mutton, veal with peas
and ham; sweetbreads and croquettes, wine and Roman punch. After
that came two pairs of canvasback ducks, two pairs of grouse, wood-
cocks and quail with salad; blanc mange, jelly, baked and frozen pudding
with ice cream, grapes, pears, apples, oranges, and ornamental sweets
from the confectioner's. Fruits and flowers were placed upon the table
before dinner, and the meal was served by family servants: three black
and two white (Irish).

If the dress, housing, means of travel, source of income, and bill of
fare of Boston families altered during the nineteenth century, so did religion, the ballast of the original state. The Calvinist was replaced first by
the Congregational, which during the eighteenth century became the
church. But as riches poured into the pocketbooks that, too, became too

rigid, too confining. In the nineteenth century the Eliots, the Channings, the Emersons, and the Lowells brought Unitarianism into high partisan flavor. But low church Episcopalianism was encroaching, slowly but surely. As the city was spreading its wings geographically, new churches were being built to satisfy the needs of small individual communities, which would eventually incorporate their turf into metropolitan Boston.

By 1820, too, a new generation of thought permeated Boston. The key to the period seems to be that the mind had become aware of itself. Man grew reflective and intellectual, being released from the search for daily bread and physical safety. He had discovered money and in so doing developed a new consciousness. The early settlers had acted under a belief that a shining social prosperity was the beatitude of man and sacrificed uniformly the citizen to the state. The modern mind believed the nation existed for the individual, for the guardianship and education of every man. The individual became the world. It was the beginning of the age of severance, of disassociation, of freedom, of analysis, of detachment. Every man for himself.

It was also the age of arithmetic and criticism. Astrology, magic, palmistry were gone, and demonology had stalked its last. In the law courts crimes of fraud had replaced crimes of force. The stockholder had supplanted the land-and-war baron. There was a fanaticism in the new philosophy of freedom. Slavery was being questioned; slave labor in the factories raised the intellectual's eyebrow. The growing city was challenged as to its right to existence, its practicality, its moral integrity. Slum areas became threadbare eyesores, and diseases common to such areas spread and claimed the lives of rich and poor alike. There was no escape, regardless of how far the children of the original founders of fortunes fled into the nearby countryside.

It was at this period in Boston that a new belief was born and the voice of transcendentalism echoed first throughout the city, then the land, and eventually the world.

Conventionally, transcendentalism has been viewed as an idyll—a pastoral moment, benign and faintly eccentric, with such idealistic and unrealistic leaders as Henry David Thoreau, and the gentle, dreamy, abstracted Bronson Alcott. Alcott tried the exasperation of those who loved him and to the "Philistines" he was a living symbol of the movement—a man with no thought of the morrow, who blithely let himself be supported by the labor of his wife until his later years, when he basked in the prosperity of his daughter's writings.

The Alcott Family. Left to right, May Alcott, Louisa Alcott, Mr. Alcott, Mrs. Alcott, Anna Alcott. From *The Ladies' Home Journal,* December 1898.

But, in actuality, transcendentalism was less idyllic than has been supposed. It in time became a religion unto itself—passionate, radical, and, in the eyes of its opponents, subversive. It faced an orthodox conformity with vigorous and determined rebellion and was the first of a succession of revolts by youthful Americans against the complacency of their elders.

The emergence of the transcendentalist group came out of individuals who gathered for "conversations." The first meetings were social in form and function. Among the original group of friends were Ralph Waldo Emerson, Margaret Fuller, George Ripley, Orestes Augustus Brownson, Elizabeth Peabody and her sisters, William Ellery Channing, and many less known but equally enthusiastic "friends." They were "like-minded" and were a new class of reformers. Instead of the fiery souls of the early Puritans bent on hanging the Quaker, burning the witch, and banishing the Romanist, these were gentle souls with peaceful and even genial dispositions. Their intellectual staff of learning was the writing of a Frenchman, François Marie Charles Fourier, a member of a bourgeois family, who conceived the idea that the passions of man would, if properly channeled, result in social harmony. To achieve this goal, the artificial restraints of civilizations were to be destroyed. The social organization for such development was to be based on the "phalanx"—an economic unit composed of 1,020 people. Members would live in the community building and work would be divided among the people according to their natural inclinations. The Boston "Savonarola" was the brilliant orator, Theodore Parker.

In their meetings there was always a leader of conversation—a pure, intellectual idealist versed in the writings of Plato, Goethe, Carlyle, and Milton. Often these conversations were incomprehensible to some of the newcomers, and the story is told of the meek, unassuming visitor who raised his hand to ask of Bronson Alcott, "Mr. Alcott, a lady near me desires to inquire whether omnipotence abnegates attribute?"

When the writings of the group appeared in *Dial,* their magazine, and their thoughts were formalized in Brook Farm, the Boston Establishment began to take serious notice of this circle to which they had referred, not without sarcasm, as the "sentimental class." The inhabitants of State Street valued inoffensive people of conventional polish—the clergyman who would live in the city *might* have piety, but *must* have taste. But when a John the Baptist, in the form of a poor printer, appeared, quite scornful of city etiquette, and openly questioned the residents of Boston as to their acquisition of the Yankee dollar and their spending of it, the citizenry began to see the transcendentalists as a group of revolutionaries whose main target was Boston itself and its poisonous environment.

What had happened in Boston was obvious. In the beginning every man had been at liberty to choose his trade. Profit had been open to him; fortunes had been made by the thousands in a proportion never before witnessed in any other city or country. But by the middle of the nineteenth century property had proven too much for the man, and men who were originally of scientific, artistic, or intellectual bent commenced to degenerate into selfish housekeepers, dependent upon wine, coffee, furnace heat, gaslight, and fine furniture. It was inevitable that the course of life would swing in another direction: that civilization had been cowed too soon; that the triumphs of the merchant princes might be treacheries; that the immense city was a big mistake; that nothing could be more vulgar than a great warehouse of rooms filled with imported luxuries. Under the circumstances, perhaps the best thing for the citizenry would be an auction or a great fire. This was Thoreau's doctrine: "Again and again I congratulate myself on my so-called poverty. I could not overstate this advantage."

In an era when materialists, zealots, and skeptics held the balance of power, the transcendentalists' beliefs in perpetual inspiration, the miraculous power of the will, and a birthright to universal good were inflammatory, to say the least.

But the impact of the "like-minded" citizens might not have been so powerful in Boston had not the rumblings of a social disorder beyond comprehension reached thunderous proportions—a civil war, which was to shake the foundations of city and country alike.

The War Between the States, 1861–1865, was not in the true historical sense a civil war, because it was not a class struggle. It was a sectional combat, politically, economically, and psychologically; it was an "irrepressible conflict" brought to the peak of bloodshed by arrogant extremists and blundering statesmen and no longer soluble by peaceful means. In the nineteenth century, when Boston reached its height as the epitome of the industrial and commercial city, its counterpart in the southern section was not a city but the plantation, with an agrarian economy that was dependent upon Negro slaves and a single commodity—cotton. Perhaps the fact that the founders of the first family fortunes in Boston had procured their wealth from trafficking in the import and selling of slaves caused their Puritan consciences to take a high moral tone in their uncompromising attitude toward the slaveholders of the south.

In Boston the transcendentalist gave impetus and support to the abolitionist movement. It is of political and psychological significance that Boston, which was having its own problems in controlling an area and population that knew no boundaries, would look to another site with problems more insoluble; in modern parlance, the neurotic seeking association with the hyperneurotic or the psychotic.

By the nineteenth century the American Anti-slavery Society had established a firm foothold in Boston. It was in nearby Nantucket in 1841 that the son of a Negro slave, Frederick Douglass (who, having been fathered by an unknown white man, took his name from Sir Walter Scott's Douglass in *The Lady of the Lake*), made his famous speech, which established him as an orator and the bellwether of the abolitionist movement in Boston. In 1835, William Lloyd Garrison, the recognized leader of the movement, suffered violence at the hands of a well-dressed Boston mob and in so doing won the moral and financial support of Wendell Phillips, a "proper Bostonian" of first rank.

Probably more than any single individual, Phillips personified the revolutionary who emerged from the established Boston aristocratic hierarchy.

A Harvard graduate, Phillips abandoned his law practice to fight for causes inimical to his own class. Revolted by the mob attack on Garrison and prodded into action by his brilliant young wife, Ann Terry Greene, Phillips delivered an eloquent protest in Faneuil Hall in 1837 on the assassination of the abolitionist editor, Elijah Lovejoy. Even when the war came to an end and the Fifteenth Amendment, which enfranchised the black people, was adopted, Phillips continued his career as an agitator for social reform, becoming a mouthpiece for such unpopular subjects as woman's suffrage, prohibition, abolition of capital punishment, and the rights of labor.

Many problems that confronted Boston following the end of the War Between the States were engendered by the Industrial Revolution. But one problem was unique to Boston. That was the existence of intruders, notably the Irish, who had descended like locusts, turning the North End, once a section of stately residences, into a dangerous, filthy slum area. In 1849 the Boston Committee of Internal Health, visiting the Irish warrens, found horrifying conditions.

> The whole district is a perfect hive of human beings, without comforts and mostly without common necessities; in many cases huddled together like brutes, without regard to sex or age, or sense of decency; grown men and women sleeping together in the same apartment, and sometimes husband and wife, brothers and sisters in the same bed. Under such circumstances, self-respect, forethought, all high and noble virtues die out, and sullen indifference and despair or disorder, intemperance and utter degradation reign supreme.

From their arrival the common ache of loneliness drew the Irish together. In the bright refuge of the corner saloon they assembled in the evenings to sing songs, tell stories, brawl, or quietly remember the blue-green lakes of their sorely missed homeland. They organized societies named for the counties from which they had come and transplanted the politics of Ireland. A consciousness began to evolve, and they took a giant step—that of linking themselves to their adopted country. Talk was natural to the Irish, and they babbled in the shops, in the streets, in the church, and in the saloons, where a man could not die of thirst. In time their talk shifted from remembered grievances to more pertinent issues, such as a badly needed ferry to link East Boston with the mainland.

Now citizens, with their feet rooted in Boston soil, some being veterans

Winter Carnival in Boston, 1882. Coasting on historic Boston Common. Crowds of enthusiastic spectators gathered to watch the sport and spills. Swells from Back Bay in high hats and fur capes mingled with gamins from South Cove. Red stockings and knickerbockers were the vogue for young Americans. From *Leslie's Weekly,* January 28, 1882.

of the Emerald Banner of Volunteers during the Civil War, they began to see the gaslit streets of Boston and their own sad plight through more knowledgeable eyes. They cast their lot with the new, rapidly growing Democratic political party. They entered in toto—a band of blarney, and full of brass. In the person of one Martin Lomasney, an orphan bootblack and a one-time city lamplighter, dubbed "the Mahatma" because of his ability to marshal the electorate of Boston's Ward Eight, they found their clan chief. In shirt-sleeves and battered straw hat, Lomasney received petitioners in his office—the "throne room"—each morning at nine o'clock, dispensing favors to the faithful and retribution to the strayed. His philosophy was simple and direct: "The great mass of people are interested in only three things—food, clothing, and shelter."

Through the seventies and eighties, the Irish mass on the doorstep of Boston stirred and groped upwards. As prescient natives had feared, the weight of numbers was beginning to tell—with a high Irish birth rate and declining mortality, due to improved living conditions, they fast approached a point where they composed half the city's population. The democratic doctrine of mass suffrage and the Irish control of the new city machine ensured ultimate success. By 1885 Hugh O'Brien was elected the first Irish mayor of Boston, and the lowly Irish were whooping across the threshold of political power. In Room 8 of the Quincy House on Brattle Street near Scolley Square, there gathered a group known as the Board of Strategy. They were the "bosses," and their group included Patrick Collins, Joseph Corbett of Charlestown, James (Smiling Jim) Donovan of the South End, John F. (Honey Fitz) Fitzgerald, the darling of the North End, and one Patrick Kennedy.

The success of the Irish in their political conquest of Boston was an inspiration to other foreign groups who gravitated there—Italians, Russian and Polish Jews fleeing Europe, and blacks, who had settled earlier after finding refuge with the abolitionists during the war. Consequently, by the end of the nineteenth century the physiognomy as well as the physiography of Boston had altered radically. The Boston merchant prince Yankee had retreated, left the antechamber, and retired beyond double-locked doors, which by the twentieth century were impregnable and could not be forced open.

The reasons for the decline of Boston at the end of the nineteenth century were complex. One reason was that man's adjustment to city life is a personal trauma presenting many hardships. Rousseau has written: "Of all animals, man is least capable of living in flocks. Penned up like sheep, men lose all. The breath of man is fatal to his fellows. . . . Cities are the burial pit of the human species." The transition of Boston from a corporate rural community to a manifold metropolitan city occurred too rapidly for plan or control. The persistence of the rural model had prevented nineteenth-century Bostonians from thinking of the city as a whole; they wished to bring to the city the commodious features of their landed estates. They expected the city to provide them with elegant squares to set off their luxurious homes, with picturesque monuments to their ancestors, with parks and boulevards to supply a backdrop for Sunday fashion parades. Mass transportation concerned them not, and when it became apparent that the ground under their feet and homes would have to be uprooted to accommodate transport lines to their mills, the cornerstones of their fortunes, they merely moved on to nearby areas where they could continue to enjoy manorial splendor.

The Italian Quarter, Boston. From *Harper's Magazine*, November 1899.

Meanwhile, a displaced peasantry seething with anxieties was not an easy problem with which to cope. Only a scattering of Boston's intelligentsia recognized the fact that these newcomers needed to interpret their lives by seeing themselves as actors in a meaningful drama, and since it was inconceivable that they should be conquering heroes, they must readily visualize themselves as victims. Victims of whom? Usually the abstract "big business."

Nineteenth-century socialism offered the factory workers and craftsmen a belief; the class struggle explained their present dilemma and offered a hope for the future. But in the city structure at the end of the nineteenth century there were hundreds of thousands of men and women whose destinies were still linked to the past—shopkeepers, clerks, casual laborers, the chaotic mass of middle-class humans who were without function but who did not seek or want the future; they wanted the security of homes and families and blood communion they had never actually had or had lost in their emigration. They sought a miracle and in their eagerness became gullible victims of nationalistic, racist, religious, or semi-religious fantasies of every sort.

By 1875 there were two distinct interpretations of the effect of the modern city upon man's personality. One saw man struggling in the city jungle where life was hard and inhuman, but where human heart and mind were so tested that emotions were deeper and reasons more acute than elsewhere. In the era that gave birth to the Darwinian concept of the survival of the fittest, it was only natural that the idea of a new, superior

The Jewish Quarter, Boston. From *Harper's Magazine*, November 1899.

man evolving in the struggling environment of the city would have appeal. The other interpretation was to romanticize the least lovely aspects of the city, its slums, its ruthless competition, and its grinding order. With the hard stone of the city streets providing the stage, the historian providing the script.

Boston was no exception to the changes cities had incurred since their founding. The classic city, according to Aristotle, was a place where men dwelt together in order to pursue a noble purpose. Athens was that city. In its original concept Boston had tried to emulate Athens. Then there came the medieval city, which, insofar as it was beautiful, was a City of God. Rome was that city. And with its churches and public buildings, Boston had also tried to copy that Rome. But Boston was, in its final form, born out of a new age—the age of industrialism, the Machine Age. Boston was indeed that nineteenth-century city, complex and contradictory.

It was a city that was to learn that its persistence as a rural model was vulnerable to an ever-changing world, where daily problems had to be faced realistically and with flexibility. The past could not be recaptured. In the twentieth century the suburb would be esteemed over the city, the house over the suburb, and the automobile over the house. The money tree of Boston was transplanted to Brookline at the turn of the century, but the hub of the area was rooted in Boston. The narrow streets would widen into expansive roads, the roads into intricate, speed-oriented highways, but they would have their origin in Boston and would ultimately have to return to the narrow cobbled streets.

4

The Adams
since the Eve

In 1636, off the coast of Cowes in Old England, a ship filled with passengers set sail for New England. The cast of travelers anticipated at best a voyage of seven weeks providing all went well, eight to ten if the wind was unfavorable. During the journey the ship would be full of signs of distress—fumes, fever, vomiting, dysentery, heat, headaches, constipation, scurvy, and mouthrot. Add to this a shortage of food, as well as such troubles as lice, which often had to be scraped off the bodies of the ailing.

The sea surged and raged so that waves of icy water swept over the ship, tossing the passengers from side to side. To survive the people tied themselves to their cots, praying aloud that their destination would be reached and once ashore they could begin a new life in a new land—America. It was this ultimate goal that encouraged the men and women to endure the long passage of suffering—a goal in which the destiny of a single man was linked to the future of many men, in many generations to come.

Aboard that ship in 1636, bound for Boston, was one young farmer, Henry Adams. In the year that the first Adams set foot in Boston, Harvard College was founded and in the crystal ball of life the future of the Adams family, the heirs of Henry, were to be intermingled with Boston, the city, and Harvard, the institution of learning. In the course of human events the three would become synonymous.

The first Adams took up his duties as a farmer in Braintree on the outskirts of Boston proper, a locale which would in a very short time be named Quincy and would become the fountainhead of the Adams family of Boston, a family which has certainly, historically, been the first family of Boston since the eve of the Revolution.

Engraving of Samuel Adams from the painting by Chappel.

Henry Cabot Lodge. Photograph
from the Clined Institute,
Washinton, D.C.

In a city whose history is based upon a familial structure, a city in
which an orphan would be predestined to ignominy, to accord the
Adamses this role of distinction is not a simple decision. When one
considers families, such as the Lowells, with notable poets Amy and
Robert; the Cabots, from merchant prince George to Henry Cabot Lodge;
the Holmes; the Appletons; the Forbes; the Peabodys—to mention just
a few—the accolade is of significant importance.

The award is bestowed not because an Adams was president of the
United States before a Cabot had set up shop in Boston, before a Lowell
had built a textile mill, and before a Forbes had shipped out to sea. The
importance of the Adams family is not based entirely upon the fact that
the family, in a space of less than two centuries, produced two presidents,
two signers of the Declaration of Independence, and three ministers to
England—a record unmatched by any single American family. The importance lies in the very being of the Boston Adamses—a family that,
since it set foot upon these shores, has not failed to produce at least one
man of outstanding prominence in each generation. The high intelligence
quotient of the family has existed from the outset (John Adams possessed
an I.Q. of 165, which placed him in the first rank among the inhabitants
of the Hall of Fame).

From farmer Henry to Reverend Joseph, it took the first Adamses three generations to make Harvard. Once Joseph became a minister— the epitome of social prestige in the seventeenth and eighteenth centuries —the Adamses were marked for social success, for Harvard was the open sesame to social recognition in Boston from the day of its founding. Within two generations the Adamses were on their way to making history.

It commenced with Samuel (1722–1803) who, more than any single man, represents the Revolution and the "radical." When we think of the town meeting hall, we visualize Samuel Adams, and when we focus upon the Boston Tea Party we see Sam, with his eggshaped noggin painted in Indian warrior streaks and covered with a headband of turkey feathers, his humpty-dumpty body half-naked, and his quivering hand wielding a tomahawk as he shouted unintelligible war whoops. We are momentarily lost in the past and are proud to glorify the radicals, who threw the tea into the Boston Harbor.

Of all the Adamses, Sam alone had the common touch. A brewer by vocation, he was an excellent organizer by avocation. He was one of the original demagogues, speaking against the crown on behalf of the discontented. He wrote furiously, protesting the Stamp Act and pamphleteering for the natural rights of man. With John Hancock he organized the Sons of Liberty and continued stirring up lethargic patriots. A price was put upon his head, but when the Revolution was over and he proudly signed the Declaration of Independence, he became governor of Massachusetts. He never lost his revolutionary spirit and was something of a problem to the other members of his family. His cousin John, a more conservative and a more likely head of the family, rebuked Samuel for being "too attentive to the public and not enough to himself and family." Of all the Adamses, Sam alone gave love to the people and in return received from them a love that was demonstrated when, as Boston's tax collector, he became forty thousand dollars in arrears to the city. Sam was honest but improvident; yet it never occurred to the citizens of Boston that Sam would not repay every cent—which he did, even though it forced him to live until his death in a state he described as "honorable poverty."

It is this quality of integrity, combined with intelligence, that stamps the Boston Adamses as a family of incredible consistency. The role of the Adams family in Boston's social history is unique, for they have never followed the vagaries of social dictum—they have consistently performed as Adamses. Of all of the families of Boston they alone have never wavered in loyalty to the homeland their forefather, Henry, chose when

John Adams. Engraving by
Copley and Stephenson.

he departed from England. There are no Tory scars, no French alliances, no southern sentimentalities. They have always put their country first, Boston and themselves second, and though they have been accused of seeking the limelight throughout America's political history, they have never basked in the light or traded upon its importance, either for social prominence or material gain.

Because of Samuel's iconoclastic personality, there has always been a veil of sadness over the Adams's countenance, and they have been regarded as the "unhappy Adamses." Actually, this is a name they brought upon themselves because of their tendency to remain aloof from society, and therefore, not to be understood. They have been considered inhibited and refined. Their lack of social graces established a characteristic so familiar that it has been aped by lesser Bostonians as being typically "Bostonian." Their proverbial tactlessness was described by James Russell Lowell, who said, "The Adamses have a genius for saying even a gracious thing in an ungracious way."

Although Samuel's cousin John had a much happier social life than Sam and a much more glamorous political career, he was pictured by a contemporary as "the most ungracious man I ever saw." He was plump, florid, and vain, and as a result of the family's intermarrying there has emerged the "Adams look." The Adamses are, for the most part, shorter than most proper Bostonians. They have "broad foreheads, sharply cut features, keen eyes, and bulldog jaws." However, their faces depict their intellectual power, iron will, and placid but grim determination. Their bodies, while shorter than their compatriots', are nevertheless built for longevity. Their average life-span is eighty-one years, and no Adams has ever been regarded as retired until he is asleep in his grave; even from the graves rumblings continue to reverberate into the present day. Theirs is not a family to be easily silenced.

John's political career began after he graduated from Harvard, moved from his homesite, Braintree, to Boston, and was assigned the unpopular task of defending the British captain tried for murder following the Boston Massacre. He was opposed to the British measures that were leading to the Revolution, but he was a conservative rebel. He was an elected delegate to the First Continental Congress and proposed George Washington as commander in chief of the Continental troops, bypassing his fellow Bostonian John Hancock, whom he snubbed with the words, "an empty barrel"—an epithet which neither influenced people nor won John Adams a friend. His real reason for ignoring Hancock and transferring the burden of revolutionary warfare from Boston was based upon his desire to bind Virginia more tightly to the patriot cause. Following the Revolution, John Adams was America's first European diplomat, but he experienced a thorny career. After his efforts to obtain loans and penetrate the British coldness he returned to Boston somewhat deflated. At home he was elected to serve as vice-president with Washington, and in the 1796 election Adams succeeded Washington as president.

Above everything else, Adams was a balance wheel between the conflicting personalities and philosophies of two men whose images loomed in gigantic proportions upon the screen of early American history—Alexander Hamilton and Thomas Jefferson. Adams's administration was one of crisis and conflict, and he steered the ship of state with honest and stubborn integrity. He was despised by the Jeffersonian Democrats, and in the flourish of Jeffersonian democracy that swept the country Adams was defeated in the 1800 presidential election campaign and retired to his birthplace, now named Quincy. (In 1946 the Adams mansion was given to the nation as a historic site.)

In his retirement, Adams wrote many political treatises and kept up a continuous correspondence with his political adversary, Thomas Jefferson. Ironically both men died on the same day—Independence Day, July 4, 1826. Adams was eighty-one years of age, Jefferson, eighty-three.

Possibly no two patriots could better illustrate the problems with which future generations would be plagued than Adams and Jefferson. From the agrarian world of Monticello, run by slaves on a little empire basis, to the confines of narrow-streeted Boston with its growing metropolitan identity with industrial power, a formidable distrust was germinating. That never the twain should meet seemed to be the handwriting both men saw on the wall of the new nation. For both men, this schism was too backbreaking a task to resolve.

In addition to his early struggle for political life, John also had a long hard courtship before he married the girl of his choice, Abigail Smith. Abigail's mother was born a Quincy and considered her daughter far too good for the likes of John Adams, a farmer's son. She did everything within her power to forestall the romance, but to no avail. Nine years after leaving Harvard, John married Abigail and brought to the Adamses their first social asset and a woman who today is regarded as the most illustrious wife any Adams has had—and one of the first "first ladies" in American history.

Abigail Adams.

Abigail was a lively, sensitive girl whose health as a child had been so delicate that she never attended school. In time she was to become the chief figure in her husband's administration and one of the most influential women in American history. "No man has ever prospered in the world without the consent and cooperation of his wife." Certainly her words bore fruit for John, her "dearest friend" as she addressed him in their now famous letters of correspondence, who prospered mightily with Abigail by his side. The Pygmalion story was reversed; instead of the man creating a Galatea, Abigail created a "natural aristocrat" out of her farmer lover.

That they were establishing an American aristocracy in the name of Adams did not go unheeded by John, who wrote to Abigail in 1780: "I must study politics and war that my sons may have the liberty to study mathematics and philosophy . . . in order to give their children a right to study painting, poetry, music, architecture, statuary, tapestry and porcelain." In the future generations the prophecy came true—but before the Charles Francis Adams trio descended upon the world there was John Quincy Adams, son of Abigail and John.

Bostonians have a habit of labeling—the Puritan of Puritans, the Yankee of Yankees, the Bostonian of Bostonians, the merchant of merchants. In such a category John Quincy becomes the Adams of Adamses. He was unquestionably the ablest of the Adamses, the most tireless worker, the most uncivil of a peculiarly uncivil family, and the most austere in personal habits.

John Quincy Adams's political life began when, as a young man, he accompanied his father on missions to Europe, and served as secretary to Francis Dana in Russia before returning home to graduate from Harvard. Washington made him minister to the Netherlands, and during his father's administration he was minister to Prussia. In 1803 he became a Federalist senator, but his independence of mind led him to support Jefferson's Louisiana Purchase and the Embargo Act. His constituents were enraged, and he was forced to resign. He was sent as minister to Russia and was extremely popular at the tsarist court, but the Napoleonic Wars eclipsed Russian–American relations. It was not until he was appointed as minister to Great Britain that his diplomatic skills were recognized. Soon his political identity rose above the limits of Boston, and even the United States. President James Monroe made him secretary of state, and perhaps his most remarkable document was the Monroe Doctrine, formulated in 1823.

Engraving of John Quincy Adams from the original painting by Chappel.

In 1824, Adams was a candidate for president of the United States, along with Andrew Jackson and Henry Clay. There was no majority and the choice fell to the House of Representatives, where Clay supported Adams and he was made president. As president his political character was solid sterling, but his personal unpopularity was unrivaled. He actually seems to have shunned popularity like the plague. Whereas his mother, Abigail, had made her husband into something of a social success and their reign at the White House was proper and even brilliant—they sponsored musical soirées and salons of social and political repartee—the reign of John Quincy and his wife followed the criterion of Boston Puritanism removed from Beacon Hill to the White House.

While in England, John Quincy married a girl who was an "internationalist," Louisa Catherine Johnson. Her mother was English, and her father American. She had spent her childhood in France and until her death felt herself a stranger in a strange land, both in Quincy, Boston, and in Washington. Louisa was no social pusher, and John Quincy was no man to be pushed. All of the rules and regulations established by Louisa's famous mother-in-law were unheeded. John Quincy was invulnerable to pleas, tears, and Louisa's pathetic attempts to adjust to what she termed a miserable life. John Quincy was no mixer. His one contribution to high life in Washington was the setting up of a billiard room—a gesture that provoked as much criticism in his day as did Truman's building of his front porch years later. People were shocked to learn that the president of the United States was a billiards fan. He played by himself, and he claimed that the game gave him a sort of "grim pleasure."

John Quincy Adams's ascetic way of life was formed in his young manhood. He was known to rise at three A.M., read five Books of the Bible, take a predawn hike of five miles and a nude, hour-long swim.[1] He refused to play cards when "stakes were so high as to constitute gambling." At fourteen, when he was in Paris, he fell in love with an actress who was scarcely older than he. He dreamed of her nightly for seven years, though he never spoke to her on or off the stage. He avoided any possible confrontation, for he felt he could not abstain from declaring his love for her. He wrote: "I learned from her the lesson of never forming an acquaintance with an actress to which I have since invariably adhered and which I would lay as an injunction to all my sons." In his policy of injunction, the sons of John Quincy Adams wishing to attend the theater in Boston had to walk from Quincy to the theater and back—

a distance of ten miles—which curtailed the danger of romantic proclivities with ladies of the stage. Another of John Quincy's rules was never to allow the family carriage to be used for recreational purposes—hence the Adams's afternoon or morning walk for pleasure became a family custom and a familiar Boston and Quincy sight.

One characteristic of the Adams men is their complete lack of identification with the masses. They are individualistic to the degree of eccentricity (the pronoun "we" rarely appears in their writings). In their political careers they have been selected by the people and have been for the people—but never *of* the people. This frigid, glacierlike quality kept both Adamses from being elected to the office of president for a second term despite their honorable, conscientious, and, in some instances, brilliant careers. They lacked the common touch of the redblooded politician. Some possibly regard their attitude as snobbery, but in the true meaning of this word it cannot be applied to the Adamses. Intellectual discrimination in selecting of acquaintances can be attributed to the members of the family—but social snobbism never. For example, the Adamses were quite aware that, with the growing social complexity of Boston, Quincy represented the wrong side of the railroad tracks—but they continued to make Quincy the seat of the family home long after other families had fled to Beacon Hill or the Back Bay area.

In a city where money has always been the prime factor in the prominence of a family and its claim to social distinction, it is interesting that the Adamses—the first family—paid little attention to the accumulation of wealth. Not until Charles Francis I, the son of John Quincy and Louisa, married Abigail Brooks, daughter of Boston's first millionaire, Peter Chardon Brooks, was the family on a financial footing of firmly rooted substance—inherited wealth.

When he left the White House, John Quincy returned to Quincy and for eight successive terms he was elected to Congress, where he served humbly and with a very small remuneration. (He refused an appointment to the Supreme Court, declaring he was unfitted for the position.) The departure from the White House had but one befitting aspect, and that was that poor Louisa had the new White House audience chamber thrown open for dancing at her last "Drawing Room." Such an occurrence had never before happened in America, and there is a special quality in the fact that it was Louisa Adams who achieved this bit of personal fame as a parting gesture. What John Quincy said at this time was not recorded for posterity. The other side of the picture was pitiable. Bankrupt, with

Louisa Catherine Adams. From *The Presidents of the United States, 1789–1898* by John Fiske (New York: Appleton, 1898).

all of his property mortgaged in both Quincy and Boston to pay off his debts, John Quincy Adams, sixth president of the United States, nevertheless served his country for seventeen years, until he was struck down by a fatal stroke on the floor of Congress.

To step into the shoes of his illustrious father and grandfather was not an easy gesture for young Charles Francis. Even if the spirits of his ancestors did not haunt him, he was encircled in the city of his birth with physical monuments to their greatness. The Smithsonian Institution in Washington became an actuality because of his father's love of science, and the family name was not only familiar in Boston, Washington, and New York but was held in high respect in London, Paris, Warsaw, and even Moscow. When young Charles graduated from Harvard—where he studied under Daniel Webster—he entered the practice of law in Boston, a city where change was occurring almost daily. And, not only was change pushing Boston into a new identity, but the same change was creating the schism between the North and the South foreseen by his grandfather.

Bearing an uncanny resemblance to his father, Charles Francis was equally taciturn and regarded as no more companionable. He was engrossed in writing, devoted a great deal of spare time to composing articles on American history, and founded and edited the Boston *Whig*. He represented his father's district in Congress, became a Republican leader of note, and was drafted for the vice-presidency on the Free-Soil ticket.

On the advice of General Seward, Abraham Lincoln appointed Charles Francis minister to Great Britain, where he executed what is today regarded as one of the masterful feats of diplomatic history—keeping England from entering the fracas of the War Between the States on the side of the Confederacy. Probably as much as any single deed outside the heroism on the bloodsoaked battlefields, this performance kept the Union intact. In a city whose physical design he knew well—much of Boston had been copied on the appearance of London—Charles Francis Adams stood alone and indomitable. With the newspapers calling for England's help to the Confederacy, with *Punch* making caricatures of Lincoln and his advocate, Charles Francis Adams, the gelid, anchoritic man remained implacable, totally undisturbed.

But, as his son and then secretary has written in *The Education of Henry Adams,* he didn't care. He seemed to possess a singular and distinct mental poise, which made it possible to see his difficult job through to the end. It is now fact that he despised English society—writing home as he did that he "had not been to a single entertainment where there was any conversation I care to remember." He remained until the end of his life "one of the exceedingly small number of Americans" to whom the titles of duke, duchess, prince, princess, even king and queen were meaningless. Victoria, Her Royal Highness, presented to Charles Francis Adams "nothing more than a slightly inconvienient person." A troublesome fly on the leathery hide of an elephant!

When Charles Francis Adams retired from active public life, he rusticated in style (thanks to his wife's fortune) and commenced to enjoy life in the true Adams manner—writing, editing, and publishing family letters and papers. He wrote the life of his grandmother, Abigail, and edited her letters; he wrote the life of his grandfather and edited ten volumes of his private papers; and he wrote his own autobiography. At the end of his life, with a satisfaction that was not smug but an honest self-evaluation, he observed: "I am now perfectly willing to go myself. My mission is ended and I may rest."

Charles Francis Adams left four sons, each of whom, in separate paths, were to add glory to the name. They were John Quincy II, politician; Charles Francis II, businessman (he exposed the corrupt financing of the Erie Railroad, and he also reformed the local public school system so that the Quincy system of education was widely adopted); Henry Brooks Adams, whose *Education* is unquestionably regarded as the greatest autobiography in American letters and one of the world's classics; and Brooks, author of *The Law of Civilization and Decay,* in which he militantly criticized his own capitalistic age. One of Brooks's earlier and lesser-known books, *The Emmigration of Massachusetts,* was as explosive to Boston as a Molotov cocktail. It attacked the works of the popular John Gorham Palfrey and his school of "filio-pietistic" clerical historians.

This burial-eulogy type of history was slain by the pen of Brooks Adams. It has never reappeared.

Of the four sons, John Quincy II was a bit of the chip of his ancestral progenitor rebel, Sam. He was one of the rare Adamses who carried a wee aura of conviviality about his person. He made friends easily and was generally regarded as a good fellow—a rare tribute for an Adams. In a predominantly Republican "society" world, John Quincy became socially conscious and joined the ranks of the Democrats. He rose, in time, to be the leading Democrat in the state of Massachusetts. In addition to all of his other eccentricities, he refused what is probably the highest honor accorded to a Bostonian, the presidency of Harvard. This was a confounding performance—even for an Adams. However, it was not the first time Harvard had been rebuked by an Adams. The old John Quincy Adams, in one of his typically tactless remarks, went out of his way to chide Harvard's honorary degree to Andrew Jackson, president of the United States, as an "insult to learning." Although Jackson was the man of the hour and the hero of the day, he was, nevertheless, in the eyes of his beholder, John Quincy Adams, an illiterate—a country bumpkin who "could hardly spell his own name."

> Under the shadow of the Boston State House, turning its house on the back of John Hancock, the little passage called Hancock Avenue runs, or ran, from Beacon Street, skirting the State House grounds to Mount Vernon Street, on the summit of Beacon Hill; and there in the third house below Mount Vernon Place, February 16, 1838, a child was born and christened later by his uncle, the minister of the First Church, after the tenets of Boston Unitarianism, as Henry Brooks Adams.

As he states:

> Had he been born in Jerusalem under the shadow of the Temple and circumcised in the Synagogue by his uncle, the high priest, under the name of Israel Cohen, he would scarcely have been more distinctly branded, and not much more heavily handicapped in the races of the coming century, in the running for such stakes as the century was to offer; but, on the other hand, the ordinary traveller, who does not enter the field of racing, finds advantage, in being, so to speak, ticketed through life, with the safeguards of an old, established traffic.

So opens *The Education of Henry Adams*, the story of the most introspective of the Adamses and the most talented from a literary standpoint.

In some of the most beautiful English ever written, Henry Adams's tour de force describes his unsuccessful efforts to achieve intellectual peace in an age when the force of the dynamo is dominant. In between the covers of this remarkable manuscript is the true story of Boston and Boston's first family: the dissensions of inbred Calvinism in conflict with the encroachment of materialism; the resistance between the natural man and a stingy, hostile universe. His is the story of a man surviving in a world where joys were few, his greatest being the pleasure of learning to love to hate. The shadow of Cromwell still loomed, resistance to something was still the law of the land, and we live through Henry Adams the dilemma of an eighteenth-century Bostonian standing in the nineteenth century with one foot stepping precariously into the twentieth.

The unpredictability of the Adams family is another trait. The fifth-generation Charles Francis returned again to the folds of the Republican party. He followed in the family tradition by becoming secretary of the navy in the cabinet of Herbert Hoover and conducting himself ably. But where his father had rejected the presidency of Harvard, he eagerly accepted the role of treasurer. And where his great-grandfather uncomplainingly faced his enormous debts following his term as president of the United States, Charles Francis III complained of his two years' service as mayor of Quincy with a salary of $1,000 per year: "I can't afford politics."

However, the Adamses of the sixth generation have a fine name in Boston for philanthropy and charity. They are now a large, sprawling family, and the role of the present-day Adamses is custodian of the family itself. Perhaps they have deserved this semiretirement, but it is almost inconceivable for any historian to anticipate a generation of American history without the name Adams in the cast of characters—if not in the lead, certainly in one of the more important supporting roles.

It is sheer irony that the city that has nurtured the Adamses, loved their contrariness, reveled in their accomplishments, was never genuinely liked by any of the members of the family. Perhaps the purity of the Adamses was too reminiscent of their Puritan past for Boston. In their intellectual honesty the Adamses could not fathom nor tolerate the hypocrisy of Boston, nor the society it encouraged. The early Adamses knew their shortcomings, especially in regard to manners and speaking. They tried, unless sore pressed, not to say the wrong thing, just to remain silent and say nothing. It is possible that the great diplomatic coups of the early Adamses were accomplished by this Adams theme. One feels their attitude toward Boston by their stubborn refusal to move into the neighborhood of Beacon Hill where they belonged.

But the younger Adamses were not so reticent about Boston. Even as a small boy, Henry Adams found himself drawn to the world of Quincy rather than the Beacon Hill world of his millionaire grandfather, Brooks. In regard to the Boston of State Street, Henry wrote: "For two hundred years every Adams from father to son had lived within sight of State Street . . . yet none had ever been taken kindly to the town, or been taken kindly by it." His brother, Charles Francis Adams II, was even more critical: "Boston is provincial. It tends to stagnate." He found Boston society "self-conscious" and "senseless." He observed, "I have summered it and wintered it; tried it drunk, tried it sober; and drunk or sober, there's nothing in it, save Boston!"

Perhaps the most successful from a business point of view of all the Adamses, this Charles Francis held his business acquaintances in Boston in low esteem. "I have known and known tolerably well, a good many 'successful' men—big financially—men famous during the last half century and a less interesting crowd I do not care to encounter." To him they were "mere moneygetters," men "essentially unattractive and uninteresting." In his summing up, he wrote: "Not one that I have ever known would I care to meet again, either in this world or in the next."

Henry in his latter days was so disdainful of Boston that he retired to live in Washington, although Washington held painful memories for him of the years he spent in residence with his wife, once one of Washington's most charming hostesses, who became mentally disturbed and committed suicide. (It is generally regarded that Henry's avoidance of mention of his wife in his *Education* is based upon the fact that the tragedy was too painful for him to write about.) Henry enjoyed thrusting barbs at Boston and Boston society. He, too, turned down an offer to be a part of Harvard in a teaching capacity. He declared that he knew "nothing of history, less about teaching, and too much about Harvard." About his peers at Harvard he wrote, "Several score of the best educated, most agreeable, and personally the most social people in America have united in Cambridge to make a social desert that would starve a polar bear."

What is the explanation of the Adamses and their relation to Boston? The answer is as inexplicable as the city itself and as complex as the individual members of the famous family. Between the two, perhaps, lies the enigma of the city character. Perhaps the Boston Samuel Adams saw in a dream failed to materialize, and the heirs, while making their contributions to the greatness of the city's reputation, sought anonymity in the nearby countryside. Boston was restraint, law, unity; winter confinement; straight, gloomy streets. Quincy, only seven miles away, was liberty, diversity, outlawry. The intense blue of the sea, the cumulus skies on a rare afternoon in June, in contrast to the cold grays of November skies and the thick muddy thaws of Boston streets were the opposites that attracted and repelled.

But perhaps the real explanation lay in the characters of the Adamses as seen through the eyes of a Virginia-bred cousin, James Truslow Adams, also a historian of note. He is very concerned with the Adamses' characteristic of self-dramatization. Since the very beginning they have always in their imaginations played the leading parts in whatever situations they found themselves and always exaggerated in their own minds the odds against them. In the *Education,* for example, Henry's critics have pointed out that much of the subject matter of the book is a single complaint on why he, Henry Brooks, is not president, fulfilling the "destiny that shapes our ends." To Henry, and to any Adams, James Truslow points out, competition is no mere matter of choice:

> A competitor is not merely a competitor; he is a malignant enemy, come from the Devil to destroy the noblest work of God. Circumstances that may oppose the plan are not accidents, they are damnable efforts on the part of society to thwart the Adams.

In the Adams family we see an almost pure, unadulterated descendant of the early Puritan ministers and Boston fathers. To them, nineteenth-century Boston was a grievance, a compromise with Satan.

> In reading innumerable entries in the *Diaries* of John and John Quincy, as well as the *Autobiography* of Charles Francis and *Education* of his brother Henry in the last generation we are reminded of the *Diary* of Cotton Mather, whose vituperative vocabulary was even more copious, whose opponents were always "vile fools" "tools of Satan" and against whom the forces of society and Hell itself were arrayed when anyone mildly disagreed with him. If indeed, it is an aspect of Puritanism, for if one is elect of God what must, necessarily, one's enemies be? The inference to be made is of the simplest sort. To identify one's self with God is greatly to complicate one's social relations. (*The Adams Family,* by James Truslow Adams)

5

A Rose Is a Rose
Is a Kennedy

In October 1848, in Duganstown in County Wexford, Ireland, one Patrick Kennedy, aged twenty-five, received the blessings of the priest from the church at Ballykelly, left the tiny thatch-roofed cottage in which he had been born, and tramped down the dirt road along the Barrow River to the seaport of New Ross six miles away. New Ross was a bustling town of fifteen thousand people, and the port, in that century, was the busiest in Ireland. Emigrants flooded the streets, carrying their possessions in bundles and wheelbarrows as they trudged to the quays and the departing ships. The going price was twenty dollars. Patrick Kennedy paid it and took steerage passage on a packet ship headed for Boston. The actual site of destination was a matter of indifference to him and to the one hundred and fifty thousand other Irish who set sail for America in 1848. The large, coarse "horse" potato or "bumper," was eaten by man and beast alike until 1845 when the crop failed, and poverty beyond human imagination swept over the land of Eire. A few families such as the Kennedys had survived, but the chances for a young man to earn a decent livelihood and raise a family were slight. Young Patrick Kennedy decided to seek his fortune elsewhere.

In addition to his twenty dollars (a fortune in impoverished Ireland), young Patrick was staking his life in a gamble in which tens of thousands lost. Most of the vessels in the emigrant traffic were fragile and pitifully small, generally in the three-hundred-ton class. The low fare, usually sent by some relative who had preceded the newcomer, guaranteed that the least seaworthy craft would be used for the passage. The greed and callousness of shipowners and the negligence of British authorities ensured that the ships would be dangerously overcrowded. As Patrick Kennedy walked up the gangplank in New Ross, there was roughly one chance out of three that he would not live to become an American citizen.

John F. Fitzgerald.

The year before, more than thirty-eight thousand Irish emigrants sailing in British bottoms to Canada died before reaching their terminal or shortly thereafter. The ships which hauled the Irish outcasts were aptly called "coffin ships."

The slow voyage westward lasted six to seven weeks in good weather. Most of this time was spent in cramped spaces below deck, where a man could not stand up without stooping. Most travelers carried their own rations—to have to seek food from the captain meant surrendering money and worldly goods. Water turned rank during the long journey and could only be drunk by adding steadily larger doses of vinegar to kill the odor. Some of the vessels stored their water supply in old wine casks in order to save money, but large quantities became undrinkable. Sanitation was primitive, and reeking privies turned the atmosphere foul and suffocating. During rough weather, passengers were imprisoned in the dark, dank steerage for days on end; nerves rubbed raw, men burst forth in murderous fights, while women and children stood by and stared with wide-eyed amazement and terror.

When Patrick Kennedy finally reached American shores, he was ill prepared to make an entrance into an advanced society. He possessed the skills of a farm laborer; but he was illiterate, as were most Irishmen, for the British had imposed illiteracy upon the Irish under the oppressive Penal Law. These laws stripped the Irish Catholics of civil and religious rights, including the right to keep and attend school. Since the seventeenth century, generations of Irish had snatched what learning they could from schoolmasters who taught secretly in fields and hedgerows. The result was a learning that consisted of myth, superstition, and tall tales of heroism and romance, burnished by the tongues of generations of storytellers, whose ramblings were intensified by the consumption of poteen—the Irish whiskey, which was illegal but plentiful.

All that Patrick Kennedy brought to Boston was the strength of his back—which was enough when he stepped ashore on Noddles Island in East Boston. He found work as a copper—a thriving trade, for most barrels held whiskey, and Boston saloons had multiplied with the advent of the Irish. On the island where Patrick Kennedy settled, conditions were not as deplorable as they were in the historic North End. There, the Irish clustered in their slums and turned inward, rejected by the natives and at the same time rejecting a strange environment.

As the Irish found reasonably steady work, they scraped together the means to put down roots. Needing a place of worship they accumulated five thousand dollars and bought the meetinghouse of the Maverick Congregational Society. Later, when they outgrew these quarters, they laid plans for a fine Gothic structure at the corner of Maverick and London streets, where the steeple, nearly two hundred feet tall, soared above the masts of the ships anchored at nearby wharves. The mainspring of the development syndicate, William H. Sumner, paid tribute to the Irish immigrants in a history of East Boston, praising the "adopted citizens . . . who, with strong arms and willing hearts, came to level the hills, fill up the lowlands, drain the marshes, erect docks, and map the island with its pleasant wide and spacious streets and squares." Life for the newcomers in East Boston was hard, but it was durable, and as one Irish settler wrote: "There is a great many inconveniences here, but no empty bellies."

On a small and uncertain salary Patrick Kennedy met and married Bridget Murphy, a girl two years older than himself. Three daughters were born and on January 8, 1858, a son, christened Patrick Joseph. A year after his son was born, Patrick Kennedy succumbed to cholera. He was thirty-five years of age. A decade in the new country had worn him out, and he died as poor as when he arrived.

Widowed, Bridget Kennedy set about to find work and landed a job as a hairdresser at Boston's Jordan-Marsh department store. Patrick Joseph was educated in the neighborhood parochial school run by the Sisters of Notre Dame. Bostonians had been annoyed by the Irish insistence upon private school for their children, but they lost the battle when it was proven that the public schools reflected a powerful Protestant bias, which taught the children to distrust the Pope and the designs of Catholic Spain. The truly devout Irish prohibited their children from attending public schools, seeing such attendance as occasions of sin. However, this Irish practice was to lose popularity in the generations that followed.

Since money was very scarce in the Bridget Kennedy home, young Patrick left grammar school and went to work on the docks as a stevedore. He was fair-skinned, blue-eyed, and strongly muscled and was called "P. J." by his friends. He had the physical strength for manual labor, but not the heart. The hard-drinking, sprawling crews with whom P. J. worked represented to him a slow life of drudgery. His aspirations were higher, but his chances in Boston in the nineteenth century were slight, to say the least. Little work except manual labor was available for a poor, uneducated Irish boy. Newspaper ads specified that only native Americans and Protestants need apply for work. Even black men faced less discrimination. The only opportunity an Irish lad found in this hard-core Yankee community was amongst the Irish immigrant community. In the world created by whiskey, P. J. found his metier. With Irish blarney and a little bit of luck, he managed to acquire a saloon in East Boston's Haymarket Square. He worked diligently and put the profits back into his business until he had acquired a whiskey business, wholesale and re-tail, with an office on High Street.

He invested in other saloons, including one in the Maverick House, East Boston's finest hostelry since its opening in 1835. This saloon was located opposite a shipyard, and brawny workers poured in, morning, noon, and night for a bit of libation and a large amount of talk. The talk turned to politics, and in his position as saloonkeeper, Patrick Kennedy became the center of a wide circle of acquaintances. He knew political office seekers, conspirators, and their intended victims. The action of words before action of deeds took place at P. J.'s bar.

P. J.'s opinion was held in great respect for two reasons. One was his physical appearance—that of austerity and propriety. With his elegantly curled moustache and his magnificent physique and poise, he was the Irish father-image—the natural aristocrat transplanted in the American–Irish ghetto. The second reason was that he did not extend his advice casually. He was—unlike his coterie of loudmouthed customers and admirers—aloof, reserved, an Irishman who seldom raised his voice. His strength lay in running a pocket-sized welfare state. The Irish, suspicious of the charity of outsiders, expected and honored help from their own people. The Irish worker was always, at best, about two weeks away from starvation. Consequently, the man who found him a job, or helped him to keep one, had the gratitude and vote of his family and friends. A round or two of free booze, a loan of a few bucks until payday, a bucket of coal for a family whose breadwinner was currently unemployed— these were the good deeds of P. J. Kennedy.

They did not go unrewarded. In 1886 he was elected by a landslide to the Massachusetts house of representatives and then to the state senate. But P. J. did not have a true proclivity for actual politics. He was not a good talker, nor a particularly good mixer. He was more of a strategist, and he threw his support behind a man whom he respected highly— Patrick Collins, the Irish–American patriot who earlier had tried to hold off a vengeful and discreditable Irish mob from conquering the city of Boston. Collins eventually became mayor of Boston. It was Collins who said:

> I love the land of my birth, but in American politics I know neither race, color, nor creed. Let me say now there are no Irish voters among us. There are Irish-born citizens, like myself and there will be many more of us, but the moment the seal of the court was impressed upon our papers we ceased to be foreigners and became Americans.

To P. J., who was above all a realist and who sought reconciliation whenever it was possible, such a philosophy meant conquest—and conquest spelled success, which was his goal. His lot had vastly improved above his ancestors and he had become a member of the Irish elite, who had already begun to label themselves either "shanty" for the luckless, the misbegotten; or "lace-curtain" for the up-and-coming. In 1887, at the age of twenty-eight, P. J. established himself through marriage with Mary Hickey, whose family stood a few rungs higher on the ladder of social success than the Kennedys. On September 6, 1888, their son was born. He was named Joseph Patrick, and he was destined to be the father of the first Catholic president of the United States.

With the nineteenth-century influx of the Irish there came a heritage of Gaelic songs, exquisite in melody, poetic in verse. Through the years they have become a part of the American heritage, although in the beginning, they were "familiars" sung in the intimacy of the family circle. "Deirin De" and "Katie Cruel," originally heard in the hold of such a coffin ship as the first Kennedy traveled on to America, one generation later was sung by the Irish mother, Mary Kennedy, while her hand rocked the cradle of her darling baby, Joseph Patrick:

> When I first came to town, they called me a roving jewel,
> Now they've changed their tune and call me Katie Cruel.
> O little lolly day; O the little lioday.
> O that I were where I would be, Then would I be where I am not;
> But I am where I must be, where I would be I cannot,
> O little lollyday; O the little lioday.
>
> I know who I love, and know who does love me;
> I know I'll go, and I know who'll go with me.
> O little lolly day; O the little lioday.
> O that I were where I would be, then I would be where I am not;
> But I am where I must be, where I would be I cannot,
> O little lollyday; O the little lioday.

✻   ✻   ✻

> Deirin De—Deirin De, the night jar calls from the grassy moor,
> Deirin De—Deirin De, the bittern booms from the red-bound shore.
> Deirin De—Deirin De, On the westward hill, the sheep will stray,
> Deirin De—Deirin De, My child will watch them from break of day.

In pure Gaelic, she sang:

> Deirin De—Deirin De, leogfad mo leanbh a pioca smear,
> Deirin De—Deirin De, ach codial go samh, so fainne an lae.[1]

In 1845 another Irishman left County Wexford, traveling first down the rutted dirt road to the seaport town of New Ross to board one of the coffin ships of the Cunard line and sail westward to Boston. When Thomas Fitzgerald arrived there was only one native Irishman to every fifty people. Those fifty were fully cognizant of the fact that in 1688 Goody Glover had been hanged in the Boston Common as a witch for saying the rosary in Gaelic while kneeling before a statue of the Blessed Virgin; the Puritans claimed she was in league with Satan and that all Irishmen were devils. The legend still persisted when Fitzgerald came

Left, James Curley. Right, John F. "Honey Fitz" Fitzgerald. Photograph courtesy of United Press International.

and settled in a paddyville shantytown. "The scum of creation, beaten men from beaten races, representing the worst failure in the struggle for existence." Senator Henry Cabot Lodge the elder said, "The latter day immigrants were inferior peoples whose prolific issue threatened the very foundations of Anglo-American civilization."

One of the "muckers," "blacklegs," "greenhorns," "clodhoppers," and "micks," Tom Fitzgerald found his wife from among the Irish "biddies," "kitchen canaries," and "bridgets" who, in their isolation, pounded away at their ambitions, shunned charity, and found real friendliness only from their Irish peers and their priests. Loyalty to family and loyalty to church were axiomatic, and the more ambitious sought escape from the Irish way of life as much as they sought parity with the Yankees. Tom Fitzgerald was the new breed of cat, and when his son John F. Fitzgerald was born February 11, 1863, in a red brick tenement at 30 Ferry Street in the shadow of the Old North Church, he had elevated himself from the role of farm laborer to manager of a grocery and liquor store. The playgrounds for his children "were the streets and wharves, busy with ships from every part of the world." It was a strange contrast of family isolation and daily contact with the enormous world of travel to strange countries populated with strange peoples, which intrigued the barefooted, patch-panted little Johnny Fitz. He soon began to make a mark upon the bustling little Irish community with its fish peddlers and tip carts, its clattering horse-drawn wagons loaded with ice and coal, fruit and vegetables.

It was also the home of the newly growing tough ward politics. Young Fitzgerald's ambitions knew no limitations, and he was a natural-born leader. He joined and led most athletic organizations in the North End and early in life demonstrated his talents for politics at picnics, minstrel shows, suppers, dances, and fairs—where his Irish tenor sang out loudly. He played football, baseball, polo, and was a sprinter of such class that boys came from all over Boston to compete with him. "I work harder than anyone else," was his code, and "what I undertake, I do; what I want, I get." In time, he was considered the best swimmer, the best sprinter, the best dancer, the best singer, and the best talker in the North End. His skills got him to the Boston Latin School, the school that had educated the sons of New England's leading families since its founding in 1635. It was no small honor for the son of an Irish immigrant to be admitted to the student body. With his athletic prowess, he managed and played right field on the baseball team and captained the football squad for two years. From the Boston Latin School, Johnny Fitz went to Harvard Medical School, but his education was cut short by the death of his father.

"My father left us a few thousand dollars. It was not enough to educate me, and I thought my life belonged to my brothers, and that I could do better outside medical school, so I gave it up and took the examination for the Custom House." He passed and became a clerk under Leverett Saltonstall, grandfather of the man who would one day serve side by side in the United States Senate with Johnny Fitz's grandsons, John, Robert, and Edward Kennedy.

Johnny Fitz married a distant cousin, Mary Josephine Hannon (called Josie) on September 18, 1889, and they took up residence at 4 Garden Court Street in the shadow of the Old North Church. Once it had been Governor Hutchinson's mansion; now it was solid with Irish Catholics. Johnny Fitz entered into the real estate and insurance business, for which he was well suited, with his large collection of friends and acquaintances. For him, the American dream was coming true. In 1890, when his daughter Rose was born, the Fitzgerald lace curtains were prim and proper and

Marriage of Joseph Kennedy and Rose Fitzgerald. Courtesy of Underwood & Underwood.

hanging in starched rigidity. They were symbolic of the new formal Irish social status, which was foreordained to set its standards, side by side, with those of the proper Bostonians.

Politics was the key, and by the time Rose was born John Fitzgerald already had been inaugurated as mayor of Boston. His prowess was celebrated in a popular ballad which more than adequately describes the "Fitzblarney" of Honey Fitz.

> Honey Fitz can talk you blind
> On any subject you can find.
> Fish or fishing, motor boats,
> Proper way to open clams,
> How to cure existing shams.
> State Street, Goo-goos, aeroplanes,
> Malefactors, thieving gains.
> Local transportation rates,
> How to run the nearby states.
> On all these things and many more,
> Honey Fitz is crammed with lore.

It was not with full parental blessing that Rose Fitzgerald became the wife of young Joe Kennedy. In fact, her father frowned upon the marriage; he thought Kennedy not sufficiently social or successful enough for his daughter. As the mayor of Boston's favorite child, Rose had been given all of the privileges Honey Fitz could bestow upon her. She was world-traveled, had been educated in Europe, and had been presented in a formal debut to the crème de la crème of Boston Irish society. She longed to attend Wellesley, but her father forbade such a notion. As she has stated, "In those days one didn't argue with one's father."

Young Joe had managed to attend Harvard, the citadel of the small world of Boston. Despite its high educational standards, Harvard's prime function in the nineteenth century was to serve as a vestibule through which young men entered Society. Generation after generation of prominent Bostonians attended Harvard, as Henry Adams wrote, "because their friends went there, and the college was their ideal of social self-respect."

For the grandson of an immigrant and the son of a saloonkeeper, Harvard could be an uncomfortable experience—and for Joe Kennedy it was. There was no crude discrimination of the bullying sort, but a subtle, cruel, typically Boston exclusion to remind him that he was an intruder in a place to which others were born. In Kennedy's class of 1912 there were some Jews and a sprinkling of Irish, but to old Bostonians change came

In the 1921 photograph above, Mrs. Rose Kennedy poses outdoors with her family. Eunice, Kathryn, and Rosemary are beside their mother; four-year-old John Fitzgerald Kennedy is sitting on the kiddy car, and Joe, Jr., stands beside him. Courtesy of Wide World Photos.

slowly—and to some Bostonians it never came at all. Equally slow to change were the old Irish, whose attitude of suspicion and enmity carried over from the days of immigration. But Joe Kennedy, although he was not eligible for the "best" undergraduate clubs, nevertheless, by his own admission, "did all right." He held his own socially, and took his fun where he found it. With his good looks, he was very popular in Boston Irish society, and because of his skill as a ballroom dancer he was a prize beau for the young Irish debutantes. And the importance of being a Harvard man was summed up in the words of the nineteenth-century Yankee, Edmund Quincy, whose father had been president of Harvard, when he tapped his Harvard Triennial Catalogue, which contained the names of all Harvard graduates: "If a man's in there, that's who he is. If he's not who is he?"

Joe Kennedy was there. He was no longer a stranger in Boston.

When Joe Kennedy and his Rose started their life together in Boston, they found themselves inhabitants of an awesomely self-satisfied city, cemented into a mold the first families found perfect and a city that they were determined to keep intact against change. Life for the proper Bostonian revolved around his grandfather rather than himself, and since his ancestors had named the city the Hub, it implied that Boston was the center of the universe. One lofty matron demanded: "Why should I travel? I'm already here!"

In the mansions on the water side of Beacon Street and the brownstones along broad Commonwealth Avenue, the lofty windows were imprisoned and the rich velvet drapes hung tight with funereal gloom. The past was incorporated into the present and, as Charles Francis Adams observed, there was "no current of fresh outside life everlastingly flowing in and passing out." In the banks and counting rooms downtown, the old leather chairs were occupied by men whose brains were crammed with ideas that were old and covered with vanishing mental dust.

In 1906, H. G. Wells, visiting in Boston, found the city as beautiful and as barren as the Common when the dawn rose and filtered the light of day over the deserted area.

> There broods over the real Boston an immense effect of finality. The capacity of Boston, it would seem, was just sufficient but no more than sufficient, to comprehend the whole achievement of the human intellect up, let us say, to the year 1875 A.D. Then an equilibrium was established. At or about that year Boston filled up.

It was in the final quarter of the nineteenth century Boston knew with cold factuality that its reign as a financial center was at an end, that New York had taken charge of the helm, of New World finance. The intellectual genius of the city, which flowered with Emerson and continued until its culmination with the demise of Holmes, had originated from the less profound but indispensable talent for making money. When that gene of genius vanished, the city commenced to die. It became the home of unimaginative men, who ate their oatmeal every day, although they hated it;[2] who carried their umbrellas under their arms whether there was a dark cloud in the sky or not; whose single claim to recognition was their impressive walk as they marched in the footsteps of their grandfathers to act out their roles as custodians of the wealth accumulated by their ancestors. These vigorous founders of family fortunes, distrusting the abilities of their heirs, consistently vaulted their wealth through unbreakable wills and spendthrift trusts. Guardianship replaced enterprise. Boston's best brains and energies shifted from commerce, manufacturing, and speculation to banking, insurance, and conservation investment. The family founders looked down from their portraits on a cold, sterile, finished society.

The cry of Honey Fitz was the shock of new blood into the corpse of Boston, hot Irish blood into cold Puritan veins. "Bigger, better, busier Boston," cried John Fitzgerald, intimidating the first families into a further retreat. "Our present Mayor has the distinction of appointing more saloonkeepers and bartenders to public offices than any previous Mayor!" moaned an Episcopal voice from the pulpit. "You have plenty of Irish depositors," Mayor Fitzgerald said to a Boston bank president. "Why don't you have some Irishmen on your board of directors?" The bank president explained that a couple of his tellers were Irish. "Yes," replied the Mayor, "and I suppose the charwomen are, too."

It was obvious to the up-and-coming Irish that money might be acquired, but money in itself was meaningless. Everyone's place had been foreordained in Boston.

"Coming of age in Boston," said one of Joe Kennedy's friends, "Joe Kennedy saw early what made the power and gentility he wanted. It wasn't talent; it was ancient riches. Power came from money. Joe had a keen mind, and it was honed against the great cynicisms underlying rank and station in Brahmin Boston."

The leading profession of the city was banking, and this was the predestined career of most of Kennedy's Harvard associates. He decided to make it his career, but he realized that a direct approach to the world of trust-encrusted wealth would be futile. Instead, he took a carefully studied indirect step and became a state bank examiner at a salary of $1,500 a year. The hours were long, but the bank examiner's job laid bare to young Kennedy the condition of every bank he investigated, and what he learned of the structure and securities of state banks was valuable to himself and others. In 1913, when bank mergers became popular, the Columbia Trust Company in East Boston was about to be engulfed. It was then that Joe Kennedy's apprenticeship ended and he became, through his maneuvering, the president of the Columbia Trust—the youngest bank president in the state of Massachusetts. A Harvard graduate and president of a bank—even though it was small and obscure—dazzled old Honey Fitz, and he consented to the marriage of his darling Rose and young Joe. They set up residence in a small gray frame house at 83 Beals Street in a middle-class neighborhood in Brookline, a house that the thirty-fifth president of the United States was to point to with the comment, "Just like Abe Lincoln and his log cabin."

In this unpretentious house in which "we were very happy, and though we did not know about the days ahead, we were optimistic about the future," neither of the Kennedys could anticipate that one day, a half century later, they would pay $55,000 to repurchase this $6,000 first home, refurnish it with everything from the original Victorian furniture to Jack's bassinet, and then turn the deed over to the government to maintain as a national historic shrine.

But the ambition, the driving forces of both Joe and Rose Kennedy, could not be stemmed by the snubs and social ostracism of the proper Bostonians. Rose, being more intrinsically Irish and Catholic than Joe, was indifferent to the Protestant world, which ignored her and which she in turn refused to accept or court. It was Joe who finally turned his back on Boston when, after he had made his first million (which he accomplished before he was thirty-five), he was blackballed from membership in the Cohasset Country Club. It was an injury to his pride that he never forgot. "Boston," he said, "is a good city to come from; but not a good city to go to. If you want to make money, go where the money is." Kennedy moved his family to Riverdale, on the outskirts of New York City, but he never transplanted the heart of Rose from her native Boston, the city in which, through her father, she had acquired the political acumen that was to be of incredible support to her sons' political careers.

Rose compromised with a summer home in Hyannis Port on Cape Cod, and under her guidance the Kennedys developed a regular routine. It was an exhausting experience, especially for the many weekend visitors. They usually came away astonished, bewildered, and in a state of fatigue from competing with the Kennedy energy. The schedule was rugged. Golf, swimming, and sailing began on Friday. Nights were devoted to home movies—easily procured through Joe's control of the movie industry. Saturday was another day of vigorous athletic events, and Saturday nights provided movies and dancing. Sunday was quiet, with church in the morning, but when the last mass had been read the afternoons were dominated by the famous Kennedy touch football games in which, according to one visitor: "Kennedys always toss the ball to Kennedys. They never, any one of them, tossed the ball to anyone else." It was a family trait. One could not win against the Kennedys, as Henry Cabot Lodge, Jr., was to learn when he was defeated for Congress by Jack Kennedy.

Ambassador to Great Britain, Joseph P. Kennedy, took his two oldest sons to England in 1938. John, left, and Joseph, Jr., right, who had engaged in fierce fights as children, had become friendly rivals. Photograph courtesy of Pictorial Parade.

"It was those damned tea parties," commented Lodge after his defeat was acknowledged. It was Rose who summed up a generation of Irish put down: "At last the Fitzgeralds have evened the score with the Lodges." The plurality vote of seventy thousand in Massachusetts, when Eisenhower was sweeping the country and the state of Massachusetts, was not a bought vote as many of the elections of old Honey Fitz had been, it was an honest reward for a family that had "worked harder than anyone else."

When Joe Kennedy was appointed by Franklin Roosevelt as ambassador to the Court of St. James, he commented to Rose as they were on their way for dinner with the king and queen at Windsor Castle, "Well, Rose, this is a helluva way from East Boston isn't it?" And indeed it was. Still to come was the founding of a dynasty to equal that of the Adamses—the Boston family most admired by the Kennedys. The Kennedys were a threatening dynasty of Irish ancestry, nurtured in the religious precepts of Roman Catholicism. As Boston began to think there was no door to be closed to the brash Kennedys, so did the world. It was now their oyster, and it appeared to be an oyster filled with pearls. But, as the pearl of the oyster is also its tear, the fame and success of the Kennedys was also the source of their tragedies. "I don't think there's any point being Irish if you don't know that the world is going to break your heart eventually. I guess we thought we had a little more time," wrote the Kennedys' friend, Daniel Moynihan, following the assassination of Jack Kennedy on November 22, 1963.

Death had claimed their firstborn son—the idol of Joe's eye—in World War Two; Kiki, Rose's favorite daughter, was killed in a plane accident over the English Channel; an institution for the mentally retarded housed Rosemary, the prettiest of the Kennedy girls; and the bullets of two assassins were to claim Jack and Bobby. Through paralysis following a massive stroke, Joe was saved much of the agony that followed the ecstasy of world acclaim. Rose alone carried the burden of grief, and in her stoic calm she joined the gallery of valiant ladies who have carved the image of the proper women of Boston. The daughter of old Honey Fitz, the wife of Joe Kennedy, the mother of the Kennedy boys and girls was a Rose whose bloom would never fade.

6

Man Does Not Live
by Little Brown Bread Alone

It was George Meredith who wrote, "Kissing don't last, cookery do!"
And it was Anthelme Brillat-Savarin who noted in the nineteenth century,
"The destiny of nations depends on how they nourish themselves." Since
its founding, America has nourished itself uncommonly well. John Adams
penned, "I know not why we should blush to confess that molasses was
an essential ingredient in American independence," for it was the British
taxes on tea and molasses that raised patriot tempers to the boiling point
of revolution. "The very discovery of the New York was the by-product
of a dietary quest," observed Arthur Schlesinger in *Paths to the Present*.

Perhaps no American city has had a greater hand in the bill of fare of
American homes and hostelries than Boston. From the hour of landing:

> And those who came resolved to be Englishmen
> Gone to the World's End, but English everyone, and they ate the
> white corn kernels, parched in the sun,
> And they knew it not, but they'd not be English again.
> Stephen Vincent Benét

The Indian "maize"—corn—was life for the first settlers. When the
Mayflower swung around the tip of Cape Cod and anchored in the sheltered harbor, one hundred and two passengers—who for more than three
months had lived on the ship's fare of hardtack, salt horse (salted beef),
fried fish, cheese, and beer, and were plagued with scurvy and intestinal
disorders—ravenously prowled the beaches for fresh food. Happily, the
pilgrims found toothsome soft-shell clams and tender young quahogs, and
they uncovered corn the Indians had stashed away for food and for seed.

Fortunately, the early fathers made a firm treaty of peace with Massasoit
and learned from the Indians how to ward off hunger and starvation by
utilizing the natural foods available. After their original year of hardship,

The Landing on Cape Cod. From *Photographing the Famous* by Alice Boughton (New York: Avondale Press, 1928).

they celebrated the first Thanksgiving—a gala occasion that lasted for three days. Games of chance and skill were played, and the Pilgrims gorged themselves on venison, duck, goose, probably turkey, clams and other shellfish, smoked eels, cornbreads, leeks and watercress, with wild plums and dried berries for dessert. The food was washed down with wine made of wild grapes. This first Thanksgiving was a huge success, and thereafter it became a New England tradition to enjoy the harvest feast. In 1863, Abraham Lincoln elevated the holiday from regional observation and officially declared the last Thursday in November as a national holiday of Thanksgiving.

The traditional Thanksgiving turkey possibly did not make its appearance until much later than the date of the original festival of the Pilgrim fathers.

The cranberry sauce served with turkey originated in Massachusetts, since most of the cranberry bogs are found on the outskirts of Boston. The raising and canning of cranberries is a large industry. The cranberry is a red, acid berry that grows in a manner similar to that of rice in a bog. They were first known as "craneberries," since cranes living in New England bogs ate the berries, and were early recognized as a good preventive of scurvy. Ships putting out to sea from Down East ports always carried casks of this "bogland medicine" in their stores.

John Josselyn, visiting New England in 1663, wrote: "The Indians and the English use them much, boyling them with Sugar for Sauce to eat with their Meat, and it is a delicate Sauce." In Josselyn's day they were also known as "bounce berries," since they were, and still are, tested for ripeness by their ability to bounce.

In 1769 a dozen fashionable young gentlemen of Plymouth organized a very exclusive club, the Old Colony. Their purpose was to elevate the social tone of the town and to honor their ancestors. The club rule required that the members be "dressed in the plainest manner, with all appearances of luxury and extravagance being avoided." But the traditional dinner was anything but plain. There were nine courses: first, a large baked Indian whortleberry pudding, followed by a steaming dish of succotash (which was a soup containing fowl), a lean pork and corned beef; a dish of clams either on the half shell or steamed; a dish of oysters and codfish; a haunch of venison, a dish of waterfowl; a dish of "frost fish" (tomcod) and eels; apple pie, cranberry tarts, and cheese. Beer, hard cider, wines, and rum were available to wash down the food, stimulate talk, and aid digestion.

By 1770 the people of Boston boasted farmsteads that furnished eggs and fowl for spit or oven. Out of the barn came milk to be drunk or served on cereals, churned into butter, or pressed into cheese. In the pastures were sheep providing lamb, mutton, and fleece to be woven for warm clothing and bedding. In the pigpen, or foraging in the nearby woods for acorns and nuts, were fat porkers, promising hams, bacon, hogback, pig's knuckles and feet, and lard for cooking. In nearby waters were fish and in the woods wild fowl and beasts. In the kitchen were the "boughten" things—salt, spices, molasses, cane sugar, and a demijohn of New England rum.

With their bellies full, the Bostonians were ready to proclaim their inalienable right to "life, liberty, and the pursuit of happiness." When John Adams signed the Declaration of Independence, he confided to his wife, Abigail, that the day of signing

> will be the most memorable epoch in the history of America. I am apt to believe it will be celebrated by succeeding generations as the great anniversary festival. It ought to be commemorated, as the day of de-

Scene on the ice, Boston Harbor. Citizens hauling the ferryboat, c. 1844. From *Romance of Boston Bay* by Edward Rowe Snow (Boston: Yankee Publishing Company, 1944).

liverance by solemn acts of devotion to God Almighty. It ought to be solemnized with pomp and parade, with shows, games, sports, guns, bells, bonfires and illuminations from one end of this continent to the other, from this time forward, forevermore.

Though the Adamses celebrated the Fourth of July each year with enthusiasm, their tastes at the dinner table—even when occupying the White House—reflected their New England thrift and simplicity; they served the traditional Boston dinner of salmon with egg sauce, along with the first new jacketed potatoes and early peas.

In the colonial days the heart of life was the common room or kitchen, with its great fireplace, often eight feet or more across and five feet high, an immense recess large enough in the seventeenth century for a person to sit inside the jambs, or side walls. Such "chimneys," as they were called, used up fuel extravagantly and smoked abominably. In the late seventeen hundreds Benjamin Thompson, better remembered by his patent of nobility, Count Rumford, called the smoky chimney "that greatest of all plagues" and, like Dr. Benjamin Franklin, he considered the design of more efficient fireplaces a subject worthy of serious study. He proceeded to become our first heating engineer and designed a cooking range and a drip coffeepot.

For more than two hundred years most of the food consumed in Boston came out of heavy black iron pots. Bean porridges were made in these pots, as were fish stews. A vivid sense of the times comes through Eleazer Moody's *School of Good Manners* (circa 1715) in which he advises: "Take not salt with a greasy knife. Blow not thy meat. Smell not of thy meat, nor put it to thy nose. Foul not thy napkin all over, but at one corner."

As the century wore on the menu expanded, and as fuel became scarcer the stoves diminished in size. Beside the fireplace hung the salt box fashioned from black cherry wood, and strings of dried peppers, apples, and squash were looped across the room. The spinning wheel whirred and the loom clacked as the Boston wife tended her other·chores, while her pork and beans, brown bread, and codfish balls cooked on the large stove or in a Dutch oven.

But around 1840–1850 a radical change took place in the style of Boston cooking. The old fireplaces were boarded up and in their place stood a simple cast-iron box with two stove lids at the top. Many good cooks believed that the cookstove caused deterioration of American cuisine. Mrs. Harriet Beecher Stowe articulated what others felt when she wrote:

> An open firepalce is an altar of patriotism. Would our Revolutionary Fathers have gone barefooted and bleeding over snows to defend air-tight stoves and cooking ranges? I trow not. It was the memory of the great open kitchen fire, its roaring, hilarious voice of invitation, its dancing tongues of flame, that called to them through the snows of that dreadful winter.

But times were changing, and there were social gains and social losses. In the growing town economy, such manufacturing as was done was handled by small enterprisers and craftsmen—the tanner, the wheelwright, the comb maker, and the cooper. The cobbler came to the New England farmsteads from Boston once a year to outfit the whole family, but as an industrial society developed in Boston, because of water transportation and the expansion of the cotton culture, the old-fashioned ways disappeared.

The great New England food was fish. The waters around Boston were

Long lines of fish drying, Gloucester, Massachusetts. From *Outing*, July 1903.

filled with cod, mackerel, bass, and lobsters. The presence of fish stimulated shipbuilding, and by the dawn of the eighteenth century skippers of pinks named *The Good Intent,* the *Harvester,* and the *Open Sea* knew the waters of the Arctic Circle as intimately as the quiet coves of their home ports and "wet down their salt" with many "trip" of fish from Nova Scotia.

The preservation of food was accomplished by heat—as in the instance of canned foods; by drying—apples, corn, and pumpkins; by smoking or brine, in the case of meats; and by the coolness of the root cellar. Ice from the ponds of Cambridge could be bought at retail in Boston in the early nineteenth century, yet due to Boston parsimony, more ice was used in the Southern states (it was shipped from Boston). Frederick Tudor, an indomitable merchant genius of Boston, became known as the Ice King. He designed a successful icehouse, pioneered the business of shipping ice, and eventually created for the home icebox a role as important in the history of American cooking as that of the cookstove.

A typical bill of fare for an average nineteenth-century Boston family commenced with clam chowder as the first-of-the-week dish. Toward the end of the week, leftovers made a platter of red flannel hash, colored by beets and accompanied by sour milk biscuits, applesauce sprinkled with nutmeg and dotted with butter, a custard so light it could hardly be counted as food, gooseberry pie, and a curd cheese flavored with tansy. Saturday was baking day. It was also fish day, to distinguish it from the Friday fasts of the Irish Catholic Papists. Codfish as cakes or balls (a delicacy that was extolled in the United States Senate when Senator George Frisbe Hoar rose during a debate upon a pure food bill to praise the excellent flavor of the codfish, salted, made into balls and eaten on a Sunday morning by a person whose theology is sound and who believes in the five points of Calvinism) reigned at the breakfast table on Sunday, and dinnertime brought the additional pork and beans which had been on the fire since early Saturday. The brown bread was made in a five-pound lard pail with the word *swift* embossed upon it, symbolically, to indicate the time in which it was consumed. The final delicacy was at sundown, but often served at breakfast, too—the traditional apple pie. The custom of apple pie for breakfast always seemed natural, inevitable, and pleasurable for Bostonians. "What is pie for?" asked Emerson, and the matter was settled beyond further question.

For beverages the merchant and professional classes, and in colonial times the small court surrounding the royal governor, drank port, Madeira, claret, and the Burgundies. The middle class relied upon fruit cordials, wines, and ciders of native growth. The yeoman farmers made their own spruce beer, elderberry and dandelion wine, metheglin, and applejack. Almost everybody took rum as a form of body heating.[1] Mixed with molasses, it was known as blackstrap; compounded with cider it was a lethal potion, aptly called "stonewall." Either way, it was a necessity at hog-killing time, when the stem and stern posts were raised in the shipyard, at the ordination of ministers, or at the ceremonies at Harvard College. At the militia training it was more essential than gunpowder. Charles Francis Adams sadly observed the Bostonian's attachment to ardent spirits, attributing the usage to the constant eating of salt meats. Children got thoroughwort tea when they were sick, and milk was so plentiful very shortly after the arrivel of the Founding Fathers that John Cotton observed that ministers and milk were the only cheap things in all of New England.

What men eat and drink, and how, is a reflection of the society in which they live. But food is more than a mirror of a way of life. It also helps shape the character of men and nations. In Boston many of the social customs originated around food and drink. Time, in Boston as in London —the city Boston copied in its social manners and graces more than any other—is of the essence. If you are invited to dinner at 7:30, you are expected to arrive exactly at that hour and not casually drift in at eight or later. There is also a well-recognized hour of departure. Ten for a seven o'clock dinner; 7:30 permits to 10:30. Ladies' luncheons usually are held at 1:00 o'clock and break up punctually at 3:30.

Tea is consumed in Boston in ritual manner every afternoon at five. What the cocktail hour is to New York or large cities, tea is to Boston. It comes in two sizes—the large, or party, tea, or the small, or daily, tea. The large tea is the occasion for a coming-out party for a debutante or the proper place to announce an engagement. The small tea is the real Boston custom. It is cozy and intimate, for family, family friends, and occasional strangers—or drop-ins. It is served daily at five, winter and summer, rain or shine. The Bostonian's "tea things" are a part of the rites just as surely as the silver chalice is an integral part of the sacramental ritual of communion. There is the crested silver service, large or small, depending upon the family wealth, and the good English teacups. The food is wholesome, but simple. Buttered toast, English muffins and marmalade, and, of course, brown bread.

Bostonians relished spices and used ginger and pepper generously, as well as cloves, mace, cinnamon, and allspice. It was this early taste for condiments that led to the establishment of one of Boston's treasured institutions, S. S. Pierce, the city's first family grocery. Founded by the Pierce family, the name was pronounced "Purse" to identify this family from lesser Pierces. Despite the family's efforts to have their name restored to its proper pronunciation, Bostonians would never consider calling S. S. Pierce anything but S. S. Purse. It shelves the finest collections of rare spices, chutneys, and marmalades of any store in existence. The Boston woman in her low-heeled shoes (almost essential for walking around the steep hills) includes S. S. Pierce on her shopping tour as regularly as she stops at her favorite Boston Beanery for a sip of tea, a slice of brown bread, or an English muffin. It is a custom—with or without manner.

The fact that food made the man is evidenced in the writings of the merchant princes and their constant complaints of dyspepsia. "The Bostonians are a dyspeptic variety of the human family. . . . The surest way of approaching most men is said to be through a dinner, but you must secure a Bostonian by telling him how to digest one." On July 5, 1794, there was born one Sylvester Graham who was destined to be the food philosopher of the nineteenth century. In 1830 he became a temperance lecturer and during his crusade against alcohol, the censor of American recklessness at the dinner table. He developed a positive program of dietary reform and its most notable features were an assault upon meats and fats and an insistence on bread made from unbolted, or unsifted whole wheat flour. This was an unorthodox attack on a long-established symbol of Western civilization—white bread. In Boston it was a dual attack, hitting below the belt on Boston's traditional brown bread.

Yet Graham's philosophy of food was especially well received in Boston. Graham incorporated his dietary laws into his daft religious precepts. God is the author of physical laws so it is not only unwise to violate them but it is an offense against true religion. Graham relied heavily upon scriptural authority, especially those passages that fitted his thesis, such as Genesis 1:29: "And God said, Behold, I have given you every herb bearing seed which is upon the face of all the earth, and every tree, in which is the fruit of a tree yielding seed, to you it shall be for meat."

The meals that were served in Boston homes influenced by Sylvester Graham included oatmeal gruel, beans and boiled rice without salt, a daily procession of puddings eaten when tepid or stone cold, and bread at least one day old. Condiments were proscribed because they encouraged a thirst for rum and wine. Fats, gravies, and sea food were out of bounds. Soups were eliminated because they provided no opportunity for chewing. (Graham insisted the teeth get a thorough workout.) Little or no water was permitted at meals to help the faithful swallow graham crackers, a kind of unleavened biscuit, made of unbolted or whole grain flour. Graham, in the tradition of the day, lectured with the passion of a flagellant, declaring in one of his lectures that man could curb sexual sin by a shift from meat eating to the cereal diet.

In a city like Boston, where masochism was a mass phenomenon, Graham's converts were innumerable until the famous "Baker's Riot." Graham's view of commercial bakers was not charitable. He considered them all cheats and adulterators. The family bread, he preached, should be baked at home, where its preparation was a kind of sacred rite. On the occasion of the attempted violence against Graham, it had been announced that he would give a lecture at Amory Hall in Boston urging the women of New England to bake their own bread and to boycott the public bakers. Threats made against the proprietors of the hall were effective and Graham found himself without a forum. But the owner of the not quite finished Marlborough Hotel, the first "temperance house" in the United States, offered the use of his dining room. The mayor warned that he could not protect the meeting with city constables, and Graham drafted police from his disciples. When the mob appeared before the hotel, a loyal shovel brigade stationed in the upper stories dumped slaked lime on the rioters until the bakers appeared to be covered with flour, "whereupon the eyes having it, the rabble incontinently adjourned."

But for all his bucolic manner and his soapbox method of persuasion, Sylvester Graham left a valuable heritage of health ideas. Generations of Bostonians heeded his thoughts about bathing, exercise, brushing the teeth, ventilating sleeping chambers, and the importance of eating in moderation. Although his place in history is largely that of a crank, barely tolerating the use of milk, eggs, or honey, and adamant against shellfish, salt, and pork, Graham, nevertheless, made Americans the most health-conscious people in the world and created a climate for nutritional quackery that has since grown to alarming proportions. But food fads flourish because people want them. The dyspeptic Bostonian was a natural target for Sylvester Graham's dietary rules. The original Graham fare was difficult to swallow, but in time it became tempered, and good taste and common sense prevailed to satisfy a palatable tongue and preserve an aching stomach.

To make Boston famous for food, the spotlight falls upon a very remarkable lady, "the mother of level measurement," Fannie Merritt Farmer, whose celebrated *The Boston Cooking School Cook Book* is as formidable a Boston structure as is the Old North Church.

Fannie Farmer was a woman of iron character who, because of a physical disability, had to conserve her time and strength. She was not impatient of pleasure nor immune to the subtleties of decoration and taste, but she would not tolerate a waste of her time and energies because of inexactitude. Before her cookbook was published, there was no such thing as a scientific cookbook. The housekeeper attempting a recipe was advised to use a "pinch" of this and a "helping" of that. What came out was anyone's guess, until Fannie Farmer set about doing something about

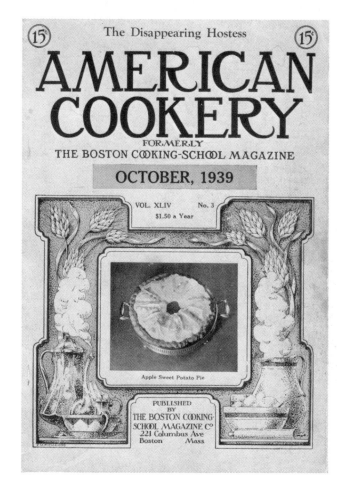

The Disappearing Hostess

AMERICAN COOKERY
FORMERLY
THE BOSTON COOKING-SCHOOL MAGAZINE

OCTOBER, 1939

VOL. XLIV   No. 3
$1.50 a Year

Apple Sweet Potato Pie

PUBLISHED
BY
THE BOSTON COOKING-
SCHOOL MAGAZINE C°
221 Columbus Ave
Boston   Mass

Cover of *American Cookery*, October 1939, formerly *The Boston Cooking School Magazine*. Courtesy of The Boston Cooking School Magazine Company.

instructions in cooking. She was thirty-nine years of age when *The Boston Cooking School Cook Book* was first published by the Boston firm of Little, Brown and Company—at her own expense even though Miss Farmer already had a distinguished culinary career.

When Miss Farmer took her manuscript to Little, Brown and Company, they told her they were not interested. It seemed impossible to them that the American housewife would be prevailed upon to buy one more collection of recipes. Miss Farmer turned about and persuaded the publisher to print three thousand copies on the agreement that she would pay the printing bill. It is probably the classic story of an unwilling publisher being talked into so lucrative a deal. Millions of copies and millions of dollars later, the firm acknowledged its original error in judgment. Fannie Farmer, deceased, is, indubitably, the reigning queen of the august house of Boston's Little, Brown and Company.

THIS department is for the benefit and free use of our subscribers. Questions relating to recipes, and those pertaining to culinary science and domestic economics in general, will be cheerfully answered by the editor. Communications for this department must reach us before the first of the month preceding that in which the answers are expected to appear. In letters requesting answers by mail, please enclose address and stamped envelope. Address queries to EDITOR, AMERICAN COOKERY, 221 Columbus Avenue, Boston, Mass.

QUERY No. 6093. — "Just recently I have lost my favorite recipe for Parker House rolls that I clipped from the magazine years ago. Would you be willing to reprint it for me?"

Parker House Rolls

Make a sponge of two cups of milk, scalded and cooled to lukewarm temperature, one yeast cake, softened in one-half a cup of lukewarm water, and about three cups of flour. Beat thoroughly, cover, and set in a warm place until light (about one and one-half hours). Add two tablespoons of sugar, one teaspoon of salt, one-half a cup of melted butter, and enough flour to knead to a light dough. Add the flour very slowly, mixing meanwhile. Knead about ten minutes and set aside to double in bulk. Gently turn upon a lightly floured board, upper side down, roll into a sheet about one-half an inch thick, cut into rounds, brush over half of each round with melted butter and fold the other half over the buttered half. Set close together in a buttered pan. When double in bulk, bake about half an hour at 400 deg. Fah. (a hot oven). — "American Cookery," June July, 1929.

QUERY No. 6094. — "Have you a tried and true recipe for Boston cream pie?"

Boston Cream Pie

Beat one-third a cup of butter to a cream; gradually beat in one cup of sugar; add two eggs, beaten light, one-half a cup of milk, and one cup and one-half of pastry flour sifted with two and one-half teaspoons of baking powder. Bake in two layer-cake pans, in an oven at 420 deg. Fah., twenty-five minutes. Put the layers together with an

English Cream Filling

Scald one cup of milk over hot water; stir one-third a cup of flour with one-third a cup of cold milk to make a smooth paste, then cook in the hot milk, stirring until the mixture thickens; cover and let cook fifteen minutes. Beat one egg, add one-half a cup of sugar, and beat again; add also one-fourth a teaspoon of salt, and stir into the hot mixture. Continue to stir until the egg is set. When cool, add one-half a teaspoon of vanilla. Sprinkle the top of the pie with sifted powdered sugar. — From "American Cookery," November, 1930.

"Queries and Answers" column from *American Cookery*, October 1939, featuring queries about Parker House Rolls and Boston Cream Pie. Courtesy of The Boston Cooking School Magazine Company.

When Fannie Farmer published her manuscript in 1896, she was the head of the much respected Boston School of Cooking which, when she first enrolled, had been merely an institute for instructing young women to be teachers of cooking—the forerunners of present-day economics teachers. Fannie was the eldest daughter of an editor and printer, J. Frank Farmer, and his wife, Mary Watson Farmer, who, according to one of Fannie's very few biographers, was a "notable housewife" at a time when housewifery was not regarded as one of the prime social female virtues. When Fannie, a typical redhead, was seventeen and a junior at Medford High School she suffered an attack. At that time medicine had not advanced to a stage where it could be properly diagnosed, although it is known it was not polio as she suffered a second one later in life that caused further curtailment of her physical mobility.

The first attack ended Fannie's high school career and chilled the aspirations her family had for her to attend college. She was confined to the family home where she gradually recovered sufficiently to assist her mother in the chores as much as her limited strength would permit. Her agile mind was immediately annoyed with the sloppiness that attended the recipes for cooking. And the cooking in the Farmer household had reached restaurant proportions, for they had had financial reverses and found it expedient to take in boarders.

At that period in Boston—and in most American cities—70 percent of all people lived at one time or another in boarding houses for an average of three years. Young people frequently started their married life in them; they could afford to live there "more genteelly" than they could in a home of their own, where they believed they would have to support several servants. Older people retired to them, and such famous and wealthy bachelors as Tom Appleton found in them permanent homes. The best ones, especially where the cooking was known to be excellent, had long waiting lists.

Fannie made the Farmer home into a residence of par excellence. It was at the suggestion of one of Fannie's younger sisters that Fannie enrolled in the Boston Cooking School in order to utilize her natural talent for cooking and to aid her thwarted desire for academic recognition. This was sound advice. Fannie was thirty-two when she graduated. Mrs. Carrie M. Dearborn, the director of the school, was so impressed with Fannie's intelligence, skill, and executive abilities that she invited her to become her assistant. Just two years later, Mrs. Dearborn died, and the board of trustees of the school elected the impressive Fannie to head the school, despite her physical handicaps. Actually, Fannie, according to Mrs. Wilma Lord Perkins, Fannie's niece-in-law, and since 1930 official editor and reviser of the famous cookbook, "was a great executive, food detective, and gourmet rather than a great cook herself."

When she was head of the Boston Cooking School, and later as head of her own school, Fannie spent as much time as she could going to the best restaurants and sampling their menus (a custom that has been carried over by such present-day followers as Julia Child, Craig Claibourne, and James Beard). Fannie's technique, when she could not divine ingredients, was to remove from her purse an engraved calling card and put a few drops of the sauce on it, fold it carefully, and take it away for future analysis and reference. Many of her pupils took great delight in reporting their taste discoveries: "Miss Farmer, you've just got to taste those rolls at the Holland House," or "They're serving a sausage at the Ritz-Carlton that you have nothing to match!" Off with her sampling cards would trot Miss Farmer to detect the missing links.

When she founded her own school—which was devoted to teaching housewives and professionals to cook, rather than instructing teachers in the art of home economics cooking—Fannie would give lectures, much in the style that other Boston ladies lectured on spiritual and intellectual food for thought. Her audiences of one hundred and fifty to two hundred eager housewives, skilled cooks, and chefs rarely had the opportunity to see the great Miss Farmer cook. "She was too impatient to cook a whole meal and while she lectured someone else cooked." Her lectures were reported in detail in the *Boston Evening Transcript* and copied by papers all over the country.

Because of her own illness, Miss Farmer's special interest was the problem of cooking for invalids. In her school there were courses in "invalid cookery." She lectured to nurses, and one year she gave a course in special invalid diets and in cooking for the sick at the Harvard Medical School. Fannie was a scientist at heart, but a practical scientist, not an abstract one. Thanks to this bent, Fannie insisted that a recipe be as accurately reproducible in the kitchen as a formula in the laboratory. Her fame spread with her cookbook from Boston to San Francisco, and she lectured across the country while she sampled the gourmet foods of her native land.

Fannie Farmer spent the last seven years of her life in a wheelchair, from which she gave her last lecture just ten days before she died in 1915 at the age of fifty-eight. Her preface in her first book was her epitaph, and a most befitting one for a lady who in death was to cease to be a person but to survive as a book. "I certainly feel that the time is not far distant when a knowledge of the principles of diet will be an essential part of one's education. Then mankind will eat to live, will be able to do better mental and physical work, and disease will be less frequent."

"I cannot find a cook in the whole city but what will get drunk," confessed Abigail Adams in 1789. But her problems were minor compared to those of latter-day hostesses in Boston, who prided themselves on the art of entertaining at home. Dining soon became an important social event in Boston homes, and there was scarcely a household that did not have on its library shelf a treasured copy of the 1880 edition of Hill's *Manual of Social and Business Forms.* Some of the rules were:

Never allow butter, soup or other food to remain on your whiskers. Use the napkin frequently. Never allow the conversation at the table to drift into anything but chit-chat; the consideration of deep and abstruse principles will impair digestion. Never hesitate to take the last piece of cake or bread; there are probably more. Never hold bones in your fingers while you eat from them. Cut the meat with a knife. Never wipe your fingers on the tablecloth, nor clean them in your mouth.

In addition a hostess was warned against a guest who used bad manners at the table. These infractions were listed:

1. Tips back his chair.
2. Eats with his mouth too full.
3. Feeds a dog at the table.
4. Holds his knife improperly.
5. Engages in violent argument at meal-time.
6. Lounges upon the table.
7. Brings a cross child to the table.
8. Drinks from the saucer, and laps with his tongue the last drop from the plate.
9. Comes to the table in his shirt-sleeves and puts his feet beside the chair.
10. Picks his teeth with his fingers.
11. Scratches her head and is frequently unnecessarily getting up from the table.

It is interesting that Hill's manual is graphically illustrated but oblivious to the rules set down by the author's occasional posers to sit with their elbows upon the table. Horrors!

The table service was a matter of great social distinction. Several items of importance were glass sugar bowls, saltcellars, and celery vases— all de rigueur at a nineteenth-century table—and preferably made of Tiffany glass, which was purchased in New York and began to replace the beautiful, simple early American Sandwich glass of the colonial homes.

The trials and tribulations of Boston hostesses involved with servants is a commentary of the class distinctions and problems that have plagued society ever since the day when man in his search for leisure used his brain to acquire the wealth with which to hire his brother to serve his bodily needs. In Boston it was especially tense, as it eventually incorporated further conflict between the Anglo-Saxon lord and master and the poor immigrant Irish man- and maidservant. But the Irish were not without their revenges. Their weapons were drunkenness, tardiness, and mimicry of the pretensions of their employers. (In a drawing by Charles Dana Gibson, a maid imitates her mistress, to the amusement of her co-workers and the Irish "cop on the beat," who foraged in the family kitchen of the upper-middle-class Beacon Hill residents.)

One of the guidebooks of hints for the hostess in the eighteen nineties was *Practical Housekeeping,* in which it suggested an oval dining table as being most sociable, and recommended that stools or hassocks be placed beneath the cloth for the comfort of the ladies. Sunday breakfasts were extremely popular.[2] Describing a summer breakfast for ten (with an illustration of the elaborate table setting) the following six courses are outlined: melon, fish, chicken with cream gravy, poached egg on toast, fillets of porterhouse steak with tomatoes a la mayonnaise, and quartered peaches. A warning was sent forth by the publication: "The worst torture that survives the inquisition is a bad formal dinner. A worse torture than any known to the inquisition is *any* formal dinner . . . inefficiently served."

The servant's means of retaliation for bad treatment was inefficient service, which humiliated the hostess and lowered her social image. The story is told of one butler, annoyed at last-minute extra guests, who took to his bottle and embarrassed his hostess to the degree that she discharged him when she saw his condition. Arrogantly, she hired another butler, not anticipating the revenge of her former chargé d'affaires. Before leaving his post he carefully unscrewed the entire gold dinner service into three hundred separate pieces and mixed them together in one heap on the parquet floor, so that they resembled the parts of a jigsaw puzzle. Unable to assemble them, the frantic hostess had to send to Tiffany's in New York, where two men were dispatched to have the service in readiness for the dinner.

Dining at home was, in truth, a battlefield, with the fight ensuing between the kitchen and the parlor. The dining table was the scene of action, and the unsuspecting guests were the spectators who reported the antics in juicy, gossipy anecdotes, which more often than not delighted in the failures and the dilemmas of a hostess rather than in the bounty of her hospitality.

Whether it was the servant problem or the innate Boston characteristic of preferring to limit home entertaining to the immediate family and very close associates one cannot determine, but Boston was one of the earliest cities to witness the success of public dining. In 1794, a French refugee, Jean Baptiste Gilbert Payplat, known locally as Julien, opened what he called a restorator or public ordinary, a cut above the general run of taverns. It was indeed a gigantic step above the rung of most taverns, since it introduced to that city truffles from Perigord, cheese fondue, and soups so delicious that Julien became known as the Prince of Soups. So renowned was the fame of Julien's Restorator that another Frenchman, the most distinguished professional epicure of his day, Anthelme Brillat-Savarin, hurried to Boston and lent his influential blessing to that establishment.

Julien's success was remarkable, considering that it occurred in a city where innovation was regarded with distrust and where Bostonians, now accustomed to the best things of life, chose to keep them to themselves. But the demand for public accommodations grew to such proportions that a group of public-spirited Bostonians pooled their resources in 1828 to build the Tremont House, probably the first class hotel (by modern standards) to be erected in the United States. Daniel Webster and Edward Everett attended the inaugural banquet, served amidst Turkish carpets, crystal chandeliers, and French ormolu clocks. For years the Tremont House furnished all guests under its roof at New Year's with a free dinner and provided diners with felt slippers, free of charge, while their boots were being cleaned and polished.

In 1855 Harvey D. Parker, whose name has been immortalized in a soft-crusted hot roll, opened in Boston's School Street, a restaurant whose instant success was based on the notion that people liked to eat meals at irregular hours. Since this was a contention of the owner, he set about proving his theory and offered an a la carte menu available at all hours. He made a fortune for himself with his idea. Inspired by the success of the pioneers in dining out places of elegance, Boston, by the eve of the Civil War, had become a mecca of fine restaurants, and dining out was as socially accepted as at-home entertaining and often less trying on the nerves of the host and hostess, the denizens of the kitchen, and the anxious guests.

Boston's list of famous restaurants is by all standards quite impressive.

Many of its establishments are still centers of protocol for eating habits and restaurant etiquette. The essentially English characteristic of the Boston-British background is self-evident. The Boston gentleman, if he does not stop at one of his English-type private clubs during the day, will pause at the typically English "for men only" spots—the main dining room at Locke-Obers or Thompson's Spa, or the Parker House Bar.

Of Locke-Obers, Lucius Beebe wrote:

> The most gracious and comforting tavern that ever survived an era of outrage, pillage, and Federal barbarism, Frank Locke's Winter Place Wine Rooms. It has been variously known as the Dutchman's, the Winter Place Restaurant, as Locke's and as Locke-Obers and even to irreverent (Harvard) undergraduates, as the Nekked Lady, but by any other name it smells the same; fragrant and holy in the souvenirs of many discerning men of several generations.

Locke-Obers is tucked up an alley called Winter Place, near Tremont Street. Except for the upstairs, there is not too much that has changed about this temple of culture since the era of the hansom cab. It is a fine, ennobling establishment, last redecorated in 1886. It smacks of ancient times and truly good living, of lobsters off the Portland boat and real class—with old-time waitresses, slightly musty private rooms with heavy draperies, and the apoplectic faces of Boston businessmen chomping away on mutton chops.

Down Tremont Street past the Hotel Touraine and left down Stuart Street is Jacob Wirth Company, a peerless German restaurant with brass rails and sawdust on the floor. The waiters are imbued with age and serving wisdom. Over the bar is a motto: *Suum cuique*—Every Man for Himself.

Since 1868 Bostonians have been gorging themselves at Jake Wirth's on bratwurst, thick green pea soup, brisket with horseradish, dark brown rye bread, New England boiled dinner, fish chowder, lobster salad (Divine!).

The Parker House at Tremont and School (recently renamed) is very old Boston, very stately, very quiet and dignified. The specialty (beyond the memorable Parker House rolls) is a honeycomb tripe a la Parker, cod-fish tongues, and cheeks.

The Union Oyster House at 41 Union Street is the home of the lobster in any form, boiled, broiled, baked, stuffed, thermidor, Newburg, fried, sautéed, and stewed. And every possible combination of clams, oysters,

The Ritz, c. 1869. Etched by Sears Gallagher.

Cape scallops, mackerel, scrod, salmon, halibut, swordfish, smelts, cod, haddock, sole, blowfish, bluefish, and lumpfish. The doors opened in 1826, and at one time Louis Philippe resided there.

Across from Faneuil Hall, amid the debris of wholesale provision markets and surrounded by shabby eighteenth- and nineteenth-century buildings groaning with fatigue, is Durgin-Park, which features long family-style tables and waitresses who, like waitresses in most kosher delicatessens, seem to resent your presence but nevertheless deliver up the food. The menu is strictly basic New England, with stews, lobsters, scrod, Yankee pot roast, old-fashioned baked beans, and honest-to-God strawberry short cake. There is no booze, no reservations, and the doors close at 7:30 P.M.

And certainly no mention of restaurants in Boston can be complete without a gentle reminder that it was in Boston that Howard Johnson started the gastronomy trend of today. Any further comment by the author is de trop!

Special consideration should be rendered the Ritz, for it has remained one of the few fine hotels. The concentration has always been on decorum, service, food, new linen, and well-modulated voices. The Ritz is one reason why so many shows on their pre-Broadway tryouts choose to come to Boston instead of Philadelphia. The producers are not fond of Boston audiences, who are so static as to appear to be in a state of somnambulism; nor of the critics, who are adept in the art of verbal destruction; nor of the climate, which is more often than not rain, turning to snow, turning to sleet, turning to rain; nor of the historic charms of Boston, to which most New Yorkers are blatantly oblivious. However, they are dedicated to the Ritz. The sign on Arlington Street in Boston is the Ritz, the interior seems removed from Boston, from the United States, a stone's throw from Westminster Abbey in London. Even Conrad Hilton has left the Ritz intact as a shrine.

By the late 1860s America was a nation on the move. Since many Bostonians traveled by train to New York for business transactions, the need for the dining car on the New Haven railroad was apparent, and in due time it became a matchless showcase for all the other services the railroad hoped to sell—the newly developed Pullman car for sleeping, ice refrigeration for the shipping of foodstuffs, among other innovations. Serving a lordly clientele of Boston Brahmins, the New Haven was famous for its scrod, Cotuit oysters, and Maine lobster, for its wine and staple groceries, all of which were supplied by S. S. Pierce. As Napoleon reputedly commented, "An army marches on its stomach," so the nine-teenth-century Boston business merchant traveled on his—in style!

What was to mold the public eating habits of Bostonians had moved a considerable distance in a period of two centuries when the early inns and taverns, the humble ancestors of the elegant hotels and dining palaces, provided more than room and board for travelers. They served, too, as law courts, centers of entertainment, meeting places for revolutionaries, clearing houses for mail, newspapers, government proclamations. Indeed about all the hostelries of the Founding Fathers did not provide were comfortable accommodations and good hosts. The consuming curiosity of tavern keepers so annoyed one traveler that he anticipated his curious host by stating: "My name is Benjamin Franklin. I was born in Boston. I am a printer by profession, and am travelling to Philadelphia. I shall have to return at such a time, and I have no news. Now what can you give me for dinner?"

The change from the rustic inns to the palaces of the people was a highly dramatic one. The earliest modern hotel does not begin to compare with the twentieth-century hotels, which are unmatched in extravagant architecture and decor throughout the world, but they were of sufficient grandeur to dazzle even the sophisticated city folk of their day. There were public rooms with mosaic floors; carpeted and curtained guest rooms and corridors; imported, carved walnut furniture; dining rooms with breathtakingly high ceilings; marble fireplaces; and menus (in French) that boasted an unlimited variety of dishes. The bridal chambers were "love bowers where Eve might have whispered love to Adam after she was expelled from Paradise without regretting the change."

The personnel of the Boston hotels had outdone the Brahmins, and an anecdote is told of a proper Bostonian who was having difficulty with his wife, who was seeking refuge in the Ritz. In a state of inebriation he demanded of the desk clerk the key to her suite. The clerk adamantly refused the scoundrel admission. "My man," said the Harvard-Porcellian aristocrat, "are you aware of who I am?" the clerk looked with a disapproving eye as the gentleman lurched forward and announced his identity and then confided, "I was conceived in the Ritz." To which the clerk retorted: "Sir, the Ritz cannot be held responsible for the mistakes of its clients." Abashed, the defrocked son of a merchant prince retreated —fully aware of his proper rebuke.

The transition marched from the Puritan Bostonian about whom

Matthew Henry reported in his *Commentaries,* published in the early eighteenth century, "It was a common saying among the Puritans, brown bread and the Gospel is good fare," to the observation that "culinary art may be said to be the distinguishing thing of civilization, and in its perfection it is the inspiration of genius. . . . The chef of a large establishment must possess at least two essential qualifications; he must be epicurean by nature, and this natural gift must be enhanced by long years of training in his profession." In the last decade of the nineteenth century and the first of the twentieth, spectacular private parties in hotels and restaurants reached their apogee. Newspapers were filled with stories of bachelor dinners at which chorines emerged from pies and danced in the altogether and of hosts and hostesses who spent thousands of dollars on masquerades. In comparison to New York, Boston retained a resemblance of Puritan influence, but the resemblance was as slight as that of the Colonel's Lady and Judy O'Grady—sisters under the skin. It was all largely superficial.

On the subject of Boston and food, the home of brown bread served with hot baked beans and tea, we cannot lose sight of the Irish day laborer, who contributed his own sustenance to the menu we have available in Boston today. For the curious we submit the most famous recipe for Boston brown bread:

1 cup rye flour	1 teaspoon salt
1 cup corn meal	¾ cup molasses
1 cup graham flour	2 cups buttermilk
¾ teaspoon baking soda	1 cup chopped raisins (optional)

Sift all dry ingredients together. Add molasses, buttermilk, and raisins. Divide batter and place in 2 buttered 1-quart pudding molds or 3 buttered coffee cans, filling them about ¾ full. Molds must be covered tightly, with buttered lids tied and taped so the bread won't force the cover off in rising. Place molds in a pan filled with enough boiling water to reach halfway up the mold and steam for 3 hours, keeping the water at the halfway mark. Serve piping hot with butter and Boston Baked Beans.

It is for baked beans that Boston came to be known as Bean Town. The Puritan Sabbath lasted from sundown on Saturday until sundown on Sunday, and baked beans provided the Puritans with a dish that was easy to prepare. The bean pot could be kept over a slow heat in a fireplace to serve at Saturday supper and Sunday breakfast. Housewives too busy with other chores were able to turn the baking of the beans over to a local baker. The baker called each Saturday morning to pick up the family's bean pot and take it to the community oven, usually in the cellar of a nearby tavern. The free-lance baker then returned the beans with a bit of brown bread on Saturday evening or Sunday morning.

6 cups tea or navy beans	1 teaspoon black pepper
1 pound salt pork	1 cup molasses
1 tablespoon dry mustard	1 small onion (optional)
1 tablespoon salt	

Pick over beans, cover with cold water, and soak overnight. In the morning drain, cover with fresh water, bring to a boil very slowly, then simmer until the skins burst ("which is best determined," wrote Fannie Farmer, "by taking a few beans on the tip of a spoon and blowing on them, when skins will burst if sufficiently cooked." Miss Farmer adds that beans tested this way "must, of course, be thrown away").

Drain beans. Scald the salt pork, which should be well streaked with lean, by letting it stand in the boiling water for 5 to 10 minutes. Cut off 2 thin slices, one to place in the bottom of pot, the other to be cut into bits. Score rind of the first piece with a sharp knife.

Mix dry mustard, salt, black pepper, and molasses. Alternate the layers of beans in the pot with the molasses mixture and the bits of pork. If you use an onion, bury it in the middle. When the bean pot is full, cover with the large lid, and bake all day (a minimum of 6 to 8 hours) in a 250° oven. Check from time to time and add boiling water if needed. Uncover pot during last hour of baking so that rind will be brown and crisp.

To this day, many old-timers believe the rich brown goodness of Boston Baked Beans is largely due to the earthenware bean pot, with its narrow throat and bulging sides. Lacking one of these pots one can use any deep earthenware casserole that has a cover.

And no chapter on Boston cooking would be complete without a Sunday menu from Harvard.

Roast Pork

Mashed Turnips   Harvard Beets*

Mixed Green Salad

Cheesecake

*Harvard Beets

2½ cups sliced cooked or canned beets
½ cup sugar
2 teaspoons cornstarch
½ cup cider vinegar
1 tablespoon butter

Drain beets, reserving ¼ cup of liquid. Combine sugar and corn-starch. Stir in vinegar. Add to beet juice. Cook, stirring over low heat until mixture is thickened and smooth. Add beets and butter and cook until beets are heated through.

Yield: Four to six servings.

Any young lady with an eye on a Harvard man's heart had better *beet* the way through his stomach!

As the city grew, working men and women found it cheaper to eat at short-order restaurants than to travel home for lunch. Ladd's Eating House in Boston offered "fast meals at all hours of the day." Dunn's handbill tempted discriminating diners with ten-course meals for a quarter. The eating habits of the working class were described: "They swallow, but don't eat; and like the boa constrictor, bolt everything, whether it be a blanket or a rabbit." (*Harper's Weekly*, 1856) The workingman's bar was almost totally Irish, devoid of frills, and a strictly male institution, featuring long wooden bars with brass rails, free lunch counters, and bartenders who were philosophers as well as pourers and mixers. The saloon became the target of the Prohibitionists and songs such as "Oh, Mr. Bartender, Mr. Bartender, Has My Father Been Here?" were supposed to wring tears when sung piteously by a wee urchin in search of a drunken brute of a father.

The saloon era ended with Prohibition, and was replaced by the soda fountain for the ladies. In 1891 *Harper's Weekly* proclaimed chauvinis-tically: "Soda water is an American drink." By that time there were almost as many soda fountains as bars in Boston. John Matthews had introduced soda water to America in 1883, and a few years later a Frenchman added syrups. In 1874 ice cream was incorporated, and the national drink, the ice cream soda, was born. The soda flowed from fountains emblazoned with statuettes of half-draped beauties, a king, a philosopher, or a spear-carrying maiden. Many ladies who were advocates

Ladd's Eating House, nineteenth century. Courtesy of the American Antiquarian Society.

of Prohibition frequented these new establishments. The fact that the decor was "racy" and full of rococo charm did not disturb their aesthetic or ascetic tastes.

In time, when Prohibition was repealed, the ice cream parlors also vanished and cocktail lounges and nightclubs replaced them. But even in Boston—famous for the Merry-Go-Round bar in the Copley-Plaza, where the twentieth-century debutante met her date and sipped, publicly, a very dry Martini—the frowning Boston matron still took to her tea and Boston brown bread at the closing hour of day—5 P.M.

7

Yes, Virginia, There Is an "A" in Harvard

Across the Charles River, in the village of Cambridge, within the sight and sound of Boston, only sixteen years after the founding of Plymouth, the Great and General Court of Massachusetts passed the following vote:

> The Court agreed to give 400 Pounds toward a schoale or a colledge, whereof 200 pounds to bee paid the next yeare, and 200 pounds when the worke is finished, and the next Court to appoint wheare and what building.

And Harvard (in Boston pronounced *Hahvud,* with a long, flat *a* and no *r*) was born. It was created primarily to make certain that the children of the Founding Fathers, their grandchildren, and their heirs unto eternity remain proudly English in their cultural aspects and not revert to an un-English tradition of ignorance and frontier barbarism.

A farmhouse was refurbished in 1636 to house the nine enrolled students, and Nathaniel Eaton, a prominent Puritan and Cambridge graduate, was selected as master. According to Cotton Mather, he was a "rare scholar" but somewhat dedicated to the old English custom of flogging. His wife contributed to the project by feeding the first students not tea and sympathy but "ungutted mackerel" and hasty pudding. But the man whose name was to legitimatize the puny institution, John Harvard, a master of arts of Emmanuel College, Cambridge, England, was in residence in Charlestown, where he was a candidate for the position of assistant minister to the Charlestown Church. Whether he ever crossed the ferry to observe the birth pangs of the first North American college is not to be ascertained, but when he died in 1638, within a year of his arrival in New England, he bequeathed half his property and his entire library to the new institution of learning. In 1639, the General Court ordered "that the colledge agreed upon formerly to be built at Cambridg shal bee called Harvard Colledge."

Only known surviving copy of the Burgis view of Harvard College (1726). Courtesy of the Massachusetts Historical Society.

It is interesting to note that this son of a butcher from the bawdy slum of Southwark was not a gentleman and scholar born, but at his death at the age of thirty years he had accumulated a small fortune and a rather astonishing quantity of books (four hundred, to be exact) and by his munificent gift had his name bestowed upon a nebulous educational fetus that was to grow into one of the world's greatest universities.

With the gift of John Harvard, subscription gifts for the college commenced; they have continued to the present day. The first president of Harvard (after the dismissal of Mr. Eaton, whose floggings and bad food brought about his downfall) was Henry Dunster, who was not only a fine teacher but a talented moneyraiser. He completed a new building, increased the enrollment, and set the standards, which were those of old England. Money came from strange sources—tolls from the Boston-Charlestown ferry, merchandise and livestock, and from every family in the New England Confederation an annual donation of a peck of wheat or a shilling (which donations were called "college corn"). Other sources of money were missionary contributions from England, including a scholarship fund from Lady Mowlson (Anne Radcliffe), who was to become—in absentia—the person for whom Radcliffe College was named.

The first commencement of Harvard took place in September 1642. In that class was one Henry Saltonstall, who later earned an M.D. at Padua,

Sir Richard Saltonstall, who with his son helped to found Watertown, Massachusetts. This portrait was supposedly painted in 1644 when he was in Holland. Courtesy of the Peabody Museum, Salem, Massachusetts.

became an Oxford Fellow, and established a family custom that is unique —they are the only family in America to have had ten successive generations graduate from one college: Harvard. The first commencement was a proud day for New England, an occasion for overeating and gaiety: "a kind of New World Holiday, another Feast of St. Giles." In subsequent years, the carousing took on bacchanalian aspects, including the discharging of firearms. In addition to the festivities there were orations, disputations, resolutions, and the presentation of degrees.

During the 1640s Harvard expanded, despite its lack of solid financial support, and what had been intended to be an institution for the education of Puritan ministers grew to be an institution of general education. New and more liberal subjects and policies were introduced. The influence of the Mathers, Increase and Cotton, waned in the eighteenth century, when John Leverett became president and introduced more liberal subjects and policies.

When Charles William Eliot was elected president of Harvard in 1869, he found himself master of an aging New England seminary, very backward in medicine, law, and science. Eliot was only thirty-five years old, and he set to work with intellectual zest and ambition. He served forty years, and during his presidency the elective system flourished, leaving the student free to follow his bent in philosophy, literature, arts and sciences, or whatever he chose to study. Possibly the most famous of all the presidents of Harvard, Eliot twice turned down an ambassadorship

The old "President's Chair" is among the most ancient relics of the past now in the possession of the college, having been used for the purpose of conferring degrees on Commencement Day since earliest recollections. It is said to have been brought to the college during the presidency of Holyoke, as a gift of the Reverend Ebenezer Turell of Medford. Turell was connected by marriage with the Mathers, by one of whom the chair is said to have been brought from England. Its variety is said to be common in the county of Cheshire, being "of wood, the seat triangular, the back, arms and legs loaded with turnery, and carved and turned in the most uncouth and whimsical forms." Harvard University, 1898.

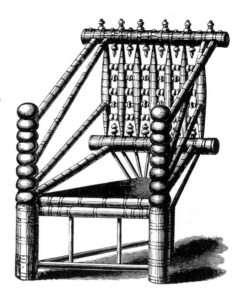

to England. He is also known across America as the editor of the Harvard Classics ("five-foot shelf"). Today, the university includes graduate schools of divinity, law, arts and sciences, education, engineering, medicine, dentistry, public administration, business, and public health. The university library, among the nation's finest, houses over six million volumes, and the Fogg Museum of Art is one of the great university museums of the world.

The importance of Harvard to Boston can only be equated by the importance of man's brain to his body. In the seventeenth and eighteenth centuries, when Boston was dominated by ministers and magistrates, Harvard was primarily a ministers' and magistrates' sons proposition. In the nineteenth century, when the merchant era began, Harvard became the merchants' sons proposition. Harvard's presidents, from the moment of inception, were dedicated to maintaining the social tone of the college. By the middle of the eighteenth century, Harvard's student body had a caste system that was unrivaled. In 1749 students were ranked according to their social standing, "to the Dignity of the Familie whereto the student severally belonged." Thus the early catalogue of student registration at Harvard was not in alphabetical rotation but in accord with family prominence. By the time President Eliot took over the helm of Harvard, the caste system had placed a pall over the institution that was deadly for public relations. But Eliot was saved the burden of categorizing the student body, because the clubs, which were to be a major factor in Harvard's social identity and in the social life pattern of Boston, had come into being.

The most famous of all clubs is the Hasty Pudding, which has its own clubhouse and stages a musical every Easter (an event for which some of America's most talented authors have contributed material). It is in the real Boston club sense not a club at all but a sort of proving ground for the election of students to one of the ten important social final clubs. These ten "finals" in social rank are: Porcellian, A.D., Fly, Spec, Delphic, Owl, Fox, Phoenix, Iroquois, and Bat. The club memberships parallel almost exactly the social ratings of Boston's first social families. The memberships of the three socially important clubs, Porcellian, A.D., and Fly, are composed mostly of Bostonians but do include some prominent New Yorkers, occasional Philadelphians, and, following the turn of the twentieth century, a few wealthy Chicagoans. For the most part, Harvard men from environs other than these, with rare exceptions, are elected to membership only in the more obscure clubs.

The Harvard clubs are modeled on the Boston social clubs, which in turn were modeled on the proper English clubs of London. Generally speaking, the clubhouses are not elaborate, and the dues not excessive. The members rarely dine in their clubs because, under the "house plan," boys at Harvard have to pay for twenty-one meals a week in their dormitories; and they never sleep in the clubs for the houses have no bedrooms. The exclusiveness of the clubs was especially evident in their treatment of female guests; except for annual teas, the opposite sex was avoided like the plague. Yet the Harvard club members made up the male attendance of most Boston female social events, in which a proper Harvard escort was a must. Club membership has always been a good recommendation for marital nomination into one of Boston's wealthy families.

The oldest of the clubs, Porcellian, was founded in 1791 and was so named because of the relish two of its founders took in the delicacy of roasted pig. The early gourmets were Francis Cabot Lowell and Robert Treat Paine. For generation after generation, Porcellian has boasted a membership of Cabots, Lowells, Cutlers, Lymans, Hunnewells, Salton-stalls, Sears, and Gardners. The clubhouse is austere, without even a game room. Its decor features a collection of pig figurines in sundry poses and a mirror, which is placed at such an angle that club members may sit in the main room and look down on the passing parade on Massachusetts Avenue without bothering to leave their chairs. The social mores of the club are exemplified in the legendary story of the stroke of the Harvard crew who was a Porcellian and of whom it was said, "He's democratic all right—he knows all but the three up front."

The importance of making a final club at Harvard is unquestionably in the eyes of the candidate. Many of the most famous alumni never were members in any of the ten finals. To some it mattered little, if at all, but to others the oversight was no mere pinprick but an open sore, forever erupting. Robert Benchley, for example, never got over the fact that he failed to make a final club. Someone once asked him if he was going back to a class reunion. "Why should I?" he retorted. "No one paid any attention to me when I was there." This was a strange reply, considering that he had been a member of Hasty Pudding, president of the *Lampoon,* vice-president of the Dramatic Society, on the Union Library Committee, a member of the Mandolin Club, the Memorial Society, the Exeter Club, Delta Upsilon, Stylus Club, O.K. Society, Student Council, Ivy Orator, and president of the Signet Society. What he meant was, "To hell with them. I never made a final club."

In order to be assured of recognition for membership in the final club, one had to conform to a life pattern decreed by the club membership. The best way to obtain this was by attending and graduating from one of the socially correct Eastern private schools. The schools fed the pabulum essential to create the Boston scholar.

The Boston English-High and Latin School, c. 1890. This pretentious structure prepped most of the younger Boston elite for Harvard and was a successor to the old Latin School. From the *American Conservationist,* August 1936.

The first such school, the Boston Public Latin School, was founded one year before Harvard and is the oldest free public school in America. For many years it was the feedbag for Harvard, and to date it has supplied that institution with four presidents and many of its more famous alumni. Of its qualifications in.preparing a student to handle the classes at Harvard, Joseph Kennedy, the father of the Kennedy clan and a graduate of the school, had this to say at the school's Tercentenary Dinner in 1935:

> To strangers I could not possibly convey the reasons for the powerful and sweet hold which the School has upon my affections. It would be like trying to explain to strangers why I love my family. The Latin School was a shrine that seemed to make us all feel that if we could stick it out at the Latin School, we were made of just a little better stuff than the rest of the fellows of our own age who were attending what we always thought were easier schools. Headmaster Fiske was not the strict disciplinarian and dry-as-dust scholar we have always pictured him, he had a human side as well.[1]

The "St. Grottlesexers"—graduates of New England's elite Episcopal Church schools, such as Groton, St. Mark's, St. Paul's, St. George's, and Middlesex—were the most likely candidates for final clubs, but only a small percentage of these were accepted. Graduates of Exeter, Andover, Milton Academy, Noble and Greenough, and Pomfret, regardless of family name and wealth, are second banana in the clubs' casting offices. Of all the schools, Groton in Boston probably takes the lead, with such notable graduates as the late Franklin D. Roosevelt. The school itself gained its reputation from its founder, the Reverend Endicott Peabody, who was indubitably the Mr. Chips of American headmasters. The Reverend Mr. Peabody, after attending school in England, returned to Boston and established what he considered the perfect duplicate of the English public school. He named the school for the site, Groton, where it was located.

It has been said of the Reverend Mr. Peabody that he ran the school on the lines of a concentration camp with games. The boys slept in cubicles, they tackled games in which the reverend himself also played, and they were saturated with chapel, hard study, and hard knocks. The Reverend Mr. Peabody has been quoted as saying that to be a headmaster you had to be "a bit of a bully." Averell Harriman ('09 Groton) remarked about the famed headmaster, "You know he would be an awful bully, if he weren't such a terrible Christian." According to Arthur

Schlesinger in *The Crisis of the Old Order,* it was Peabody himself "who put his stamp on the school, infusing the routine and the discipline with an awful moral significance." Cold showers upon arising toughened the sleepy adolescent for the brutal awakening to the cruel, cold facts of adult life.

And no one could impress Headmaster Endicott Peabody. He observed of his most illustrious student, F.D.R., "There has been a good deal written about Franklin Roosevelt when he was a boy at Groton, more than I should have thought justified by the impression he left at the school." Off from Groton went Franklin Roosevelt to Harvard, to be accepted in Fly, to edit the *Crimson,* and to observe: "Recalling Harvard years it seems to me that it used to take me the better part of a day just to take my shirts to the Chinaman and buy a new squash ball."

Architecturally, Harvard is a hodgepodge of buildings constructed around the famous Yard. The Yard is filled with elm trees, supplemented by sporadic plantings of bushes. Here among these New England bricks

View of Harvard University, Cambridge, Massachusetts.

there is no opening for knots, mazes, terraces, pergolas, temples, fountains, flower-banked walks, or topiary hedges. It is not odd that the physical layout is similar to that of Boston built around the Common, for the same architect constructed both—Charles Bulfinch, whose University Hall, built in 1815 of white Chelmsford granite in the middle of the Yard, is considered one of the "most beautiful" buildings.

Charles Bulfinch, graduate of the Boston Latin School and Harvard University in 1781, is recognized as America's first professional architect. In 1793, he was responsible for the old Federal Street Theatre, the first playhouse in all New England bringing to Boston the devil in person in the form of actors, actresses, stagehands, and stage managers. His next important work was the State House on Beacon Street at Park, across from Trefry and Partridge, up the street from the Boston Athenaeum. Bulfinch then provided the Elizabethan city of Boston with new drainage and street lighting and "straightened and widened the streets." (What streets he straightened and widened is still a mystery.) Of his University Hall, Charles W. Eliot told the students of the School of Architecture: "Here is the great architectural effort of the College in the early part of the nineteenth century."

Many famous architects have left their stamp on Harvard. Sever Hall is one of the Romanesque creations of Henry Hobson Richardson. It sits about 450 feet away from the Dana-Palmer House, which was built in 1820 and was the home of Richard Henry Dana, the father of the author of *Two Years Before the Mast*. This pleasant clapboard house was the site of the first Harvard astronomical observatory and the home of many presidents, notably the illustrious James Bryant Conant.

Harvard has seen a number of famous buildings torn down and replaced by newer and (supposedly) more beautiful edifices. One of the traditional and romantic buildings that was demolished and replaced by the Widener Library was Gore Hall, the original college library. It was a Walter Scott type of construction in the form of a fourteenth-century Gothic Latin cross, with towers, pinnacles, and buttresses. Charles W. Eliot lamented the passing of Gore Hall in 1909 when it was leveled to earth, "despite the fact that it bore the name of Christopher Gore, eminent citizen, governor, and one of the largest benefactors Harvard had ever had [$95,000] in 1831."

But Gore Hall was not the only building to feel the ax of changing architectural fashions. In 1912 President Abbott Lawrence Lowell razed the President's House, which had been the gift of Peter C. Brooks in

Charles Bulfinch. From *Memorial History of Boston*, ed. by Justin Manor (Boston: Osgood, 1880–1881).

President Abbot Lawrence Lowell of Harvard.

1846, to house his son-in-law Edward Everett. President Lowell wished to give the university a larger and better president's house than the mansard-roofed Brooks homestead. The house President Lowell placed on the same site is a very handsome colonial house built on a grand scale. It cost $155,000 to erect, and President Lowell footed the bill out of his own personal fortune. Lowell fulfilled "the most rigid conditions which the most august member of the Harvard corporation could require. He is of the Brahmin caste; he is distinguished in letters, he has had experience in financial affairs and administrative boards; he is an inheritor of reasonable wealth." (The New York *Sun,* October 6, 1909) It might also be added that he was the brother of the cigar-smoking poetess Amy Lowell.

In addition to the old colonial buildings that compose the physical Harvard, there are also several dreary nineteenth-century dormitories, one of them being Matthews Hall, which was built in 1872 and was considered at the time to be "the finest college dormitory in America," its majestic Gothic style being admired for its "ornamental" qualities. Across from it is Weld Hall, also of 1872 vintage in the "Elizabethan style," with two towering skylights. Erected in this same period (1870) is Thayer Hall, the gift of Nathaniel Thayer, a Boston merchant who contributed $100,000 for this massive conglomerate of brick. As a building it is totally lacking in character and bears an uncanny resemblance to the textile mills that helped furnish the cash that bought the bricks that inspired the architect to build Thayer Hall. It was in Matthews Hall that the first bathroom was installed in a Harvard dormitory. Up until 1860 there had been no water in the Yard, nor was there any sewer. For bathing purposes the students carried water to their rooms in buckets from one of the two pumps in the Yard. They might have heated some water in their own fireplaces, but in the best Boston tradition of austerity, they probably bathed in nice cold water. Consequently, "the amount of bathing being done at the college was very limited."

In recent years there has been a grand remodeling program going on in the Yard. Following World War II, when Lowell House was used as headquarters for Navy units stationed at Harvard, $50,000 was spent to make it again habitable for the esoteric. Most of the money reputedly went to sweep out cigarette butts and paint out graffiti on the walls. The evidence of the New Architecture of Le Corbusier in the Leverett House Towers and the New Quincy House, in which glass and steel predominate, makes it apparent that although the body of Harvard may be ancient, the face is either new or being skillfully lifted by the plastic surgeons of contemporary design. As George Santayana said, "Harvard has freedom, both from external trammels, and from pleasant torpor of too fixed a tradition. She has freedom and a single eye for the truth, and there are enough to secure for her, if the world goes well, an incomparable future."

> So it's cheer, cheer, cheer
> At the jolly Book and Bell,
> And it's three times three for Harvard
> With a yell, yell, yell.

From its founding, Harvard has been a sports mecca, and this enthusiasm has carried over to Boston's grip on the national professional sports of baseball, hockey, and basketball—played in the Boston Gardens on a parquet floor, no less! In a school where intellectual pursuits are and always have been the essential business at hand, in this day of highly competitive sports it is surprising that Harvard rates as high as it does in Ivy League sports' competitions.

The oldest sport at Harvard is the noble and honorable art of rowing. It is only natural that Harvard, patterned after Oxford and Cambridge and situated on the Charles River, should imitate her English counterparts in aquatic pursuits. Until 1826, the college maintained a sloop, *Harvard,* which made periodic trips to bring firewood for the college to its own pier. From the earliest times students skated on the Charles River, swam in it, and even drowned in it, but real boating, organized boating, did not begin until 1844, when a regular boat club was formed by members of the class of '46 with the six-oared *Oneida,* "a plumb stem, undecked lapstreak, thirty-seven feet long, three-and-a-half-foot beam." The oldest college contest in the United States is the Harvard-Yale crew race, which antedates football by seventeen years. "Rowing has always stood high at Harvard and the boats have been manned by men of admirable quality," says John Hays Gardner in an Oxford Press publication titled *Harvard.* Some of the men who carried their salty sport into areas of national and even world prominence are: Nathaniel Bowditch; Richard Henry Dana; Harold Vanderbilt; Charles Francis Adams; Rear Admiral Samuel Eliot Morison, the official historian of naval operations, World War II; Assistant Secretary of the Navy Franklin Delano Roosevelt; and Lieutenant, j.g., John F. Kennedy of PT boat 109.

Football at Harvard is designated in two words—The Game. The

Rowing on the Charles River.
Photograph courtesy of the Society
for the Preservation of New England
Antiquities.

Game refers, among Harvard and Yale graduates, only to the Harvard-Yale football classic, played on alternate years at the Yale Bowl, which is roughly ten minutes from the Yale campus in New Haven, Connecticut, and at Soldiers Field, on the banks of the Charles River in Cambridge, Massachusetts. At one time Harvard used to be a power in football, and the Harvard-Yale game was observed with respect by sports lovers. Now it is a social brawl in which man's cup runneth over. At one point, Harvard was regularly represented on the All-American teams. The formation called the flying wedge was invented at Harvard, and the forward pass was the innovation of Percy Haughton, the famous Harvard coach, about whom Charles A. Wagner once said:

> Percy Haughton was without question the greatest creative mind of American football. Other names may challenge the designation, or draw more familiar recognition, still others may, through the circumstance of promotional prestige, be called forth above his own on the roster of regency. It is fable. Haughton was the supreme artist of American football coaching. He approached the art with the deviousness of a Leonardo; all science, all knowledge, even life itself was the slave of his creativity.

Haughton was made coach in 1908, and his teams in eight years won 85.54 percent of their games, lost 8.43, and tied 6.03. Of football

Haughton had his own words: "Football is poetry. The same rhythmic skill, the same startling and significant expression." And, that's the way a Harvard man talks about his game-plan!

The English game of "rounders," slightly modified and now known as baseball, came to Harvard during the Civil War. Oliver Wendell Holmes said that he played a "good deal of baseball" while at Harvard in 1829, but the first organized ballgame was played in Cambridge by some students who entered from Phillips Exeter Academy. They called it the New York Game, presumably operating under the set of rules laid down by the Knickerbocker Baseball Club of New York in 1845.

It is impractical to analyze each and every sport indulged in at Harvard but there are

facilities and organization for every level of athletic ability . . . there are 49 tennis courts, 71 squash courts; the Indoor Athletic Building which contains two swimming pools (there is another in one of the Houses), three basketball courts, and rooms for wrestling, boxing, and fencing. . . . Just across the Charles on Soldiers Field are 70 acres of playing fields. Dillon Field House is there and the Briggs cage and the stadium, which was the first college stadium built (1903). A new enclosed artificial ice hockey rink was completed in 1955. (*Harvard Crimson*)

In addition to the standard sports there are varsity teams in sailing, skiing, lacrosse, and rugby. There is also occasionally informal cricket, bowling on the green, curling, cockfighting, falcony, and tossing the caber. Is it any wonder that it has been said that nothing except being in love is as exciting as being an undergraduate at Harvard?

But Harvard is not what it is because of the final clubs, nor because of the architectural contributions, nor the athletic facilities. Harvard has managed to survive as the intellectual spearhead of America. The patrician families of Boston regarded Harvard as a family responsibility. They sent their sons as a matter of course. And they considered it a family duty not only to endow and foster it in the interests of the meritorious poor, but to maintain its standards and oversee it. They founded chairs that bore their names, such as the Boylston chair, the Eliot chair, and the Smith professorship.

Who would have respected wealth in Boston if wealth had not respected learning? In the beginning the true Harvard man was the Boston man, possessing a clear, distinct mentality; a strong distaste for nonsense; steady composure; a calm and gentle demeanor; stability; good principles; intelligence; a habit of understatement; a slow and cautious way of reasoning; contempt for extravagance, vanity, and affectation; kindness of heart; purity; decorum; and profound affection, filial and paternal. A noble type, severely limited, which Boston celebrated in marble busts. That the ideal man bore a strange resemblance to John Quincy Adams is no accident, but of original intent. It was what the supporters of Harvard expected the college to produce—a pattern suited for the merchant, the lawyer, and the man of God, after the Boston fashion.

But the mind of Harvard bypassed the model and produced many leaders of intellectual powers above and beyond the narrow breadth of vision of the original founders and donors. In the Law School of Harvard we find the names of three Supreme Court justices who have radically altered the due process of law as we know it in the United States. Oliver Wendell Holmes, "the great dissenter," while lecturing at Lowell Institute advanced his theory of judicial restraint, in which he advocated that common law must be a response to the needs of the society it represents. In the early twentieth century Louis Brandeis broke the pattern of conservatism in the Supreme Court when, with the famous Brandeis Brief, he revolutionized the practice of law by presenting before the court evidence from doctors, factory inspectors, and social workers of the disastrous effects of hard labor and over-long working hours upon women. Known

Surpreme Court Justice Oliver Wendell Holmes at the age of 89. Photograph courtesy of Wide World Photos (1930).

as the "people's attorney," he was also one of the first prominent Americans to be conscious of the plight of Jewish people, and he became a leader of the Zionist movement. In the later years Harvard Law School could claim Justice Felix Frankfurter, the "braintruster" of Franklin Delano Roosevelt's presidential terms. Frankfurter was not only a great teacher of law but also the organizer of the American Civil Liberties Union. He is best remembered for his defense in the famous Sacco–Vanzetti case, which ripped the Boston Establishment at the seams and produced the traditional breach between the town and the gown.

During the Civil War, Charles Sumner of Harvard and Boston became one of the country's loudest voices in the Abolitionist movement. In his speech, "The Crime Against Kansas," he verbally attacked Senator Andrew Butler, only to be physically assaulted by the southern senator's nephew, Preston Brooks, in the august chambers of the Senate. It took Sumner three years to recover, and when he did he and Thaddeus Stevens questioned the executive power of the presidency and brought about the impeachment charges against President Andrew Johnson.

It was not only in the Law School that Harvard stretched toward the heavens of man's intellectual scope but also in the holiest of holies, the

Professor Louis Agassiz of Harvard. Photograph courtesy of Culver Pictures.

Divinity School. In 1837, Ralph Waldo Emerson first called for American independence of European cultural influences, thus sending a reverberation of shock through Boston cultural circles; but in 1838, while teaching at the Divinity School, he suggested that man could find redemption within his own soul—a premise that was regarded by Boston theologians as a repudiation of Christianity. Emerson was removed from the Divinity School and was ignored by Harvard until 1866, when the university conferred an L.L.D degree upon the man who has become one of Harvard's most revered graduates.

Jean Louis Rodolphe Agassiz was another noteworthy Harvard graduate. Swiss-born Agassiz opposed the new theories of Darwin, urging a direct study of science through nature. One of the few things President Edward Everett of Harvard did of eternal merit was to appoint Agassiz professor of geology and zoology, since he completely revolutionized the study of natural history in America. In addition to his scientific gifts Agassiz was a warm, lovable character who, after the death of his first wife, married Elizabeth Cabot Cary, one of the brilliant and intellectual women of that Boston era. Elizabeth Cary was a great teacher and became the first president of Radcliffe College, which she had helped found, using the corner-stone endowment of Anne Radcliffe. In addition to being the president of Radcliffe, Elizabeth Cary was a collaborator with her husband on *A Journey in Brazil;* and with her stepson, Alexander, she wrote the biography of her renowned husband. It was no doubt partly her influence that convinced Alexander to perpetuate his father's memory by richly endowing the university with the Museum of Comparative Zoology, which his father had founded.

The role Radcliffe women have played in the lives of Harvard men is attested to in the matrimonial biographies of Harvard alumni. Since its founding, Radcliffe has maintained a high scholarship reputation, a tribute, no doubt, to the intellectual strength and vitality of such early leaders as Elizabeth Cabot Cary Agassiz.

To the city of Boston, the real importance of the foundings of the Boston Public Latin School and Harvard College was the establishing of Boston as a "culture city" in the pattern of the culture cycle as described by Oswald Spengler. Boston fits into the pattern that Spengler accords to Florence, Bruges, and Weimar; and no other American city can be accorded their accolade. The establishment of the schools stimulated the further establishing of more schools in and around Boston. Among the many institutions of higher learning centered in Boston and its environs are Boston University (1839); Boston College, a Jesuit coeducational college (1863); Emerson College (1880); Simmons College (1889); Emmanuel College, a Roman Catholic college for women (1919); Northeastern University (1898); Tufts University (1852), which incorporated Jackson College for Women (1910); the Crane Theological School; the Fletcher School of Law and Diplomacy (1933); and Brandeis University (1948).

The Massachusetts Institute of Technology, chartered in 1861 and opened in Boston in 1865, has long been recognized as an outstanding technical college. Among its facilities are five high-energy accelerators, a large nuclear reactor, and a noted nuclear engineering laboratory. Today, the institute operates a research center near South Dartmouth, Massachusetts; the Lincoln Laboratory at Lexington, Massachusetts; and an engineering practice school at Oak Ridge, Tennessee. Significant among its more than seventy special laboratories are an instrumentation laboratory, a computation center, and a spectroscopy laboratory. The institute also has cooperative arrangements with the Woods Hole Oceanographic Institution.

Primarily a technological institute, it maintains a center for international studies and, with Harvard University, a center for urban studies. The institute maintains the Boston Stein Club Map Room in the Hayden Library and the Hart Nautical Museum.

In addition to Radcliffe, which is a part of Harvard, Boston is also the home of one of the most famous women's colleges in America—Wellesley. Founded in 1870, Wellesley was the first woman's college to feature scientific laboratories. Situated on Lake Waban in four hundred acres of wooded hills, the campus of Wellesley is renowned for its physical beauty. Its Jewett Art Building has a collection of classical and medicinal art, in addition to a library that houses one of the largest Browning collections in the world.

Then there are the preparatory schools, which were founded on the ancient pattern of a public school—they drove the boys with switch and ferule and even drove the girls—when the boys and girls were children of learned families. The children were all precocious, and only a dunce could fail to be ready for college at fourteen or fifteen.

Even the tiny tots were given special attention by one Elizabeth Palmer Peabody, the eldest of the famous Peabody sisters. (The second sister, Mary, became the wife of Horace Mann, the early tutelary saint of coeducation, and the youngest sister, Sophie, a painter, married Nathaniel Hawthorne.) Elizabeth founded a girls' school in Brookline, which was originally called Muddy River. Elizabeth, who was an inspired teacher, was not a businesswoman, and the school went bankrupt. Elizabeth then joined Bronson Alcott in his temple school as a teacher but left to open a bookshop in Boston. There she found herself operating a meeting place for such transcendentalists as Emerson, Hawthorne, and Thoreau. She became a publisher as well and published Margaret Fuller's translations, several of Hawthorne's early books, and the *Dial* magazine. She involved herself deeply in the abolitionist movement, and traveled to Richmond to plead for the life of one of John Brown's aides at Harper's Ferry.

In 1861 Elizabeth Peabody opened the first kindergarten in America. She studied the Froebel methods in Germany, and in 1868 she established a Froebel Union. With her sister Mary, she wrote *Moral Culture of Infancy and Kindergarten Guide.*

In the early days there was a joyous awakening, an unconscious pride expressed in the founding of institutions, intellectual, humanitarian, and artistic. There was a moment of equipoise, a flowering of imaginations in which the ideas and feelings of Boston thinkers found expression. Together, these early intellectuals made up the mind of Boston, the culture city, which dominated and became the mouthpiece of the country. "Men are free," wrote D. H. Lawrence:

> . . . when they are in a living homeland, not when they are straying and breaking away. Men are free when they are obeying some deep, inward voice of religious belief. Obeying from within. Men are free when they belong to a living, organic, believing community, active in fulfilling some unfulfilled, perhaps unrealized purpose.

What could better describe the impetus of the early intellectual days of Boston? What could better delineate the individual minds living in Boston? These early teachers, educators, and bringers of light enacted a Promethean role.

But in time the poetic urge, which had controlled the mind of Boston and inspired it to great heights, grew more prosaic, over-intelligent, cautious, and even doubtful. The early self-confidence vanished, and a presentiment of future failure appeared. The scholars and historians lost themselves in their documents; the freedom and originality of the countryside poets became engulfed in the analytical and the precious. What was vital grew provincial, and in time the culture city surrendered to the world city. Boston took a back seat to New York and capitulated to Spengler's next cycle of cosmopolitan deracination. The original cultural roots are rent asunder, the flowers that do not wilt and die must now bloom in a sophisticated sunlight of integration.

Today, Harvard is no longer restricted, geographically, to Cambridge and Boston. It has spread physically over much of Massachusetts and New Hampshire. It houses a center for Byzantine studies at Dumbarton Oaks in Washington, D.C. The mind of Harvard has assumed its universal scope. As President Nathan Marsh Pusey has said, "Harvard College simply cannot stand still. In curriculum and research the process of re-evaluation simply must go on. A community like Harvard is alive with new ideas." Of such a cellular brain structure was the original mind of Boston made. It desired to build a city, a nation, to civilize it and to humanize it. Harvard was the cornerstone of its foundation. Fortunately, Harvard is richly endowed.

At the time of writing this book it is only fair to note that despite the fine scholastic records of such institutions as Harvard, M.I.T., Radcliffe, Wellesley, etc., these prestigious schools are as foreign to the children of

Boston's workingman as are the suburban Yankee patricians who have preached school integration for the city while practicing snob zoning in the suburbs. The school busing problem of Boston is a rather frightening spectacle. It's sad to witness on national television mobs of frenetic parents shouting "nigger," to let the rest of the country know how little they care about the school integration laws of the country. What happened in Boston, 344 years old and three-quarters of the way into the twentieth century—the confrontation between the police and the Irish and Polish-American kids supported by their parents—was an example of what could be expected when the yellow school buses came into South Boston emptying black students. The spectacle did Boston no good and shocked a large part of the United States, which had erroneously believed Boston to be a "liberal" city—especially in regard to tolerance of blacks and support of public education. Hadn't aging Mrs. Peabody—the widow of Endicott Peabody—personally come south to march on behalf of southern black children being denied admission to white-attended schools? The truth lies in the facts, which, for the sake of public relations, have, through the years, silenced the voice of violence of the Boston mobs. Boston, the very center of reform, seems badly in need of reform itself.

It must have been somewhat satisfying to many southerners to watch Boston's busing agonies after years of encountering latter-day abolitionists from the North lead the civil rights revolution. But the irony is that the people whose agonies the southerners have been enjoying are not the Boston liberals, the intellectuals, who have always been representatives of Boston's national image, a population from the start replete with literary giants, railroad investors, Brahmin statesmen, and stern-faced clergy. The descendants of these people moved to wealthier suburbs and left behind whites and blacks lacking the luxury of time and education for high-minded thoughts and good deeds. The other Boston, composed of the workingmen (quite often unemployable) of varied nationalities, were the whites who were opposing the school integration.

The basic problem goes beyond the school issue. It goes to the very pattern of the settling of Boston. It commenced when the first Yankees abandoned the older sections of the city to the invading Irish. As immigrants from other nations, especially Italians and Russian and Eastern European Jews arrived, the character of the city altered from its original Puritan composite. In time the Irish had to fight the newcomers, and the neighborhoods became power bases of the opposing ethnic groups. The smart politicians saw to it that patronage was distributed not only in the ward rooms of South Boston but in the Jewish clubhouses of Roxbury and Dorchester and in the Italian counterparts in the North End. These neighborhoods revolved around the church, the parochial school, the small store, the public school, and the local politicians.

But many changes have taken place in the neighborhoods. The parochial schools are heavily in debt; the small stores have been replaced with supermarkets and shopping plazas. The public schools are being integrated. The local politician has found himself with little or no control over the forces that are shaping the fate of many American cities. Boston, with its school predicament, is no exception. A simple example of what is happening can be found in Roxbury, Dorchester, and Mattapan where the Jews are moving out, leaving behind a black population, made up of almost 35 percent of its public school children. The crime rate is high and the poor whites, struggling to keep jobs they do not like, are in open conflict with the migrant blacks, seeking jobs that do not exist. In the enforcement of school integration, the suppressed hostilities had a cause for unification.

We cannot overlook the overwhelming presence of one woman, who is contradictory to the Boston women we have already noted. Her name is Louise Day Hicks. She is a member of the City Council and one of the founders of ROAR (Restore Our Alienated Rights). Mrs. Hicks emerged from her working-class Irish South Boston neighborhood a few years ago to become a leader in the antibusing forces. In running for mayor, she lost twice to Mayor Kevin White. In person, she seems to be a sensible grandmother, busily attending to her City Council job but dead set against busing. Mrs. Hicks explains that ROAR is a combination of several neighborhood groups, which have been fighting busing for more than a decade. "I thought we could bring them all together," she says, "I was going down to the Cape one day, and I thought, what if our voices could be heard as a roar?"

Later she decided on the words the letters ROAR would represent. Then "I had a press conference or something else and I said a new organization had been formed called ROAR."

As is the case with many such movements, the story broke before there was an official organization. But the neighborhood groups gathered behind Mrs. Hicks, the organization sprang into being, and its roar has now been heard around the world. A symbol was chosen—a ferocious lion with his paws on a bus.

Obviously, in the final analysis, the children are the victims, not only in facing the problem of education under such conditions, but also in being inculcated with race hatred during a very formative part of their development. Until the matter is resolved, education in Boston is a far cry from the original intent of the Founding Fathers, who established a public school almost as soon as shelter was provided.

8

The Mighty Quill
of Beacon Hill

"In the beginning was the Word and the Word was with God and the Word was God." *John 1:1*.

In the beginning of Boston, the word was written almost before a single brick was laid. The writing was in the form of a letter from Governor Thomas Dudley to Bridget, Countess of Lincoln, dated "Boston in New England, March 12, 1631," nine months after the arrival of emigrants at Massachusetts Bay. The document had been called "the most interesting as well as authentic document in our early annals"—that is, in the annals of New England. The fate of the original manuscript remains unknown, but a shortened version of the letter, evidently made from a manuscript copy of the original, was published in Boston in 1696. The complete letter was printed in full by John Farmer of Concord, New Hampshire, in 1834, and in 1846 Alexander Young of Boston published a modern version in his *Chronicles of the First Planters of the Colony of Massachusetts Bay*.

The letter in itself is a noteworthy manuscript, a quiet and unadorned account of the simple human sacrifices upon which the Bay Colony was built. Dudley himself was a nobleman who spent much of his adult life as a steward to the earl of Lincoln, and his letter conveys data of his new situation to an old friend, the wife of his former employer. While quite a young man, Dudley had come under Puritan influence, and the intensity of his religious faith may be measured by the fact that at the age of fifty-four, when most men were looking forward to retirement, he left his native land to found a new commonwealth on a strange and unknown shore. Not only did he survive the ordeal of colonialization he so vividly describes in his letter, but he lived on for a quarter of a century in the Bay Colony, serving four terms as governor and thirteen as deputy governor. His letter is one of the first writings from the pen of a settler of New England, and it reflects an event of utmost importance in the seven-

The "Stockbridge Bowl," or Mountain Mirror. Cottage in which Hawthorne wrote *The House of Seven Gables*. From *Harper's Magazine*, November 1871.

teenth-century history of the English-speaking world. Thomas Dudley wrote:

> But bearing these things as we might, we began to consult of the place of our sitting down; for Salem where we landed pleased us not. And to that purpose some were sent to the Bay to search up the rivers for a convenient place; who upon their return reported to have found a good place upon Mystic, but some others of us seconding these to approve or dislike of their judgement we found a place liked us better three leagues up Charles River. And thereupon unshipped our goods into other vessels and with much cost and labour brought them in July to Charles Town; but there receiving advertisements by some of the late arrived ships from London and Amster-

dam of some French preparations against us (many of our people brought with us being sick of fevers and the scurvy and we thereby unable to carry up our ordinance and baggage so far) we were forced to change counsel and for our present shelter to plant dispersedly, some at Charles Town which standeth on the north side of the mouth of the Charles River; some on the south side thereof, which place we named Boston (as we intended to have done the first place we resolved on) some of us upon Mystic, which we named Medford; some of us westward on Charles River, four miles from Charles Town, which place we named Watertown; others of us two miles from Boston in a place we named Rocksbury, other upon the river of Saugus between Salem and Charles Town. And the western men four miles south from Boston at a place named Dorchester. This dispersion troubled some of us but help it we could not, wanting ability to remove to any place fit to build a town upon, and the time too short to deliberate any longer lest the winter should surprise us before we had builded our houses. The best counsel we could find out was to build a fort to retire to, in some convenient place if any enemy pressed thereunto, after we should have fortified ourselves against the wet and cold. So ceasing to consult further for that time they who had health to labour fell to building, wherein they were interrupted with sickness and many died weekly, yea, almost daily.

Literary pens of Boston women flowed freely at an early date. One of the earliest female settlers was Anne Dudley Bradstreet, born in Northampton, England, who traveled to America with her father, Thomas Dudley, in the Winthrop Puritan group. She married Simon Bradstreet who later, like her father, became one of the first governors. Anne Bradstreet originated a tradition that was upheld for many years in Boston . . . she raised a large family, and she took to writing as well. If not the first poet in America, she was the first from the new world to be published. Her *Tenth Muse Lately Sprung Up in America* was published in London in 1650. Her second volume, *Several Poems,* published in Boston in 1678, contains "Contemplations," which is regarded as her best work. Her writing was remarkable for so new a settlement and coming from a woman whose household chores in the primitive new world were enormous, considering the size of her family and the rigid Puritan pattern of life.

The Puritans, setting aside the traditional organization and structure of the Catholic church, evolved during the late sixteenth and early seventeenth centuries an elaborate theological system of their own. It was in this intellectual and philosophical framework, in a context of Christian thought and morality, that American culture was to evolve. Puritanism, whether we want to admit it or not, has had a deep influence on the fabric of American thought and society ever since. It is pivotal to the understanding of American intellectual and revolutionary heritage. The fact is illustrated by the extraordinary emphasis that Americans, right from the beginning, have placed upon written law, upon government by the book rather than by the man.

The Puritan immigrants laid a special emphasis on written law, since they were part of the wider Protestant movement that had jettisoned the total authority and pretensions of the Catholic church, which had ruled through the power of precedent, custom, and ritual and through the very personal influence of bishop and priest. Protestantism rejected all authority except the Bible as the written word of God, a divine revelation for the faithful. For this reason the promotion of literacy and biblical instruction played a major role in the Puritan concept of education. The Bible was enshrined in the center of the Boston meetinghouse, and the Puritan child learned, as he grew older, to respect and revere the higher law of God, a law that was written down and could be looked up for reference. The early Puritan minister was a kind of lawyer, whose function was to translate and expound the law to his congregation.

In 1641, the Body of Liberties was composed for the Massachusetts Colony. In this first written document of human rights, the Puritan mind was in total control. The preface connotes the fraternal bondage of spiritual morality that pervaded the colony and the colonists. It states:

> The free fruition of such liberties immunities and priveleges as humanity, civility, and Christianity call for as due every man in his place and proportion without impeachment and infringement, hath ever been and ever will be the tranquility and stability of churches and commonwealths. And the denial or deprival thereof, the disturbances if not the ruin of both.
>
> We hold it therefore our duty and safety, whilst we are about the further establishing of this government, to collect and express all such freedoms as for present we forsee may concern us, and our posterity after us, and to ratify them with our solemn consent.
>
> We do therefore this day religiously and unanimously decree and confirm these following rights, liberties and priveleges concerning our churches and civil state, to be respectively, impartially, and inviolably enjoyed and observed throughout our jurisdiction forever.

The rights of men, women, children, foreigners, strangers, servants, even the "brute creatures" were prescribed. The Capital Laws and their punishments in the event of failure to execute such laws was clearly defined, as were "liberties the Lord Jesus hath given the church."

Since Boston was a city founded upon the laws of a Puritan God, it was only consistent that God's adversary, the devil, should be called to account. When the siege of witchcraft, which had long existed in Europe and in the mother country, finally penetrated New England, it became necessary to define the devil. What, indeed, was the devil? To the Puritan, the question had become no less important than what was God. Could good exist without evil to define its proportions? When the question arose, most Bostonians were reading John Milton's *Paradise Lost,* in which the blind poet had created Satan in his own image—doomed, but not without his grandeur. One could loathe and fear this creature, but one could not despise him.

It took one Cotton Mather to dispute this concept of the devil and offer in its place a poltergeist, a devil of the early miracle plays, a comic creature, yet a creature who dared to come into God's very presence and challenge him. Such a devil had once besieged Job, and such a devil had come to Massachusetts in the presence of the Salem witches. Could it be that God used the devil to bring a new element to earth—that out of the testing of men's faith and love eventually good would come? What good did the devil's presence forebode for Boston?

In his indefatigable writing, Cotton Mather put together a jumble of materials on the ecclesiastical history of Massachusetts, attempting to prove in his document that the establishing of the colony and the founding of the city of Boston, even the North Church where he was pastor, were the workings of God's will. He entitled his thesis *Magnalia Christi Americana* (1702), and its influence in his day was widespread. His concern with diabolism led him to produce two pieces of writing, *Memorable Providences Relating to Witchcraft and Possessions* and *Wonders of the Invisible World,* which helped to bring about the wave of hysterical fear that possessed Salem and Boston.

In reading his manuscripts one cannot help but be somewhat alarmed at Mather's childlike, marveling credulity. His writings reveal much of his true nature, which was concealed by his clerical robes. The details of witchcraft, of horns sounding across Essex County at midnight, the airborne excursions to Parris's pasture—all were not so much horrors and abominations as exhibitions of the drama of life. Mather could not have avoided his encounter with witchcraft any more than Macbeth could have avoided his encounter with the three sisters of doom and evil. Mather was thrilled to have been a spectator of the collision of good and evil, the battle between heaven and hell.

Actually, Mather was an early sponsor of education and learning, and he helped to make Boston a cultural center. He was deeply interested in science and was the first native-born American to become a member of the Royal Society. He persuaded Zabdiel Boylston to inoculate against small-pox and supported the inoculation even when his own life was threatened. His life disappointment was his failure to be named president of Harvard, as his father, Increase, had been. In his rejection he became vindictive. He wrote in his diary, "The Corporation of our miserable College do again treat me with their accustomed indignity," when he was by-passed the fourth and final time. With some other ministers, all graduates of Harvard, who thought the college was going downhill insofar as theology was concerned, he founded the Collegiate School of Connecticut. In 1718, Cotton Mather wrote to Elihu Yale, a wealthy Boston merchant, suggesting the school be named for him in return for financial support. Yale donated a parcel of goods, which when sold brought 562 pounds, the largest single donation until 1837. The college moved to New Haven, Connecticut, and was named Yale by Harvardman Mather.

As the city of Boston became established, preoccupation with religion receded into the background. Puritanism's original and passionate impulse waned, and the churches commenced to lose all but superficial contact with the people. The ruling ministers became narrowly complacent and catered only to a small segment of the community. As the population expanded, the demands of a hard, practical world crowded in upon men. Daily they had to face up to the ordeals of labor on the farms and frontiers, the ever-recurring strife with the French and the Indians, the lure of wealth through farming, commerce, and speculation, and the constantly increasing immigration from Europe. Scots, Irish, Germans, French, and Dutch were continual passengers on the Cunard ships. How to assimilate them into the nondemocratic community presented a major problem.

The early man of Boston lived on the edge of eternity; his need for spiritual consolation and peace of mind was great. By background and tradition, the Puritan was not groomed for inner security. He needed the faith of his fathers to lean upon, the laws of his church to support his actions, the words of his ministers to guide his wavering soul. In the activity of the new settlement there was considerable confusion. From this situation and the decay of religious life, there sprang into being a new movement, which was to have a strong effect upon the future not only of Boston and Massachusetts but of the entire new world of North America. It commenced slowly, in the homes and in the places of work —outside the formal structure of the church proper.

The Great Awakening, as it was called, occurred in the 1740s. It was a burst of fiery evangelism that swept the American mainland colonies from Georgia to Maine. It was carried forward not only by great and itinerant ministers but by preachers who spoke to people wherever they could find an audience—in meetinghouses, in the streets, on the commons, in the open fields, and even in the forests.

The Great Awakening preached the message that all men could be saved if they would repent and throw themselves on God's mercy and believe in him. In so doing, the Great Awakening struck a telling blow at the Old World concept that religious establishments were a necessary foundation of the social order. It contributed powerfully to America's awakening sense of nationalism, for it taught a democratic creed—the brotherhood of man in Christ—that leaped over narrow provincial boundaries and brought to the people a revolutionary faith—a faith that inspired the struggle for national independence against an oppressive, decadent authoritarian and outmoded dynastic rule. The writings of Jonathan Edwards, notably *The Life and Death of Abigail Hutchinson* (1736), emphasize the complementary aspects of Edwards's thinking: his hellfire and damnation, which was the sounding knell of eighteenth-century Protestantism; and on the other hand his love of ordinary men and women and his deep belief in the possibility of human redemption through faith and repentance.

To the enthusiasts the Awakening, with its mass audiences, tears, groans, footstamping, handclapping, swooning, fits, shrieks of joy and agony, appeared to be the work of God, who had brought the masses to witness the salvation of their souls and their conversion. But to ministers of the old, established congregations, the revival was a plebeian movement that encouraged boisterous and passionate exhibitions, which were frowned upon in Boston. The revival challenged the theology that was fashionable in Boston's centers of learning. By the middle of the eighteenth century, an enlightened rationalism was replacing the stark doctrines of medieval damnation with which the Puritans had begun. Revivalism directly challenged the liberal heresies of Bostonian respectability.

The leading exponent of Harvard theological liberalism of his day was Charles Chauncy, who countered and pointcountered Jonathan Edwards in one of the most famous theological controversies in American history. His letter to George Wishart, transcribed in 1742, is an interesting account of the spirit of the Awakening previously presented from a hostile point of view. He wrote:

> The goodness that has been talked of, 'tis plain to me is nothing more in general than a commotion in the passions. I can't see that men have been made better, if hearby be meant, their being formed to a nearer resemblance to the divine being in moral holiness. 'Tis not evident to me that persons, generally, have a better understanding of religion, a better government of their passions, a more Christian love to their neighbour, or that they are more decent and regular in their devotions toward God. I am clearly of the mind they are worse in all directions.

This voice was drowned out by Edwards's forthright question: "How will you stand on the lay of Judgement?"

> O sinner man, where are you going to run to?
> O sinner man, where are you going to run to?
> O sinner man, where are you going to run to?
> All on that day?
> Run to the moon, O moon won't you hide me?
> Run to the moon, O moon won't you hide me?
> Run to the moon, O moon won't you hide me?
> All on that day.

Who knows the power of God's anger?

Many historians have seen in the Great Awakening the sowing of the seeds of the American Revolution, but there were several paths to the Revolution: the liberal theologians and the orthodox, the Puritan and the Anglican, the religious man and the secular. The Revolution came more easily because England and America had developed two different societies, the first a sphere of mundane aristocracy and worldly establishment, the second a locale of ascetic Protestantism and proletarian ethics. As the century wore on, Americans increasingly regarded England as abandoned to corrupt morals and as losing its liberties and came to think of America as the future both of Christianity and the freedom of real Englishmen.

During the prerevolutionary and Revolutionary days of Boston, this moral tone and note of righteous indignation prevailed in the pamphlets of Samuel Adams and in the anonymous articles of John Quincy Adams, which appeared in the *Boston Gazette*. The handwriting inscribed upon the wall of early American history was the foreordained destiny of the infant nation. Without this impetus it is doubtful if the Revolution could have succeeded, considering the power of the armed forces England was able to command against the colonies. Thus proving again the adage that the word is more powerful than the sword.

It is, however, a mistake to presume that in a (in retrospect) prerevolutionary city such as Boston revolution was the preferred course. It was no more true than that the Great Awakening, with its common-man democracy, was more favored than the established aristocratic theocracy upon which the city was founded. American Loyalists—and there were a great number in Boston—suffered the fate of those who lose the contest; history has relegated them to footnotes or brief paragraphs, at best. By refusing to repudiate their monarch, loyalists condemned themselves to exile during the Revolution and oblivion afterwards. Two writers for the Loyalist cause were Thomas Hutchinson, governor of Massachusetts, and Andrew Oliver. Their articles and letters were compiled by an Englishman, Israel Maudit, who never visited Boston but whose family had business connections there, which he represented in England. In *A Short View* compiled in 1774, Maudit infiltrated Boston with the principles of the Loyalist cause as seen by Hutchinson and by Oliver, his lieutenant governor.

Following the Revolution many veterans dwelt to the east, west, north, and south of Boston—but remained Bostonians. John Quincy Adams dwelt in the home of his father and mother, John and Abigail, in Quincy, where he rejoiced in his life's thesis that statesmanship was the noblest of human callings. In the peaceful homestead, the Adamses—like hedgehogs —retired and wrote their memoirs and histories.

In Cambridge, a village so quiet that one heard the booming of the revolutionary guns in the navy yard at Boston, a few old houses stood around the trim Common. One of them, a gambrel-roofed dwelling, was the home of the Reverend Abiel Holmes, author of the *Annals of America*. On Dana Hill stood the Dana mansion, built by Chief Justice Francis Dana. Richard Henry Dana, his son, was a critic, a poet, and the editor of the *North American Review*. He is best known for his poem "The

Buccaneer," which was published in 1827. His son, Richard Henry Dana, after spending two years at Harvard, shipped as a common sailor around the Horn to California. The narrative of this voyage, published as *Two Years Before the Mast* in 1840, was written to secure justice for sailors. It has become an American classic. Richard Henry Dana returned to Harvard, graduated in 1837, and entered into the practice of law, where he handled many maritime suits and in 1841 published *The Seaman's Friend*, now a standard manual of the law of the sea.

In Cambridge, the first printing press of the commonwealth was brought from England in 1638 and produced for twoscore years all the printing in the colonies, including John Eliot's Indian translation of the Bible and the *Freeman's Oath.* It was not without national pride that Bostonians pointed to their printed words, which were beginning to attract notice in London where, earlier, critics had commented: "Who, indeed, reads American authors?" Now the world was reading the writings of Nathaniel Bowditch of Salem, author of *The Practical Navigator*, a book that had saved many lives and that had helped make American vessels the swiftest ever to sail. And, in time, the son of the old revolutionary hero of Bunker Hill, William Hickling Prescott, compelled by a serious eye injury (probably a detached retina) to give up the practice of law, wrote *History of the Reign of Ferdinand and Isabella the Catholic* (1838) and followed it with a *History of the Conquest of Mexico* (1843), a classic in literature. Although time has seen Prescott's research superseded, he has survived as one of America's greatest historians.

With the Ghent Treaty of Peace, following the War of 1812 the second war with England, Boston had become rich, and the leading citizens could not imagine why Boston should not be the finest town in the world. It had taken the lead in the Revolution, it had put the best cruisers on the seas, and the Yankee rifle in Yankee hands had set a new standard for marksmanship. The dream of a Puritan commonwealth lingered in the Boston mind.

In the spring of 1815, with the budding of the first crocuses, America's greatest intellectual and literary period was born out of Boston. It is generally known as the period of the "Flowering of New England." Its richness in letters, men and women of gigantic personalities, make it impossible to adequately etch such a mammoth canvas. The writers ran the gamut from such historians as John Lothrop Motley, whose early history of Boston has some of the romantic quality of Shakespeare's *As You Like It*, with its tales of Miles Standish, John Alden, and Priscilla—all

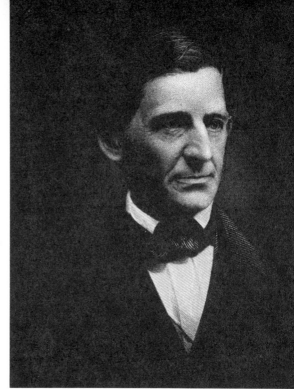

Ralph Waldo Emerson.

vague, misty characters, neither real nor unreal—to the philosophical writings of Ralph Waldo Emerson.

The most interesting factor is that, for the most part, the participants were the children of the "codfish aristocracy," or they were sponsored in their artistic endeavors by such heirs.

There were many strains in this Boston mind that were to produce the new literature. There was still a warm and chivalrous Tory strain, a passionate strain of rebelliousness, a strain of religious fervor, even a sybaritic strain, in contrast with a cold strain of asceticism.

Some people on Beacon Hill were quite patrician. The Cushing house on Summer Street, for example, was surrounded with a wall of Chinese porcelain, peacocks strutted about the garden, and the Chinese servants wore their native dress. In the Otis household, Harrison Gray Otis, at the age of eighty, after forty years of gout, breakfasted every morning on paté de fois gras. Here, every afternoon, ten gallons of punch evaporated out of the Lowestoft bowl that was placed on the landing. One of the Perkins brothers, in reply to a minister who advocated total abstinence, doubled his children's portions of Madeira.

The reading fare was traditional—Hume, Gibbon, Shakespeare, Milton, Dryden, Addison, the *Arabian Nights, Don Quixote.* Their minds were closed on certain lines, and they could hardly be called lovers of originality. But the merchant princes were prepared to humor their sons and daughters. Boston was filled with quixotic souls, visionaries, and non-conformists. The population was said to have two intellects and half a heart. The prevailing mind was cautious, excessively formal, singularly obsessed with its own importance, bigoted in its fear of political change.

This prototype was to survive in literature in John P. Marquand's satire, *The Late George Apley,* which won the Pulitzer Prize in 1937. Following the opening in Boston of the play based on this book, a leading member of one first family approached another and commented, "Very amusing, wasn't it?" The other paused for a moment and then, rather painfully, replied, "No, very exaggerated!"

In the spring of 1815, two young Boston men embarked on a voyage of discovery. They were George Ticknor and Edward Everett, and they set forth to investigate reports that had come to Boston regarding the prodigious progress of German scholars. They sailed for Liverpool along with a party of other Boston friends, including the two sons of John Quincy Adams.

George Ticknor was a rich young man with very engaging manners. While not a genius, he was a man of remarkable talents of a utilitarian nature. Everett was better known. He was a recognized prodigy and had already preached for more than a year in the most fashionable of Boston pulpits. John Adams called him "our most celebrated youth." The two friends had much in common. Both were excellent students; both were vain and unquestionably gifted. Both had been fascinated by the writing of Madame de Staël, whose book, *De l'Allemagne,* had been suppressed by Napoleon in France. (For her writings, Bonaparte had exiled the lady of letters, and she took up her new residence in upstate New York, near Ontario.) In their evangelical tour the two men traveled over Europe, meeting writers and publishers.

The importance of the journey of these two men cannot be underestimated, because never before had anyone invested with such glamor the life of the poet and the man of letters. Their influence is still felt. In addition, when Ticknor returned in 1819, he unpacked his rich collection of books—which in time would become famous, establishing a precedent for the creating of great libraries, destined for eventual public use by wealthy Americans. In his travels, Ticknor made many friends among writers and publishers, and an outgrowth of his travel abroad was that publishing of English and European authors commenced in America and American authors found representation abroad. In time, the prestigious house of Fields and Ticknor in Boston would make Boston the stronghold of American publishing—a role the city did not happily relinquish when New York became the citadel in the twentieth century.

It was an auspicious time, because Boston was dominant and potent. Everyone labored to be foremost. Even the women were superior, culti- vated, witty, dominant—meeting the qualifications of Abigail Adams, who had written: "If we mean to have heroes, statesmen, and philosophers, we should have learned women."

At that time, Ralph Waldo Emerson was able to write of Boston:

> What Vasari said, three hundred years ago, of the republican city of Florence might be said of Boston; "that the desire for glory and honour is powerfully generated by the air of that place, in the men of every profession; whereby all who possess talent are im- pelled to struggle that they may not remain in the same grade with those whom they perceive to be only men like themselves, even though they may acknowledge such indeed to be masters; but all labour by every means to be foremost." (Emerson, *Natural History of the Intellect*)

The time and place were ready for a magazine which became an outlet for the writers who were cropping up in every corner. The publication grew out of the *Monthly Anthology* and was modeled on the erudite British reviews. The new *North American Review* was the child of George Bancroft, and, probably more than any single publication, pinpointed Boston and Beacon Hill as the home of the American literati. It was George Bancroft who used the *Review* to preserve and publish the docu- ments of the Revolution period through the writings of such men as Jared Sparks, "the American Plutarch," author of *The Library of American Biography*, and editor of the magazine. It was in this circle that the literary geniuses came into full bloom.

The most original mind was Ralph Waldo Emerson, an anathema to the Boston pundits. Everett sneered at Emerson's "conceited, laborious nonsense." The Cambridge theologians reviled him, he was a pantheist and a German mystic, and his style was strangely Neoplatonic. His life appeared aimless. He had bypassed all open avenues of success, followed none of the rules of common sense. He seemed to be guided by some strange star that no one else could see. He had traveled in Europe to confirm his intuitions, his inner power. The currents of the universal being seemed to circulate through him and he was part of nature—the laws of life, justice, truth, love, and freedom appeared to be revealed to him. Observing the rocks, the grasses, the fishes, the insects, the birds, the animals, he predated Darwin with his theory of evolution. In his early development he was influenced by his eccentric but brilliant aunt, Mary Moody Emerson, who fed him the sacred books of the East. Naturally, he was in open rebellion against the Puritan mind and manner.

Emerson focused attention on the fact that the feats America boasted about were of no great moment. He was the first American writer to point out the flaws in the swaggering, shallow, avaricious being who in time would become the Ugly American, the man who gambled away the charters of the human race for petty, selfish gain. For compensation, he offered no reward beyond the joy of exercising the highest functions of human nature—the reward of virtue. Emerson feared vulgar prosperity, which he sensed would eventually retrograde into barbarism, but the reward he offered was, for a long period of time, too complex in its simplicity, too unyielding in its strength to attain immediate attraction.

The mind of Emerson was laid to rest with the advance of fascist technocracy. It has only now, in the last half of the twentieth century, begun to be explored by a new generation, disillusioned with the disasters of the living world they see about them—pollution of the very elements man needs for survival, disintegration of all morality from the lowest echelon to the highest. Today, Emerson is alive—a frail ghost, perhaps, but then the man who walked the streets of Concord was also frail in appearance, although strong in spirit.

In Emerson's house on the Boston turnpike Henry Thoreau took up residence. He was a little man, little but tough, with the nose of a Pinocchio and the mind of a giant. His long arms swung in simian fashion as he stalked. His hands were the hands of a workingman; his feet were meant for walking. Thoreau studied under Emerson at Harvard and became "Emersonized." Their friendship evolved when Emerson's sister-in-law, who was boarding at Mrs. Thoreau's, told Emerson that young Thoreau had thoughts similar to his in the journal he was keeping. Emerson sought out this young man who was a master woodsman; shrewd as a fox; a modern-day Ulysses who charmed the snakes and the fishes; and upon whose scrawny looking shoulders the wild birds roosted. Emerson realized he was a scholar of unusual distinction.

Henry Wadsworth Longfellow, c.
1840, by C. G. Thompson and
S. A. Schoff.

In 1845 Thoreau built himself a small cabin on the shore of Walden
Pond, near Concord, where he remained for over two years "living deep
and sucking out all the marrow of life." A supreme individualist and
idealist, he sought an existence free from the world, concentrated and
simple. He earned his daily needs by his work as a handyman. In 1854
he wrote the book which was to make his name world famous, *Walden,
or Life in the Woods.*

If Emerson was the Plato of this golden age of classical Boston,
Thoreau was the Socrates. Henry was a commoner, but he was also a
poet—"if with light head erect I sing," the man for whom the bloom
of the Puritan Bible had faded. In its place the Bhagavad-Gita had
blossomed from some remote Eastern mountaintop, and his words incorporated a wisdom beyond the comprehension of the Beacon Hill
mind. Today, Thoreau is recognized as one of the major figures of
American literature and thought—a mystic, a naturalist, and a social
critic, who championed the individual against sodality and materialistic
civilization. His essay, "Civil Disobedience," which espoused the doctrine
of passive resistance, was the inspiration for the twentieth-century
Mahatma Gandhi.

The written word of the New England renaissance was closely linked
to the past, and its authors sought environments in which to write that
would more closely identify them with the background and lore of their

ancestors. Tory Row, in Cambridge, was Henry Wadsworth Longfellow's choice. Following his marriage to heiress Fanny Appleton, he purchased Craigie House, now Longfellow House, where much of the memorabilia of the author and the Appleton family are to be found.

The house itself had been the home of Mrs. Craigie, a well-known beauty and hostess, who lent her residence to George and Martha Washington for their wedding. Following the Revolution hard times fell upon Mrs. Craigie, and she was obliged to take roomers, among whom were some of Harvard's most famed scholars. The setting was ideal—a place where every sound and odor had a meaning. The gardens were filled with sturdy marigolds, hollyhocks, and larkspurs, in addition to the humbler garden vegetables, carrots, parsnips, beets—all planted to remind the occupant that the good earth provided not only beauty, but food.

In Craigie House, Longfellow established himself, his wife, and their children. In his study he wrote such masterpieces as "The Children's Hour," and through the centuries his millions of readers have become acquainted with every nook and cranny of the old mansion.

If the past hovered, its ghosts claimed one author, Nathaniel Hawthorne, a descendant of the hated Magistrate Hathorne of Salem witchcraft days, with the *w* inserted by the time Nathaniel was born.

Meanwhile, Salem, like many other seaports, had lapsed into quietude. The waterside streets were no longer glutted with sailors in their blue jackets, checkered shirts, well-varnished straw hats with flowing ribbons, duffel bags filled with riches from the Caribbean islands or India or China. Grass choked the cobblestones, a few idle seafaring men leaned against the posts of the wharf, eyeing a lone Nova Scotia schooner and telling tales of bygone days.

Behind the bolted doors of the old mansions on Chestnut and Federal Streets the household legends were narrated, getting more grisly with each generation. There were whispers of locked closets, their doorways now bricked up, in haunted houses where skeletons had been found. Houses, where poisons were brewed from formulas brought from the Caribbean, were occupied by old maids who dwelt in solitude, or by old misers who counted their gold when all the rest of the world slept.

The Hawthornes lived on Herbert Street. They had lived a special kind of life since the death of Nathaniel's father, a Salem skipper who died of yellow fever in faraway Surinam. Upon hearing of the news Nathaniel's mother and his sister retired to the second floor and were never seen after that day until her death. Inside his room, Hawthorne filled his notepad with observations of Salem. He somehow managed, after twelve years in his haunted chamber, tortured with thoughts of suicide and madness, to escape. He entered a publishing house, Peter Parley, where he edited the *American Magazine*. Eventually Hawthorne left Salem and went to Boston where he worked in a customhouse, but he never lost the other half of his split personality. His stories, written almost as if in a trance, procured his fame, but his practical life at the customhouse was where his reality lay.

It was in Boston that Hawthorne fell in love. The object of his affection was the youngest of the famed Peabody sisters of Salem, girls who believed themselves to be descended from Boadicea, British Queen of the Iceni. The girls were imbued with a store of nervous energy, and they incorporated it into the "higher" things of life. Elizabeth, the oldest, was William Ellery Channing's literary assistant; the confidante of Washington Allston, the artist; Bronson Alcott's aide at the Temple School; and founder of the first American kindergarten school—all adventures she was to record for posterity in her books of reminiscences. Mary, the second sister was the wife of Horace Mann. Sophie, the youngest was a neurasthenic invalid who was witty, clever, and an excellent linguist. Her avocations were purely artistic. One of her hobbies was making medallions, and one day she found herself illustrating one of the stories of the young author Nathaniel Hawthorne. Her style copied John Flaxman, the English artist. It was a style that lent itself

Sophia Peabody Hawthorne.   Elizabeth Peabody.   Mary Peabody Mann.

The famous Peabody Sisters of Boston. Courtesy of the Picture Collection, The Branch Libraries, The New York Public Library.

magically to the eerie tales of Hawthorne. After meeting, Sophie and Nathaniel became engaged and were married, thus giving Boston its own version of an Elizabeth Barrett–Robert Browning romance.

In 1850, Hawthorne published his masterpiece, *The Scarlet Letter*. This novel and his next, *The House of Seven Gables* (1851), are filled with the gloomy atmosphere of Puritan New England—the days of Cotton Mather—and its dark psychological effects. In 1852, Hawthorne wrote *The Blithedale Romance,* a novel based upon his experiences at Brook Farm. In reality, it is a biography of Margaret Fuller, who is scarcely masked as the heroine, Zenobia, a champion of women's rights, who fell in love with the blind leader of an ideal community, then lost him to her younger, prettier sister, and committed suicide by drowning. Hawthorne would not publicly acknowledge Margaret Fuller as his real-life model. But the book was published after the tragic death of Margaret Fuller, who drowned with her lover (it is not known whether their union was ever consummated in marriage), Angelo Ossoli, and their small son, also Angelo; and Miss Fuller's many admirers castigated Hawthorne for his portrait. It was known that Hawthorne had intensely disliked Miss Fuller. He thought she was disconcertingly aggressive for a woman, overly clever, and improperly frank on the subject of sex. He wrote in his journal:

> She had not the charm of womanhood. She had a strong and coarse nature, which she had done her utmost to refine, with infinite pains; but of course it could only be superficially changed. She was a great humbug. But she had stuck herself full of borrowed qualities. There was never such a story as her whole story—the sadder and sterner, because so much of the ridiculous was mixed up in it, and because she could bear anything easier than to be ridiculous. It was such an awful joke she should have resolved—in all sincerity, no doubt— to make herself the greatest, wisest, best woman of the age.

Actually how could a woman of genius, such as Margaret Fuller, conform to the world about her, or find her mysterious impulses understood? She saw herself as the goddess Isis, and her ideal men were Alfieri, the Countess of Albany's lover, and Count Rudolstadt, George Sand's lover, aristocratic democrats who shared the culture of the fortunate classes but longed for the welfare of all. Bostonians censured her because she filled the girls who flocked around her with her own romantic ideas. She made them wish to marry Alfieris, as if State Street lawyers, cotton merchants, and codfish packers with an eye on the

James Russell Lowell and Leslie Stephen in the front study at Elmwood a year or so before the poet's death. From *Country Life in America*, January 1903.

legislature were not good enough. They laughed at her superstitions, her faith in demonology, omens, foresight. They giggled behind her back when she said that Margaret meant "pearl," the gem that is cradled in slime, in disease and decay, like all that is noblest in the human soul. They laughed, but they never forgot either Margaret Fuller or her literary counterpart Zenobia.

The atmosphere of mysticism is evident in the works of such poets as James Russell Lowell, whose trances engulfed him every June (the miracle month that ambushes New England), "with one great gush of blossom." Lowell was essentially an English poet writing in New England but his *The Biglow Papers,* which voiced his radicalism, has remained as a permanent landmark of the New England mind. In this work, the literate and the illiterate meet on a common ground; they are at one in essential matters, religious and political alike, and their regard for human rights, their hatred of war and false ideas of empire, springs from their common principles.

In the Harvard class of 1829 two poets graduated. One, Samuel Francis Smith, wrote the words for "America"; the other, Oliver Wendell Holmes, son of Dr. Abiel Holmes, historian, wrote a poem called "Old Ironsides." He composed it with a pencil, standing on one foot in the attic of his old house in Cambridge. The Battle of Bunker Hill had been planned in this house, and the dents of muskets were still on the floor. The frigate *Constitution* was about to be dismantled and abandoned. It lay prostrate in the nearby Boston Navy Yard. Young Holmes's poem was reprinted on handbills from a Boston newspaper and scattered about the streets of Washington. It saved the ship and made the poet famous.

Upon his graduation, Holmes was determined to study medicine. His father sent him to Paris. Here he learned the gracious art of living, which taught him a sense of the contrasts of life that sharpened his innate critical spirit when he returned to his native home. He established himself as a doctor in a modest street in Boston, and in his spare time gave lectures on the English poets in neighboring country towns. His own poems were happy poems "in which genius poured / And warmed the shapes that later times adored." They told of the homeliest facts of the Yankee world—washing day, the spinning top, the katydid, the gale, the dinner bell, the oysterman, the churchyard, the family portrait, the unmarried aunt—all familiar scenes of and about Boston and its environs, subjects touched upon beautifully by an unhackneyed and vigorous mind One of the doctor's whims was to think of all America, as well as Boston, as a large and friendly boardinghouse, a house with an ample breakfast table at which, for a number of years, he was to preside. The role of an autocrat was thrust upon him by his incandescent mind, natural wit, and his chosen profession. Did not a doctor cope with life and death in terms of reality? Did not a doctor have to know how to diagnose his patients' ills, prescribe the proper dosages, and then persuade his patients to take his medications to feel better? Was a doctor not a person of authority, an absolute ruler? In time, Oliver Wendell Holmes, M.D., became the "Autocrat of the Breakfast Table."

Possibly more than any man who ever lived in Boston, Dr. Holmes knew and loved it. He knew every elm on the Common. To him the

DECEMBER 8, 1885.   PUBLISHED BY HARPER & BROTHERS, NEW YORK.   PRICE FIVE CENTS.

ADVERTISING RATE, for Cover Pages, each insertion, FIFTY CENTS A LINE. Average, eight words to a line, twelve lines to an inch.

Louisa May Alcott on the cover page of *Harper's Young People*, December 8, 1885.

State House was *the* standard of architecture. Boston was the hub of the solar system, though it might possibly be like other towns—except that its fish markets were superior, its monthly publications more erudite, its fire department more admirable, and its spoken word better English. Dr. Holmes knew Boston through and through and when he settled in his last "justifiable homicide," he had reached the ultimate in happiness; he could see Bunker Hill from his window facing the bay and Cambridge across the river. "All the gay and young / Love the light antics of the playful tongue," wrote the little doctor. Of himself: "From the crown of my head to the sole of my foot, I'm alive, I'm alive!" he replied in acquiesence to the observation that he was the most intellectually alive man—"I am, I am!"

At the time when Thackeray wrote to his American publishers, Fields and Ticknor, "I always consider Boston my native place," he was referring to the period of the efflorescence of Boston, the Yankee Athens. He was referring to the Saturday Club, where the leading intellectuals of the Boston world gathered. This literary center was like the Mermaid Tavern of Shakespeare's day, the coffeehouses of Addison and Steele, Samuel Johnson and his Boswell, Goldsmith and Gibbon. In the marble-floored Parker House the bodies convened in rich dark leather wing chairs, while the minds circumambulated the entire universe. They fed, as a group, on genius.[1] The results of the gatherings were visible in the contributions to the city, such as Ticknor's gift of Spanish and Portuguese literature and the libraries of Nathaniel Bowditch and John Adams, all housed in the Boston Public Library.

Times changed, especially with the Civil War. Many of the best literary minds of Boston fled to Europe, where their impact was felt. Harriet Beecher Stowe, who had lived as a girl in Boston, wrote her classic *Uncle Tom's Cabin,* in which she crystallized the sentiments of the North and propelled the world into assuming a position on the question of slavery. Never had any book been so widely read. Over three hundred thousand copies were sold the first year after publication, and the reputation of this spiritually imbued woman was international. On a visit to Europe in 1853, she wrote, "Why do foreign lands regard us with this intensity of interest? Is it not because the whole world looks hopefully toward America as a nation especially raised by God to advance the cause of human liberty and religion?"

The eminent Bostonians of the 1840s and 1850s confronted England with imperturbable self-possession, convinced that America had a mission. Theirs was a different approach from that described by T. G. Appleton as existing in the Yankee mind: "Europe is the home of his protoplasm, of the long succession of forces which make him what he is."

Edith Wharton does not belong to Boston by birth, but the impact and effect of her marriage to a Bostonian upon her personal life and her writing career cannot be denied. She was born Edith Jones of a wealthy Manhattan family[2] and she, like two other New Yorkers, Julia Ward and Isabella Stewart, married into a "proper" Boston family. Her husband was Edward Wharton, an amiable fellow ten years her senior, a moderately well-to-do but essentially directionless human being. The themes of her writing are universal: "domination, entrapment, the longing and the failure to escape, along with considerations about the nature of artistic commitment . . . and the varieties of relationship—nourishing or

Edith Wharton. From
Outlook, 1906.

suppressive, loving or self-centered—between generations, between older
and younger people, between parents and children." These themes
of Edith Wharton's work were also the themes of her life. Her Boston
marriage was a disaster sexually (the marriage was not consummated
for three weeks), and when it culminated in divorce, Edith Wharton
removed herself from the narrow confines of Boston's Beacon Hill
and Manhattan's Fifth Avenue and became a citizen of the world, residing
in Paris until her death. In *Ethan Frome* (1917) she switched from her
customary social setting to depict, against a stark rural New England
background, the tragic fate of three doomed people.

Boston's female writers customarily have been identified with nineteenth-century wealth, which gave them the opportunity to express their
artistic leanings. Amy Lowell was born into the famous Lowell family
in Brookline in 1874. The minds of both Amy and her brothers,
Percival and Abbott, were cast in the pure Brahmin mold. Abbott became
president of Harvard, and it was he who established the "house plan"
based on the type of intellectual cohesion he had experienced in the

English universities. Percival became a famous astronomer, establishing the Lowell Observatory in Flagstaff, Arizona. He also traveled with a special commission to Korea and Japan and wrote about the Far East in *Chöson—The Land of the Morning Calm* (1885) and *Soul of the Far East* (1888). Becoming convinced that there was life on Mars, he wrote a book, *Mars and Its Canals.*

Amy was, like her brothers, an intellectual—and an iconoclast. Her personal social patterns were inconsistent with the structure of the society into which she had been born, and at times her eccentricities overshadowed her considerable talent and true intellectual capacities. She was known for her masculine attire, her cigar-smoking habit, and her general disregard for social protocol. In 1912, she produced her first collection of verse, *A Dome of Many-Coloured Glass.* After its publication

Amy Lowell. Sketch by Foutz. Courtesy of the Picture Collection, The Branch Libraries, The New York Public Library.

William Dean Howells, c. 1903. From the United State Library of Congress, Prints and Photographs Division.

she became involved with the Imagists. Her poetry was rooted in classical and French symbolism and her poetic ideas were expressed in subjects, not merely with the effusive, exuberant, and somewhat sentimental observations of earlier poets. Amy's poetic stature increased with the publication of *Men, Women, and Ghosts* (1916), *Can Grande's Castle* (1918), and, posthumously, *What's O'Clock* (1925), *East Wind* (1926), and *Ballads for Sale* (1927). Her most famous poem is probably "Patterns." In addition to being a poet of considerable influence, Amy Lowell was also a splendid critic, as her two-volume biography, *John Keats* (1925), testifies.

The demise of the mighty quill of Beacon Hill came about through an outside force—that of realism in literature. In 1900 Theodore Dreiser published *Sister Carrie*, and the curtain was drawn on the New England scene, even though it still was represented by such men of eminence as William Dean Howells and boasted such publications as *The Atlantic Monthly* and *Harper's*. The die had been cast, and the twentieth century would honor the Dreiser school and its followers, from Hemingway to

George Santayana, 1936. Courtesy of Charles Scribner's & Sons.

Mailer, and leave to nostalgia the glories that had belonged to Boston in the magical days of Elizabeth Peabody's bookstore on Beacon Street.[3] Once the monumental authors and their works were real, alive. Now they, too, are relegated to another era of ghosts. Their works alone survive to tell the curious about themselves and the lives they led or of the imaginary people and lives they wrote about.

The moral solidarity of the Boston literary mind is what aligned it to the literary mind of Europe just before, during, and after the Civil War, up into the twentieth century, when many writers living in exile found the reform atmosphere of Europe more rational than that of their own country. One author, George Santayana, the philosopher whose novel *The Last Puritan* was a portrait of a Bostonian of the late nineteenth century, retired to a convent in Italy, where he lived until his death in 1952. In order to escape from the turmoils of the twentieth century he became a recluse, detaching himself from any involvement either with people or the social events of Fascism and Communism, both of which he dismissed as mere milestones in the history of mankind. It is quite possible that Santayana, in his rejection of organized religion but retention of a deep religious sense, became in his self-imposed confinement the true embodiment of Boston's last Puritan.

9

Jack-in-the-Pulpit

Here's to the town of Boston
And the turf that the Puritans trod,
In the rest of mankind
Little virtue they find,
But they feel quite chummy with God.

When the Puritans came to Sparta City, as Samuel Adams called Boston, they were for the most part members of the recently organized Congregational church. This type of Protestant church organization was one in which the local church had free control of its own affairs. The underlying principle is that each individual congregation has as its head Jesus Christ alone, and that the relations of the various congregations are those of fellow members in one common family of God. Bishops and presbyteries were eliminated in Congregationalism. The movement to which the name came to be applied began in the sixteenth century in England in a revolt against formalized worship, unregenerate membership, and state control of the established church. In 1582 Robert Browne, an Englishman, published the first theoretical exposition of Congregational principles.

For these Founding Fathers, law, literacy, education, the sense of history and of the future all found their focus in the Bible. The faith of these first settlers inculcated a democratic and revolutionary lesson as well as a purely religious one. Boston was the hub of the Massachusetts Bay Colony, from which sprang all other important New England settlements. And the church was the center of law, order, and religion.

One of the first ministers to the newly settled flock was Richard Mather, pastor of Dorchester, Massachusetts. He coedited *The Bay Psalm Book,* which was published in Boston in 1640, the first work to be printed in the colonies. Later American critics have attacked the language of *The Bay Psalm Book* for its clumsiness, comparing it unfavorably with the

Warren Street Chapel, Boston. Illustration by Major. From *Gleason's Pictorial Drawing-Room Companion*, 1853.

King James version of the Psalms of David. The Bay Colony translation was rendered into meter appropriate for singing to simple tunes; the question of prose balance and structure was irrelevent. "If," wrote John Cotton in the preface, "in our English tongue we are to sing them, then as all our English songs (according to the course of our English poetry) do run in metre, so ought David's psalms be translated into metre."

For melodies, the Puritans borrowed much from the French and English tradition, following as they put it, "the graver sort of tunes of our own country songs." The songs were put to use in a diversity of practices. In the Sunday meeting, the congregation sang them in unison, although in the course of time different groups developed their own special styles of singing and harmonization. In the evening they might be sung to the lighter more lyrical melodies of leading English composers. They were sung in the field, on the road to battle, or in the hour of trial. Old Hundred, or the Hundredth Psalm, was one of the most popular and beloved of these devotional songs:

Make ye a joyful sounding noise
Unto Jehovah, all the earth:
Serve ye Jehovah with gladness
Before his presence come with mirth.

Know that Jehovah he is God,
Who hath us formed it is he,
And not ourselves; his own people
And sheep of his pasture are we.

Enter into his gates with praise,
Into his courts with thankfulness:
Make ye confessions unto him,
And his name reverently bless.

Because Jehovah he is good
Forever more is his mercy;
And unto generations all
Continue doth his verity.

One of the molders of the Congregational Church was John Cotton, a firm believer in the right of the Congregational minister to dictate to his faithful. Consequently, he is regarded as one of the strong upholders of theocracy—the form of government under which the early city developed. Cotton's daughter married Increase Mather, the son of Richard, and the first Congregational dynasty was established.

Old South Meeting House, Boston. Photograph by M. H. Halliday. Courtesy of the Society for the Preservation of New England Antiquities.

If song was in the hearts of men, oratory was on their lips. In Boston, the first mark of culture was a man's ability to express himself. Increase Mather assumed the pulpit of the North Church in 1664 and retained that position until the end of his life. "If ever a woman feels proud of her lover, it is when she sees him as a successful public speaker," wrote Harriet Beecher Stowe many years later, when the art of public speaking had reached an apex in Boston culture. Certainly Mrs. Mather had every reason to be proud of Increase, and afterwards of her son, Cotton. Their speaking was not limited to the pulpit; during the Salem trials both men spoke volubly, denouncing "spectral evidence."

Referring to the period, Emerson said,

> The books read, the sermons and prayers heard, the habits of thought of religious persons were all directed on death. All were under the shadow of Calvinism, and of the Roman Catholic purgatory and death was dreadful. The emphasis of all the good books given to young people was on death. We were all taught that we were born to die; and, over that, all the terrors that theology could gather from savage nations were added to increase the gloom.

It was upon this medieval theme of education of fitting people to die that the early Congregationalists founded first Harvard College then Yale, and many more seats of learning. The Puritans demanded learned ministers, not Jesus-shouters; men who could "expound the Sacred Scriptures from the original Hebrew and Greek, and be cognizant of what the Church Fathers, the Scholastic Fathers, the Scholastic Philosophers, and the Reformers had written, in Greek and Latin." They needed and would need for 150 years the brightest, brainiest, cleverest, and most educated they could produce to deal with the mysteries of English colonial policy, to establish trade, to keep the domestic peace, cope with the redskin, establish industry, collect the taxes, quell disturbances, uplift the fainthearted, provide for the poor,[1] control transportation, lay out the law, discourage excesses, command the uncouth, and be pillars of intelligence and honor for all to behold and admire. In short, to transport old England to New England, culturally.

In an analysis of such a religious atmosphere, it is only logical to realize again that such an incident as the Salem witchcraft would arise. It was as obvious and as precise in its enactment as a Greek tragedy, with a beginning, a middle, and an end. It was based upon the assumption that the children of the elect would inherit salvation along with the family household goods. The preaching from the pulpit described in gory details the punishments of those damned to hell by their activities on earth. It had the same intrigue to a young mind as the excitement of a hanging, a lynching, or an enormous fire. If arson was not instigated, the flames of the torture of an inquisition were substituted. The young girls of Salem sat watching the preacher in his pulpit, impressive in his black robes, talk of the devil, that archcriminal in the continuous crime novel enacted by the church. In a short time, they fell—as many young girls have continued to do—in love with the devil incarnate. They offered themselves to him, secretly, as disciples. They allowed—or so they thought, in their vivid imaginations and hallucinations—the dancing dervishes of his creation to wiggle in their sexually frustrated bodies, and to use their mouths for his accusations, his foul damnations. The end result was a purge. A purge not only of those afflicted, but of the church that had helped foster such behavior. Gradually the early Calvinism vanished and the Great Awakening occurred.

From the hysteria, exhortations, confessions, and promises of redemption, there began a replacement of theological ideas in the religious mind of Boston, and Calvinism was replaced by Unitarianism. The Divinity School at Harvard was established on a Unitarian basis, and the college was considered dangerously lax and liberal by the remaining representa tives of the old orthodoxy. Even so, in its inception it was a far cry from being an institution of high academic standards. The college was an adequate nest for a Boston lawyer, a merchant who desired a well-trained mind, or a minister who did not indulge in raptures. It filled the Unitarian pulpits of Boston with men who preached on Plutarch, who encouraged the sharpening of one's reasoning factors, of accepting a new kind of Christian faith that knew where to draw a fine line.

This new form of Christianity, which appealed to the Boston mind, was a form that denied the doctrine of the Trinity, believing that God exists only in one person. There had been many antitrinitarian movements in the early Christian Church, but modern Unitarianism traces its origin to the period of the Protestant Reformation. John Biddle has been called the father of English Unitarianism, but the development of a separate Unitarian body came about gradually through the efforts of men, such as Joseph Priestly.

In Boston, Unitarians took over the liberal wing of the Congregational Church and built King's Chapel, where in 1785 trinitarian doctrines were removed from the liturgy. In 1815, when Henry Ware was named head of the Divinity School at Harvard, the group took the name Unitarian. In a sermon by William Ellery Channing in 1819, his statements of belief became the platform of the new denomination. In 1825, the American Unitarian Association was formed.

A congregational form of government prevails in Unitarianism, each congregation having control of its own affairs. Neither ministers nor members are required to make profession of any particular doctrine. No

William Ellery Channing.
From *Le Magasin
Pittoresque*, 1861.

Theodore Parker. Engraved by S. A. Schoff
from a daguerrotype by Allen & Horton.

creed has been adopted by the church. The covenant in general use is simply, "In the love of truth, and in the spirit of Jesus, we unite for the worship of God and the service of man." It was under the influences of Ralph Waldo Emerson and Theodore Parker of Boston that American Unitarianism eventually became a religion of reason. Reason and conscience were considered the only guides to religious truth; complete religious tolerance, the innate goodness of man, and the universal salvation of man were preached.

The sermons that were preached were marked by grace and by force. This exacting scholarship, which became expected of any man in the Unitarian pulpit, was taught by Dr. Edward Tyrrel Channing, brother of the famous theologian.

> Channing with his bland, superior look,
> Cold as a moonbeam on a frozen brook,
> While the pale student, shivering in his shoes,
> Sees from his theme the turgid rhetoric ooze.
>   Holmes

Dr. Channing had an eye for the highfalutin, the swelling period, the emphatic word. He exemplified Puritan instincts as clarified by a sensible classical culture, and his influence was felt in every word that dropped with the sound of beauty from every Boston orator-minister's mouth. For the church, it was the shining hour of the spoken word of God.

Unquestionably, the Demosthenes of this new faith was William Ellery Channing, the man of genius in the movement, a poet in his theology from the day he stepped into the pulpit of the Federal Street Congregational Church in Boston, which he served until the day of his death in 1842. In his denunciation of war, his discussion of labor problems, and his views on education, he was generations ahead of his time. Although he did not ally himself with the abolitionist movement, his writings and preaching on slavery helped prepare for the Emancipation. He demanded of his congregation a large degree of intellectual and spiritual understanding. "A learner," he said, "must have something great in order to receive great lessons." His inspiration provided Bostonians with a situation and the will to cope with it. They had inherited the responsibility of a nation from their fathers. As Emerson wrote: "I do not speak with any fondness, but the language of coldest history, when I say that Boston commands the attention as the town which was appointed in the destiny of nations to lead the civilization of North America."

This was a notable school of self-respect, and they had all the virtues they professed. The idea of provinciality did not exist. The members of Dr. Channing's congregation were absorbed in public interests, in the creation of a classical center to be shared with all western Europe. They were self-confident, for to date their republic had proven a triumphant success. The dark sky of Civil War had not yet burst forth in a storm, and the wealth and population growth of their city was prodigious in its expansion. The Boston leaders saw themselves as commanders of a great forward movement of the human race. They were exhorted to glorify their city with beautiful buildings, works of art, collections of libraries, salons of music, and as the millionaires increased so did the physical beauty of the city.

Perhaps the dream of religious idealism was too stringent. From his pulpit in the Spring Street Unitarian Church, in West Roxbury, Theodore Parker preached a doctrine so radical that the Boston Unitarian clergy withdrew from him, even though he remained a member of their association until his death. His voice was heard throughout the country, where he lectured in lyceums—as was the fashion of the day—and spread his antislavery doctrines and other platforms of social reform. Ill health forced him to retire, and like so many of his contemporaries he, too, withdrew to Florence, where he died.

The behavior pattern began to tax the Boston mind. It acquired a zest for European art, although the unpretentious magnificence of the simplicity of the New England churches hardly lent itself architecturally to the munificence of the transplanted treasures of the Medicis and the Borgias.

A practical, low-church Episcopalianism began to penetrate Boston's original Unitarianism. The definite ritual and a returned belief in the divinity of Jesus Christ became acceptable to the liberal pocketbooks of many Boston millionaires—notably, William Appleton.

The original Puritans settling Boston had proscribed all that was Anglican. However, in 1686, when the colonial charter of Massachusetts was revoked, Church of England clergymen were appointed in that colony. In 1689, King's Chapel in Boston was opened, but during the American Revolution a great number of the Anglican clergy of Boston, who were openly Loyalists, fled with members of their congregations to Canada or England. For a long time the church was bruised by the battle scars of the revolution, although a majority of the founders of the new American nation were Episcopalians. After the war one of the first objectives was to establish a native episcopacy. The new ecclesiastical body was called the Protestant Episcopal Church, a name approved in 1789 by the first general convention, which adopted a constitution and a revised version of the *Book of Common Prayer.*

The success of the return of Episcopalianism revolved around the handsome young bachelor minister Phillips Brooks, who in 1869 began his memorable ministry at Trinity Church in Boston; a statue by Saint-Gaudens bears witness to Brooks's influence in his time. His ringing rhetoric was singularly important in placing Episcopalianism on a par with Unitarianism in becoming the favorite religion with the wealthy and socially important strata of Boston. His charm, even more than his gifts as a preacher, his spiritual qualities, and his generous sympathies, won him his esteem, but even so, he was regarded as "an Episcopalian —with leanings toward Christianity," by many stark-pure Unitarians. Another great strength of the Episcopal church in Boston came from its sponsoring of many excellent boys' schools, which were staffed by Episcopal clergymen whose influence seeped down to the third and fourth generation.

Of the other Protestant sects, the Baptists (or Anabaptists, as they were sometimes called) were, to the Puritans, the anarchists of their day, "the incendiaries of commonwealth." Roger Williams founded the first Baptist church in America in Rhode Island, after he had disagreed with the local Puritan establishment both on specifics and generalities of doctrine and had left the Massachusetts colony to settle in Providence. In 1665, a group of Baptists organized a church in Charlestown, which later moved to Boston but had little following. But, by the beginning of the nineteenth century, there were two strong Baptist churches in Boston. Dr. Samuel Stillman, a popular extemporaneous preacher, ministered at the First Church.

Boston Baptists were very concerned with being "heralds of salvation" and preaching in "heathen lands." A missionary society was founded by the early Baptists, and in 1871 a national foreign mission was formed in Boston. The churches grew rapidly, and there was a special program for the building of churches for black members. Daniel Sharp Ford, the publisher, spent lavishly to advance Baptist interests. He left a million dollars to the Baptist Social Union to foster better conditions for the laboring classes. They built Ford Hall and established the controversial Ford Hall Forums, which eventually moved to Jordan Hall. The Baptists especially began to adjust to the needs of the twentieth century, and their results are symbolized in the careers of two black Baptists: singer Roland Hayes; and Martin Luther King, Jr., who trained at the theological school of Boston University.

Presbyterians had some difficulty in making much of a religious impression in Boston, being too close to the Congregationalists. Although the Presbyterians from Scotland were among the earliest settlers (establishing the country's oldest charitable groups with their Scots Charitable Society founded in 1657), the identity with the Congregational Church was too strong for the group to decide to make a definite split. In 1825 the First Presbyterian Church was founded in Boston, but its influence was never very strong. One hundred years later there were ten active Presbyterian churches, including the Gloucester Memorial Congregation of Negroes, but the Great Depression and the population changes caused by increased moving from urban to suburban centers diminished the importance of the Presbyterian Church among the religious groups in Boston.

In 1736, John Wesley's brother, Charles, paid a visit to Boston, since many Methodist evangelists included the city as one of their preaching stopovers. In 1790, Bishop Francis Asbury, chief founder of Methodism in America, visited Boston, and the first Methodist church was built between 1795 and 1797. It became known as the "Mother of Bishops," because of the number of clergy who were raised to that office. The Tremont Methodist Church has been called "the cradle of the Women's Foreign Missionary Society." This growing Methodist group started a weekly newspaper, *Zion's Herald,* in 1823—a paper that denounced the violent "mob" that attacked William Lloyd Garrison in 1825. The most popular Methodist minister was Edward T. Taylor, who opened a nonsectarian home for sailors and was the model for Melville's preacher in *Moby Dick.* In 1839 the Methodists founded Boston University, which, though nonsectarian and coeducational, bears a strong Methodist imprint in its theological school.

Lutheranism came to Boston with the German immigrants, who founded a church in 1839. Today, there is one major Lutheran church housed at the corner of Berkeley and Marlborough streets, but the principal project of the Boston Lutherans is the operation of the Lutheran Brook Farm Home (once the Martin Luther Orphan's Home) on the site of the original Brook Farm in West Roxbury. It works with emotionally disturbed children.

Before the middle of the nineteenth century there were few Jews residing in Boston, but in 1842 there were enough to form the first congregation, which was formally organized in 1843 and incorporated as the Congregation Ohabei Shalom, with Henry Selling as its rabbi. The first members were mainly of Polish extraction. In 1854 one group (mostly German Jews) withdrew to organize what is today the Temple Israel, and another group formed Mishkan Israel in 1858. Under Solomon Schindler as rabbi, Temple Israel reformed and Americanized the old-world rituals. Rabbi Schindler introduced the family pew, the choir, the organ, a new prayer book, and eliminated the wearing of hats. He tried to erase prejudices between Jew and Gentile, even sanctioning intermarriage. His tenets were carried further by Rabbi Joshua Liebman, whose *Peace of Mind,* published in 1946, was a best seller in its day.

Like other congregations serving small ethnic groups, the Jewish synagogues became a part of the larger Boston community, expanding to the adjoining communities as their members moved to nearby Brookline, the Newtons, Roxbury, and Dorchester. With the Jewish synagogues came the associated Jewish organizations—the B'nai B'rith, the Zionist groups, the Federation of Jewish Charities. Brandeis University, named for Boston's famous Justice Louis Brandeis, became, under the guidance of Dr. Abram Sacher, one of the country's leading universities.

Among the early Protestant movements was Universalism, which appears almost as a home-grown Boston religion, with emphasis on social reform. It grew out of revisions of Calvinism, and in 1852 the group founded Tufts College on Walnut Hill in Medford. Here a noted minister, Alonzo Ames Miner, who became president of Tufts College, was one of the nation's chief advocates of temperance. Prison reform was another social objective of the leaders. But again, as the Boston population changed, most Universalist churches closed or moved to the suburbs, and in time the denomination merged with the Unitarian, leaving only one active Universalist church in Boston—an experimental group that met in the Charles Street Meeting House.

It is interesting to note the segregation problems of all churches in Boston. Since there were blacks in Boston as soon as there were whites, and since the Puritans required everyone to attend church, the question

Afro-American Meeting House, South Court, Boston. Photograph by Arthur Hoshell. Courtesy of the Society for the Preservation of New England Antiquities.

arose as to where the black slaves and servants could sit. Since the precepts of church membership did not depend on wealth, social status, or skin color, blacks were occasionally admitted to the company of "visible saints." Because Negro slavery was legal in Boston until after the Revolution, though its practice had been dying out, it was difficult for the church fellowship to accept Negroes as fellow Christians. Separate worship originated about this time. The old African Church on Smith Court off Joy Street on Beacon Hill was built by Afro-Americans and dedicated in 1806. In its sanctuary the American Anti-Slavery Society was founded in 1833, and it was backed by such notables as Frederick Douglass, Harriet Tubman, and Sojourner Truth.

Once begun, separatism grew. White churches did not welcome blacks. When a Boston merchant escorted a black gentleman into his church in the 1820s there was a great flurry until it was explained that the black worshiper was worth a million dollars. The Yankee's love of the almighty dollar was more powerful than his love of the Almighty, and the black man was not ousted; but all rich black worshipers did not fare so well, since most churches had a clause in their pew deeds stating that they could only be held by "respectable white persons."

With the increase of the black population, various denominations began to be organized to serve their religious needs. Churches such as the Charles Street African Methodist Episcopal Church were erected. As the times changed, so did the purpose of the black churches. During the Depression Father Divine had a Peace Mission on Canton Street that featured chicken dinners for fifteen cents; today Muhammad's Mosque No. 11 has its Shabbazz Restaurant, where it permits no smoking or drinking. The present-day black churches in Boston have been mostly concerned with civil rights movements. In the works of Allan Rohan Crite, black faith has been depicted in watercolors that show the Madonna and child living in the area of the Boston black ghetto slums.

The story of the Roman Catholic Church in Boston is almost as involved as the history of Boston. There are three periods in the history of the church. The first was when the church was considered by the pre-dominantly Protestant faith as being merely another Christian sect with special forms of prayer and ritual. The French were the sponsors of this early attempt to make the church important in the new world around Boston. Their efforts were mostly among the New England Indians; but the English victory in the French and Indian War brought this effort to an end, and it stigmatized Catholics as being both religious and political enemies of Puritan Protestantism. This attitude continued until the Revolution, when the anti-Catholic prejudices of many were softened.

Two names survive this period—Father Francis Anthony Matignon and Father Jean Louis Anne Madeleine Lefebre de Cheverus. Together they were quite indomitable. They raised the money to build the Cathedral of the Holy Cross on Franklin Street, which was designed, free of charge by Charles Bulfinch, and was contributed to by John Adams. In 1810 Cheverus was ordained bishop of the diocese of Boston.

The church seemed destined to survive, but the vast immigration of the unwanted Irish changed the destiny of the organization radically. The rising Protestant sects stood strongly against Popery and Papists, and the antagonism against Roman Catholics reached such proportions that violence broke out—the most dramatic event being the burning of the

Ursuline convent on Mt. Benedict in Charlestown in 1834. The outburst was a native American movement, and it focused on the Irish and their religion. "Catholics were constantly exposed to vituperation, invectives, assaults, and arson. Groups of rowdies frequented the streets of Boston . . . eager to insult and beat up 'Paddies.' " Fears of racial and religious war penetrated Boston, and until 1875 the ruins of the convent were allowed to remain as a visible symbol of the effects of prejudice.

Bishop Joseph Fenwick, who took over the diocese when the Catholic population had been 5 percent of the population and who died when it had increased to 25 percent, tried to maintain a calm through the critical years. He was succeeded by Bishop John B. Fitzpatrick, who had to endure the Know-Nothing Movement of the 1850s when the Boston School Committee, in the hands of the Protestants, set up compulsory Bible readings and school prayers that were anti-Catholic. The bigotry reached a peak in 1859, when a young Catholic student, Thomas Wall, was brutally whipped for refusing to repeat the Ten Commandments in a Protestant translation. The incident was commonplace, and when the boy's father brought charges, the School Committee defended the teacher! Yet it was during these years that Bishop Fitzpatrick continued to build churches, started the parochial school system, and in 1857 began the plans for Boston College.

Ironically, it was the Civil War that helped to cement relations between the Catholics and Protestants. Now the immigrants who poured into Boston were mainly Catholic but not predominantly Irish. Boston-born Archbishop John Williams began his long reign, and churches, schools, seminaries, monasteries, convents, orphanages, hospitals, asylums, societies all multiplied under his quiet but firm control. The prominent role of Catholics in the city's life soon became synchronized under William Cardinal O'Connell, under whose power Catholic prestige increased in every direction, culminating in the political career of the tough Irish politician James Michael Curley.

When O'Connell died he was replaced by Richard Cardinal Cushing, a man with a very different personality but with equally great qualifications for leadership. Cushing was not the aristocrat O'Connell had been, but he was warm and witty and possessed a human quality his predecessor had lacked. He danced with the children, he read the first mass ever televised, and he performed the first nuptial mass on TV. He became a close personal friend of the beloved Pope John XXIII and was a prominent member of Vatican II, fighting for the deletion of anti-

Semitic references and for the Schema of Religious Freedom. (He was the first cardinal in the United States to address a Masonic lodge.) Cushing was friendly with the Kennedys, and through them he acquired much financial support for Catholic charities. He also suffered their personal tragedies and triumphs. When he died in 1970 he left to the seventh head of the Boston archdiocese, Humberto Sosa Madeiros, an establishment of 401 churches, 2,511 priests, 5,915 nuns, 12 hospitals, 7 colleges and universities, 338 parochial schools, and a Catholic population of nearly 1,900,000.

That Boston has been much preached at, no one would deny; nor would anyone deny the strong impact of the female sex upon the life of the churches. The auxiliaries, the charities, and the social tones of the churches have been set for the most part by formidable Boston women. One Boston woman established a new strain of religious thought that was to become worldwide. She was Mary Baker Eddy. In 1875 she wrote *Science and Health,* which was to become the manual and textbook of the newly founded Christian Science religion.

Although not a native-born Bostonian, Mrs. Eddy was a New Englander. Frail health prevented regular school attendance when she was young, although she did study for a while at Holmes Academy in Plymouth. Her ill health led her to explore the mental healing of P. P. Quimby in Portland, Maine. She benefited from his treatments and became his pupil, although she later discarded his methods and created her own.

The year 1866 (in which Mrs. Eddy was divorced from her second husband, her first died shortly after their marriage) marks the actual beginning of Christian Science as she saw it. Extensive reading of the words and works of Jesus Christ led Mrs. Eddy to the conclusion that "the starting point of divine Science is that God, Spirit, is All-in-All and that there is no other matter or mind. Spirit is immortal truth; matter is mortal error . . . Spirit is God and Man is His image and likeness. Therefore man is not material; he is spiritual." To the Christian Scientist, all that is eternal, indestructible, true, is real; all that is contrary to the nature of God, unreal. By understanding, love, prayer, and faith in the goodness of God, followers of Christian Science work to overthrow evil, disease, and death, and to save all mankind. They apply the principles of Christian Science to all problems of human existence.

In 1879, Mrs. Eddy established the Church of Christ, Scientist. In Boston, in 1892, she organized the Mother Church, of which Christian Science churches all over the world are branches. Each individual church is self-governing and self-supporting, but all accept the tenets framed by Mrs. Eddy and incorporated in the *Church Manual* (1895). The extremely strong organization created and headed by Mrs. Eddy until her "passing" (Christian Scientists never refer to death as dying), has enabled Christian Science to grow steadily in numbers and in its scope of activity. The most important of the numerous publications issued is *The Christian Science Monitor,* an influential daily newspaper with worldwide readership, published in Boston. There are no individual pastors in the church (Mrs. Eddy's pastorship was "spiritual"). Services are conducted by two readers, one reading from the Scriptures, the other from *Science and Health*. All churches read the same lessons at the same time.

The evolution of the religious mind from Boston's founding to the establishment of the Church of Christ, Scientist, is extremely important in the psychological-historical study of the city and its inhabitants. The words of the church ministers have had an impact upon its human behavior, for much of the action of man is motivated not only by the doctrines of the church but within its walls—baptism for redemption, marriage for the consummation of the human sexual relationship and producing of children, and funerals for the final exit of man from life. In Boston all of these celebrations were and are actively observed, but of the three the Boston funeral is the most faithfully attended. A Boston funeral, of whatever religion, is mandatory for family and friends.

In Boston funeral attendance has long been one of society's favorite pastimes. No detail is overlooked, and strict attention is paid to every wish of the deceased, no matter how extreme. The obsequies run from high Episcopalian to low Unitarian, and range from the somber solemnity of the Protestant mourning to the conviviality of the typical Irish wake.

The funeral of Mrs. Jack Gardner reached the ultimate high with two complete ceremonies: a private one in the Spanish chapel of her Italian castle and a public one in the Church of the Advent. Following the church services, her body, covered with a purple pall, was returned to lie in state in her palace. Under a huge black crucifix between tall candlesticks were prie-dieux where nuns, relieving one another at intervals, maintained constant prayer for four days and nights before the body was interred. This was in contrast to the Unitarian low church service,

The Mathers' tomb, Copp's Hill Burying Ground. Photograph by
W. H. Halliday. Courtesy of the Society for the Preservation of
New England Antiquities.

typified by the funeral of Ralph Forbes of Milton, whose service was
held in the parlor of his home, without music and with one minute
of reading from the Bible and a full hour of Emerson.

In Boston, the funeral is not the end; equal emphasis is laid upon the
burying ground. The most historically famous burying ground is Old
Granary, which was laid out in 1660 and was part of the original Boston
Common. It takes its name from the town granary, which at that time
was situated where Park Street Church now stands. The oldest marker
in the cemetery is that of one Hannah Allen, and the oldest upright stone
is that of John Wakefield. For years this cemetery has been regarded
as the Westminster Abbey of American history. Three signers of the
Declaration of Independence are buried there: John Hancock, Samuel
Adams, and Robert Treat Paine—in addition to Paul Revere, James Otis,
and Peter Faneuil. There is also the grave of Mary Goose, wife of Isaac
Goose—better known as Boston's Mother Goose, said to have written
the nursery rhymes for her grandchildren.

King's Chapel Burying Ground was probably established soon after
the settlement of Boston. Governor John Winthrop's *Journal* records:
"Captain Welden, a hopeful young gent, and an experienced soldier,
dyed at Charlestowne of a consumption, and was buried in Boston with
a military funeral." The earliest interment on record was that of Governor Winthrop in 1649. Tombs of **William Dawes, Jr., Mary Chilton,**

and Robert Keayne also are to be found in this first Boston burial ground.

It is said that the land was owned by Sir Isaac Johnson, an important man in the colony, who came to Boston with the governor. On his death-bed, Sir Isaac expressed the wish that he be buried on his land—and he was, on September 30, 1630. Before long, somebody else died and wished to be buried alongside Brother Johnson, and was. But when frequent applications for the same privilege were made to the authorities, we see the notation in the old record: "Brother Johnson's is getting to be a poor place for vegetables." The garden is now King's Chapel Burial Ground. In 1688 Governor Andros took one corner of the old burying place for the first Episcopal chapel in New England. Graves of the early settlers were disturbed, and stone memorials removed from the site.

The second burial ground in Boston in the North End is Copp's Hill, which was named for William Copp who dwelt nearby and is interred there. There are over 225 tombs in this burial ground, the oldest having been erected in 1717. In one tomb are buried "The Reverend Doctors Increase, Cotton and Samuel Mather." Both Robert Newman, the sexton of Christ Church (the Old North Church of Paul Revere fame), who displayed two "lanthorns" at Revere's order, and the patriot Daniel Malcolm, "who desired to be buried ten feet deep, safe from the British musket balls," are buried in the old ground. It was from Copp's Burial Ground that Generals Clinton and Burgoyne witnessed the Battle of Bunker Hill and directed the fire of the battery.

Forest Hills, between Milton and Mount Auburn, is the so-called "Gateway-to-Heaven," and the little Walnut Hills Cemetery in Brookline is crowded with the bodies of many of Boston's proper citizens. In addition, there are the special Jewish and Roman Catholic burying grounds. In the sweet summer days, there blooms all around Boston the fair "rose where some buried Caesar bled."

In the history of a city founded upon religious principles and pursuing the variations upon the theme of religion as they developed in Boston, three churches have special historical significance. The Park Street Church (Congregational Trinitarian Evangelical) at the corner of Tremont and Park Streets occupies the site of the granary where the sails for the frigate *Constitution* ("Old Ironsides") were made. It is the best re-maining example of Boston's early nineteenth-century ecclesiastical archi-tecture and was designed by the English architect Peter Banner. The Ionic and Corinthian capitals of the steeple are the work of Boston's own Solomon Willard, the construction engineer of the Bunker Hill

Park Street Church, Boston, by Filliner. From *Gleason's Pictorial Drawing-Room Companion*, September 3, 1853.

Monument. The church stands on Brimstone Corner, so called from the storage of brimstone in the basement for the manufacture of powder in 1812. Here "America the Beautiful" first was sung in public; William Garrison gave his first public address in Boston against slavery; and Charles Sumner gave his great oration "The War System of Nations," at a meeting of the American Peace Society in 1849. The story of the legend of Brimstone Corner, in *Boston Common Scenes from Four Centuries,* by Mark Antony DeWolfe Howe, is a delightful fantasy that tells why the wind always blows on Brimstone Corner, the whereabouts of his Satanic majesty, and why the name Brimstone Corner:

> The Devil and a Gale of Wind
> Danced Hand in Hand up Winter Street
> The Devil like his demons grinned
> To have for comrade so complete
> A rascal and a mischief maker
> Who'd drag an oath from a Quaker.

> The Wind made sport of hats and hair
> The Ladies deemed their ornament
> With skirts that frolicked everywhere
> Away their trim decorum went
> And worthy citizens lamented
> The public spectacles presented.

> The Devil beamed with horrid joy
> Till to the Commons rim they came.
> Then chuckled, "What you here, my boy,
> For duties now my presence claim
> In yonder Church on Brimstone Corner;
> Where Pleasure's dead and lacks a mourner.

> "But play about till I come back"
> With that he vanished through the doors,
> And since that day the almanac
> Has marked the years by tens and scores
> Yet never from these sacred portals
> Returns the Enemy of Mortals.

> And that is why the faithful Gale
> Round Park Street Corner still must blow
> Waiting for him with horns and tail
> At least some people tell me so—
> None of your famous Antiquarians
> But just some wicked Unitarians.

King's Chapel, which was the first Episcopal Church in New England, due to the character of changes made in *The Book of Common Prayer* is often referred to as the first Unitarian Church in America. It was established in 1686 by the Reverend Robert Ratcliffe, the Private Chaplain of King James II, who had come from England commissioned to establish the Church of England in the colony. Services were held in the Town House (where the Old State House now stands), for no Congregational meeting house would permit the Church of England service to be read within its doors. In December 1686, Sir Edmund Andros came to Boston, the first fully commissioned governor of the province. Within four months Governor Andros took the keys of the Old South Church from the sexton, and for nearly two years the Episcopalians held possession of the Old South on Sunday mornings, the Congregationalists having to wait until a later hour to hold their services.

Andros tried to buy a site for the Episcopal church, but none was available. He finally succeeded in setting aside one corner of the burying ground and erected a wooden edifice, where King's Chapel still stands. In 1710 it was enlarged, and the present edifice was dedicated in 1754. The granite walls were built right around the wooden building, and the granite came from Quincy, where the first granite was quarried in America. The bell in the tower was recast by Paul Revere and Sons in 1816.

Christ Church, the Old North Church of Paul Revere fame, is the oldest church edifice in Boston, a substantial handmade brick structure of about 70 feet long, 51 feet wide, and 42 feet high. Its walls are 2½ feet thick. The steeple is 190 feet high. It is the work of master builders Thomas Tippin and Thomas Bennett, designed after the manner of Sir Christopher Wren. The clock in front of the gallery was made by Richard Avery in 1726, and the case was made by Thomas Bennett of Pew #36. It still keeps good time. It was here that Paul Revere, at the age of fifteen, came as a member of a guild organized to ring bells. The eight bells, which were cast in Gloucester, England in 1744, "the first ring of bells cast for the British Empire in North America," still are played before a Sunday morning service.

A large collection of organs also exists in the churches. Although the Puritans had a horror of musical instruments being played in the Lord's house, singing with "heart and voyce" was approved. The singing with instruments was unsanctified and left to the Anglicans to introduce. The

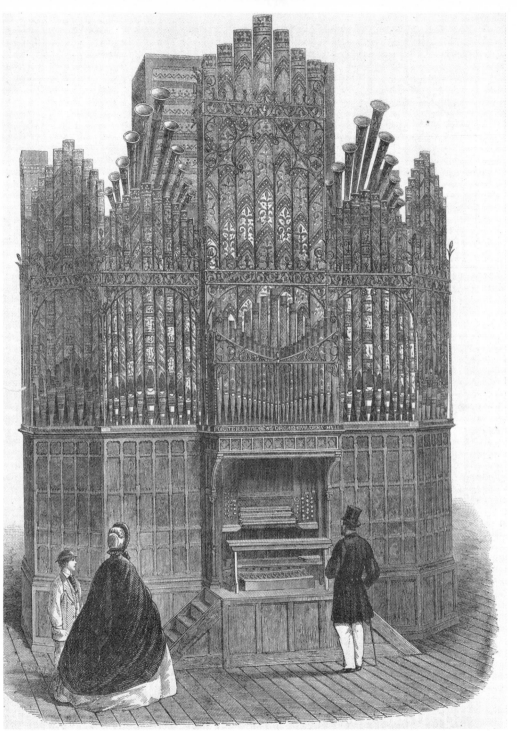

Church organ built by Messrs. Forster and Andrews of Hull. Engravings by J. L. Calcomb. From *Illustrated London News and Sketch, Ltd.*, September 20, 1862.

first organ used in Boston was in King's Chapel in 1714 and was the bequest of Thomas Brattle, who brought it from England in 1708. Most of the early organs were imported from England; but in 1752 Thomas Johnston became the first American organ maker of note. The most famous was William Marcellus Goodrich, whose instruments were preferred to those of foreign make.

By the middle of the nineteenth century, Boston, with sixty-four organs, had more such instruments in proportion to its population than any other city in the country. The German style of organ-building dominated at the time of the Civil War. In 1863 the great organ of the Boston Music Hall was brought from Bavaria. In 1885 it was purchased by the New England Conservatory of Music and later removed to Methuen, Massachusetts. All of these early organs suffered from unsteady wind pressure, but the later introduction of the electric motor solved this problem. The first electric action was used in the organ in the Church of Christ, Scientist, in 1895 and the first electric motor in Trinity Church in 1900. Boston's dominance in the field of organ manufacture existed until the twentieth century, and recently the building of organs has had a revival.

Some of the famous organs in Boston churches today are in King's Chapel, The Church of the Advent, and All Saint's Lutheran Church. In St. Stephen's (Catholic) there is an 1830 Goodrich. Immaculate Conception has an 1863 Hook, which is reputedly hard to equal for playing French romantic music, and in Most Holy Redeemer there is an 1856 William Simmons, which according to one prominent organist "possesses a grandeur usually found only in larger instruments." In addition, there is in the Museum of Fine Arts a 1792 Avery chamber organ that has been fully restored, and the State House now owns the organ that was once the property of Oliver Holden, Boston's famous hymn writer.

The contest between the preacher in the pulpit and the organist in the stall was resolved in Boston's old Trinity Church, where one of the city's most famous organists played. Each Sunday Dr. George K. Jackson dressed in the full regalia of an English doctor of music: plum-colored coat, yellow breeches, and square cap. He played elaborate church music; when the minister asked him to shorten his recitals, he told the minister to shorten his sermons. The following Sunday, Dr. Jackson picked out the psalm tunes with one finger. The Reverend Dr. Gardiner asked for his resignation and got it. Jack-in-the-pulpit had, in Boston, the last word.

10

A Slab of Culture

Culture is defined as that quality in a person or a civilization that arises from an interest in and an acquaintance with what is generally regarded as excellent in arts, letters, manners, scholarly pursuits, music, and so on. From its origin, Boston's citizens were determined that it be a city of culture. The order was large and eventually could have produced the line attributed to Hermann Göering: "When I hear anyone talk of Culture, I reach for my revolver." Culture with a capital *C* in Boston was an acting out of the lines of Matthew Arnold, who described culture as "the passion for sweetness and light and (what is more) the passion for making them prevail."

Boston is a complex city in its dual role. It is, first and foremost, the Puritan city of revolutionary origin—the city that is America. Just as Voltaire saw the city of London as representing England and England's sense of social order, the visitor to Boston must see this Puritan-revolutionary aspect of the city. Second, Boston exemplifies the economic power of industrial wealth, in which the city's aesthetic needs were supplied by the newly founded aristocracy's pleasure in taking on new refinements. Thus we find two still-existing cultures, one built upon the other; with each represented in the existing arts and artifacts related to the times and the talents of its men and women.

Despite the rapid changes of modern times, Boston has managed to retain many of the cultural aspects that existed before the American Revolution. Many of the artifacts have survived: furniture and household articles made of wood, pewter, copper, silver, and glass are on hand for the visitor to see in museums, and its early printed words can be studied in the Paul Revere House in the North End of Boston: There are also "primitive" paintings, which record the time as seen by the living eye of the inhabitant. In those early days men created their own art

The Paul Revere House in North Boston. For a long time this part of Boston was cut off from the rest of the town by a ship canal. It was the most elegant section of the city. Photograph by Arthur Griffin. From *Boston Book* by Esther Forbes (Boston: Houghton, Mifflin, 1947).

culture, for in their exit from the old world they transported few if any worldly goods. It was their longing for the familiar things of their past lives that caused them, as soon as they could afford it, to bring from Europe to their newly found city some of the Old World art, which they felt was essential to a cultural way of life.

That they were creating a culture—new and unique—did not occur to many of the early settlers. They felt that they were sacrificing culture for a new city where moral order did, in truth, exist—although from the beginning they realized the frailties of human nature and discovered that any city, being human in design, inspires both good and evil. When the revolutionary spirit had died, and the stern Calvinist moral order had mellowed with the acquisition of wealth, Boston set about imitating the culture of the old world by buying its art; introducing the early glories of Greece, Rome and China. From the very beginning it was an imitative culture, created with nineteenth-century money—doomed to die, perhaps, when the twentieth century demanded a new order compatible with a society of free enterprise.

Probably the first organized art show in Boston was the work of one John Smibert, a Scots portrait painter who, after serving an apprenticeship to an Edinburgh house painter, went to London and from there to Italy to study art. He had a small London success but left with Dean (later Bishop) Berkeley to teach in his college in Bermuda. Smibert arrived in Boston in 1730 where he assembled an art show. If the show was not a great success in any other area it was in the field of matrimony, for Smibert met an heiress, whom he later married. She was influential in his obtaining commissions. In time he became an eminently prosperous portrait painter of top-drawer social standing. Among his works are portraits of Judge Edmund Quincy, now in the Museum of Fine Arts in Boston, and Peter Faneuil in the Massachusetts Historical Society in Boston. Harvard and Bowdoin also possess examples of his formal, faithfully produced portraits. Yale owns the first important portrait group painted in America, Smibert's *Bishop Berkeley and His Entourage,* executed in 1731, into which Smibert slipped his own self-portrait.

Smibert influenced the works of John Singleton Copley, who was Boston born and bred. Copley also studied with his own stepfather, Peter Pelham, a colonial artist, and with Robert Feke, an early American portrait painter, born in Oyster Bay, New York, but a resident of Boston. Feke's most familiar portrait is that of John Royall and his family, now owned by Harvard University. Feke's works are best known for their charm and detail of elegant costume. Feke and Smibert shared studios, where young Copley worked.

By the time he was twenty, Copley was a master portrait painter with a mature style remarkable for its brilliance, clarity, and forthright characterization. In 1776 his *Boy with a Squirrel* was exhibited in London and drew the attention of Benjamin West, the Quaker-born Pennsylvania master, who received the patronage of George III and who had a remarkable influence on all leading early American artists. West persuaded Copley to come to London to study, which, after eight years of exhaustive work in Boston, New York, and Philadelphia, he did, never to return. In England his style gained a subtlety and polish but lost some of the vigor of his prime work. He was finally admitted to the Royal Academy. One of his best canvases, a unique forerunner of romantic horror painting, was his rendering of a contemporary disaster, *Brook Watson and the Shark*. It now hangs in the Boston Museum of Fine Arts, which owns many of Copley's works. Among the pieces on display are his portraits of Samuel Adams and Paul Revere. Harvard has his portraits of Nicholas Boylston and Mrs. Thomas Boylston.

Another of West's protégés was Washington Allston, who, after graduation from Harvard, went to live in London for a few years to study with West. While there, Allston, who was also a poet, painted Coleridge. Later he returned to Boston to live. His involvement with the art world of the city was complex (he married William Ellery Channing's sister, and then, upon her death, Martha Dana, the sister of Richard Henry Dana). Allston's own work became somewhat confused, his efforts expended in colossal but never completed compositions such as *Belshazzar's Feast*, now in the Boston Athenaeum. His paintings, usually biblical or classical in subject, show the influence of the Venetian school. Despite his preference for monumental figure formations, Allston's most successful works were his romantic landscapes or seascapes, such as the *Moonlight Landscape,* now in the Museum of Fine Arts or his magnificent chalk drawing, *Ship in a Squall,* now in the Fogg Museum.

One of Allston's Charlestown-born pupils was Samuel Finley Breese Morse, the inventor of the telegraph, who was also a quite well known portrait painter and one of the founders of the National Academy of Design. It was Morse, with John Draper, who brought the daguerreotype to the United States, a process which in time altered the method of recording human events from that of the pen and the palette to that of the camera.

At the time of the Peace of Ghent, Gilbert Stuart was a Boston resident. Another of Benjamin West's protégés, he had lived with the artist in London during the Revolution and became a member of the Royal Academy with his *Portrait of a Gentleman Skating*. Famous in London and in Dublin, no one questioned his talent in Boston. In art circles his word was law; he was the arbiter of painting. He did three portraits of George Washington from life. The first, the so-called Vaughn type (1795) is a bust with the right side of the face shown (there are at least fifteen replicas of this piece); the second was the Lansdowne type (1796), painted for the Marquis of Lansdowne, and is a full-length study of the first president (the original is in the Pennsylvania Academy of Fine Arts); the third, unfinished, is in the Boston Athenaeum and is called the Athenaeum head. It was commissioned by Martha Washington, who

John Singleton Copley,
from a painting by
Gilbert Stuart.

never received the original, and only one of the seventy-five replicas. The portrait has been immortalized by the engravings on the one-dollar bill. Stuart's brilliant style, modeled after the work of Sir Joshua Reynolds and Gainsborough, is seen at its best in his portraits of the Appletons and other Boston merchant princes and their families. Most of these paintings can be seen in Boston museums.

Stuart was a mischievous man whose personal charm almost exceeded his talent. In his lordly style he was quite familiar with the social elite of Boston. Bostonians enjoyed his dipping of snuff, his taste for Madeira, and his flowing conversation. They delighted in repeating the story that when one of his sitters fell asleep he painted him with asses' ears; but what they liked most was what they saw on canvas. It was the golden age of portrait painting, and Stuart was fourteen carat. One of the world's most famous artists, he was sponsored by Bostonians because his presence added to their pride in themselves and because it was an age of family pride.

Actually, from a critical point of view, it is evident that Bostonians of Stuart's day lacked a sense of perception and did not realize that Stuart was perpetuating, for the world to see, the inner man with his petty ego and his superficialities. They chose not to see what the mirror on the wall was saying. What they heard and saw was that "the fairest one of all" was in the Stuart portrait.

Boston's wealthy art patrons traveled to Europe and were impressed

Paul Revere as a young man, by John Singleton Copley. Courtesy of the
Museum of Fine Arts, Boston. Cheek photograph.

by the flourishing schools of art in existence on the continent. The influence of these schools is evident in the existing art works now in the galleries and private collections in Boston. The studying of painting was a high form of cultural achievement for nineteenth-century Bostonians— ladies worked in pastels and painted china as a hobby, men had studios and painted or sculpted.

Most popular was the Barbizon—an informal school of landscape painting that derives its name from the village of Barbizon in France near the forest of Fontainebleau, a favorite habitat of the artists belonging to the school. Theodore Rousseau was the principal figure of this group, which included Corot and Millet and such landscapists as Jules Dupré, Constant Troyon, and Charles Daubigny. These men reacted against the conventions of classical landscape and advocated a direct study of nature. With their unpretentious rendering of landscapes, they paved the way for the Impressionists. Their works became favorites with Boston collectors, and the Barbizon influence is seen in many works of Boston artists of the era, the Museum of Fine Arts in Boston has an outstanding collection for public display—especially the Quincy Shaw assemblage of Millet.

For a century, artists sprang up around Boston with the alacrity of a fungus mushroom's growth. In painting, the post–Civil War period produced works of enduring worth and striking individuality. Four giants appeared on the American scene. Three were Boston-oriented—James Abbott McNeill Whistler, Albert Pinkham Ryder, and Winslow Homer. The fourth, Thomas Eakins, was from Philadelphia. The four are strikingly dissimilar. Whistler, who was born in Lowell and became an expatriate, cultivated a delicate art of suggestion both in his oils and in his etchings. Ryder, a hermit, produced a significant visionary art, deep and abstruse. Eakins painted with uncompromising honesty a world filled with the people he saw and knew. Homer, whose powerful and dramatic watercolors of the sea about him have never been equaled, had been an illustrator for *Harper's Weekly* and gained his original fame with his Civil War sketches and his drawings of Negro life in the South.

In the collections of art in Boston, the works of John Singer Sargent are prominently displayed. Sargent was an American born in Florence, Italy. He made sundry trips to the United States, Africa, and Spain but finally settled in London where he spent most of his life painting portraits of American and English social celebrities. In 1890, he was commissioned to paint a series of murals, *The History of Religion,* for the

James Abbott McNeill
Whistler by Chase.

Whistler's grandmother. From
Critic, February 1906.

Boston Public Library (founded in 1852 through a gift of Joshua Bates).
The building on Copley Square, designed by McKim, Mead and White
was completed in 1895. In addition to the Sargent mural, completed
in 1916, the main hall is decorated with murals by Puvis de Chavannes.
Other rooms exhibit Edwin Abbey's *Quest of the Holy Grail* panels. In
addition to the Ticknor Spanish and Portuguese collection and the libraries of Nathaniel Bowditch and John Adams, the library boasts the Albert
H. Wiggin collection of rare paintings and etchings.

Sargent was a tenacious and prolific painter, particularly brilliant in
his treatment of textures. In his portraits he showed considerable
virtuosity in his handling of the brushstroke, quickly capturing the likeness and vitality of his sitter. One of his most prestigious portraits is
that of Mrs. Jack. After 1910 Sargent deserted portrait painting in order
to do impressionist landscapes in watercolor. Most are of Venice and
Tyrol. The Boston Museum of Fine Arts has a superior collection of these
canvases.

Of all the arts, perhaps the least cultivated in colonial days was
sculpture. Apart from the anonymous carvings of tombstones and ships'
figureheads, most native sculpture existed in the form of portraiture.
John and Simeon Skillin of Boston and Samuel McIntire of Salem were
masters of the art of wood sculpture during the eighteenth century. They
specialized in carving furniture and architectural details, portrait busts,
and ship figureheads and relief plaques. John Frazee graduated from
tombstone sculpture to portrait sculpture, and his busts of Daniel Webster and John Marshall are among the first such works to be found. It
was Boston-born Horatio Greenough, a protégé of Washington Allston,
who started the American colony of sculptors in Italy. The atmosphere
and taste of Greenough and his group have been immortalized in Hawthorne's *The Marble Faun*. They had fled from "cold roast Boston," as
T. G. Appleton had named his birthplace. These artists had deserted
Boston, where they were expected to be men of business, to live in the
land of the myrtle and the orange, where they came as strangers and
hoped to remain strangers, reveling in a world that was tumbling to
pieces. One of them, William Wetmore Story, wrote:

> Nature abhors what houswives love—the clean,
> And beauty hides when pail and brush come in.

These sculptors were greatly influenced by Thorvaldsen, the neo-
classicist. Their work was not so significant for Boston as the Halian

Portrait plaque of
George Washington,
attributed to Samuel
McIntire of Salem,
Massachusetts. Courtesy
of Old Sturbridge
Village. Photograph by
Charles Klamkin. From
Wood Carvings by
Marian and Charles
Klamkin (New York:
Hawthorn, 1974).

Figures of Peace, Plenty, and Virtue on pediment of chest-on-chest. Carved by John
and Simeon Skillin. Late eighteenth century. Courtesy of The Mabel Brady Garvon
Collection, Yale University Art Gallery. Photograph by Charles Klamkin, from
Wood Carvings by Marian and Charles Klamkin (New York: Hawthorn, 1974).

collections gathered under the careful eye of James Jackson Jarves, son of Deming Jarves, the glassmaker. The elder Jarves, utilizing the excellent Cape Cod sand, founded the glassworks at Sandwich and became known as "the father of American glass." His son used his fortune to collect Tuscan paintings—for which he was ridiculed during his lifetime. Jarves wrote many art books and advocated art teaching, museums, and schools of design. He exposed the fraudulent art being foisted upon rich Bostonians and denounced the time in which he lived as "an epoch of monstrous plaster figures, daubed with crazy paint, of mammoth cast-iron wash basins, called fountains, of cast-iron architecture and clumsy gateways to public parks, of shoddy portrait statues and inane ideal ones." He praised the clipper ship and the old-fashioned farmhouses, which were appealing and true because they were suited to the necessities that created them and were made of materials at hand. To him they were as successful as a Greek temple or a Gothic cathedral because the American merchants and farmers had taken pride in work that met their needs.

> Build me straight, O worthy Master!
> Staunch and strong, a goodly vessel,
> That shall laugh at all disaster,
> And with wave and whirlwind wrestle!
> Henry Wadsworth Longfellow

What Boston patron of painting and sculpture had expressed such depth of feeling as the merchant in Longfellow's "The Building of the Ship"?

In 1856, when Thomas Crawford, living in Rome, executed a bust of Beethoven for the Boston Music Hall, it was the first statue raised in America to an artist of any kind.

Following the Civil War, there was an increased demand for commemorative work. John Quincy Adams Ward introduced a strong note of realism into a tradition suffering from the somewhat vapid classicism of the sculptors of the Italian colony, who had been flooding Boston homes and museums with histories in granite and romances in marble, such as *Greek Slave* and the *Libyan Sybil*.

Ward's student, Daniel Chester French, devoted his talents to monumental sculpture. From his *Minute Men* to his *Lincoln Memorial,* his work has been viewed by more Americans than that of any other American artist. Born in 1850 in Stockbridge, Massachusetts, French spent most of his life in Concord, the friend of Longfellow, Emerson, Thoreau, and Louisa May Alcott. In fact, his first teacher was May Alcott, Louisa's sister, an artist in her own right. He later studied with William Rimmer, a physician who trained him in anatomy. As a result, French usually sculpted his figures in the nude and later added clothing. When he did his famous bust of Emerson, Emerson observed, "The more it resembles me, the worse it looks," to which French asked: "But is it a good likeness, Mr. Emerson?" And the philosopher replied, "Well, it's the face I shave."

William Rimmer, French's teacher, who decided to study medicine at the age of thirty, practiced in Boston, and did an occasional portrait or a painting of a religious subject. In 1855 he began to carve in granite. His *Despair* is in the Museum of Fine Arts, where he was professor of anatomy and sculpture. But the leading American sculptor of the day was Augustus Saint-Gaudens, whose *Shaw Memorial* in Boston established a standard of classical elegance and excellence.

Jarves had declared that American architecture would eventually be America's only great art. In Boston, it had developed early with the work of Charles Bulfinch, America's first architect. Many of the tremendous number of buildings he created have been demolished, but his chief monumental works still remain—the State House, University Hall at Harvard, and the Massachusetts General Hospital. He designed a memorial column on Beacon Hill, the Massachusetts State Prison, a number of courthouses, and the Franklin Crescent, which was a long curved row of sixteen residences inspired by the work of Robert Adam in England. The First Church of Christ in Lancaster, Massachusetts, is one of the few remaining churches that Bulfinch designed and is one of his finest productions. The elegance, repose, and refinement of Bulfinch's works rank among the best products of America's formative years. The influence of the brothers Adam is keenly expressed in Bulfinch's Boston and is the reason, perhaps, why so many visitors compare the physical Boston to Edinburgh, Scotland.

Very early in the publishing life of Boston there appeared books on architecture—notably the works of Asher Benjamin, one of the city's first architects. Much of the original architecture looked to the ancient classical world for its inspiration, but as early as the late eighteenth century the "castellated Gothic" of the English diletanti began to have imitators. Just before and during the Civil War the influence of Ruskin can be seen. There was a brief splurge of Victorian Gothic, but it was short-lived.

Museum, Peabody Academy of Sciences, Salem. From *Harper's Magazine*, March 1878.

The two decades following the Civil War were confused years, and the confusion was expressed not only in politics but in architecture and culture. Consummate strides in industrialization altered the building methods and techniques. A new study of the functional basis of house design brought many experimental forms into being. New wealth sought expression in unbridled ostentation, and increasing foreign travel brought acquaintance with all types of European building, overwhelming existing local traditions of taste and traditional doctrines. Up until the Civil War, the engineer designed the structural elements that the architect decorated; in the process they both forgot the basic principle of oneness of visible form and structure.

In spite of the importation of European ideas in architecture, some architects rebelled against the ruling taste for senseless details. One of these architects, Henry Hobson Richardson,[1] expressed his ideas in Trinity Church in Boston and in the New Brattle Square Church. About this time, the influence of William Morris in craftsmanship was evidenced in the structural designs of the city's edifices. It was when Walter Gropius started teaching at Harvard that modern functional architecture assumed its importance in the more recently constructed buildings of Boston. In Le Corbusier's Visual Art Center at Harvard we have an example of an architectural form that is as satisfactory emotionally as it is physically. However, the protests of men like Richardson and Morris bypassed Boston and were best exemplified by Louis Sullivan and Frank Lloyd Wright in the Chicago School.

The citadels of culture in Boston have embellished the city and shown the talents of the people who created them and the civil dedication of the Bostonians who endowed such institutions as the Boston Athenaeum, the Boston Public Library, and the Symphony Hall—to mention a few landmarks. The twentieth century's significant cultural development was the expansion of art museums necessary to house the growing collections of private connoisseurs and the establishing of art schools where new teaching techniques flourished.

However, one of the most fanciful museums in Boston resulted from a doctor's suggestion to Mrs. Jack Gardner (following a nervous breakdown) that she develop a hobby. She did. She erected a complete Florentinian palace in the marshes of Boston's Fenway, in the upper reaches of Back Bay. Mrs. Jack bought the palace abroad and had it shipped piece by piece for reconstruction, which she personally supervised. The purpose of the palace was to house her sumptuous art collection. Never lacking in wealth, Mrs. Jack had purchased art since girlhood, and she owned Titian's huge *Rape of Europa,* Vermeer's *The Concert,* and many other priceless paintings. During her lifetime, Mrs. Jack made the museum her home, but upon her death it was willed to the city and today is open for the public. There are few of her paintings whose authenticity has been questioned, but even those that are controversial have to remain hanging on the walls, so restricted are the requirements of her will. Fenway Court, which is one of Boston's showplaces, stands intact as a monument to a very remarkable lady.

From its founding, Boston has always had a song in its heart. The city's musical heritage is vast and complex. Much of it remains to be assimilated into the cultural picture of Boston, for in the beginning the song was folk music brought from England, Scotland, and, later, Ireland. These songs constitute the original foundation upon which American

Fenway Court, Boston, c. 1904. Photograph by Thomas E. Mort.

musical expression was to grow. The ballads and lyrics were in many cases a heritage from medieval times; others, of religious significance, were from the Psalms of David. From the homes, churches, and taverns of Boston songs such as "Strawberry Lane," "Western Wind," "The Two Sisters," and hundreds of others of similar vein proved very popular with westward-moving people and have been traced to the California shores with variations on the original themes.

> Are you going to Scarborough Fair,
> Parsley, sage, rosemary and thyme.
> Remember me to one who lives there;
> Once she was a true love of mine.*

Song reverberated in the husking bees and socials of the busy colonists, and simple music accompanied the early folk dances. Naturally, as people had more leisure, music became more sophisticated. Musical instruments were brought from the old country, and some instruments crudely executed in the new. Harpsichords were in the drawing rooms of the first Boston socialites, and a John Broadwood piano found a place of lodging on Beacon Hill.

As the Revolution approached, the singing voice of Boston was almost as strong as the voice of the orator. It has been said that, if one wishes to understand the Revolution as a human experience, the best way to approach it is through its songs. These played a very important part in the struggle, helping to spread news, ridiculing the enemy, summoning courage from men's souls for the ordeal before them. Most of the revolutionary songs were "broadside" ballads. When printing was first invented in the sixteenth century, English balladeers began to print ballads on single sheets, or broadsides. The tradition was carried on to the colonies. The Revolutionary War witnessed a blossoming of broadsides, as songs about battles and naval encounters multiplied and were sung by soldier and civilian alike.

The Revolution, furthermore, witnessed an evolution in American song, for the Americans created new lyrics adapted to the revolutionary experience. From the fusion of this with the traditional melody, a uniquely American song was born. "Young Ladies in Town" was first published in the *Boston News-Letter* in 1769 as a result of the boycott of British goods that followed the passage of the Townshend Laws in 1767. The boycott was very successful in Boston, and the song is notable not only for its propaganda message but for the appeal to women to place love of country above love of personal finery:

> Young ladies in the town, and those than live round,
> Wear none but your own country linen;
> Of economy boast; let your pride be the most
> To show clothes of your own make and spinning.
>
> What if homespun they be not quite so gay
> As brocades, be not in a passion;
> For once it is known 'tis much worn in town
> One and all will cry out, "Tis the fashion—"

Another popular ballad, "The Rich Lady over the Sea," is a song written about the Boston Tea Party of December 16, 1773. It narrates in an unmistakable manner the conviction that the American people had come of age:

There was a rich lady lived over the sea,
And she was an island queen;
Her daughter lived off in the new country
With an ocean of water between,
With an ocean of water between.

The old lady's pockets were filled with gold,
But never contented was she;
So she ordered her daughter to pay her a tax
Of thruppence a pound on the tea
Of thruppence a pound on the tea.

O mother, dear mother, the daughter replied,
I'll not do the thing that you ax;
I'm willing to pay a fair tax on the tea,
But never the thrupenny tax,
But never the thrupenny tax.

You shall! cried the mother, and reddened with rage,
For you're my own daughter, you see;
And its only proper that daughter should pay
Her mother a tax on the tea,
Her mother a tax on the tea.

She ordered her servant to be called up
To wrap up a package of tea;
And eager for three pence a pound, she put in
Enough for a large family,
Enough for a large family.

She ordered her servant to bring home the tax,
Declaring her child must obey;
Or, old as she was, and woman most grown,
She'd half whip her life away,
She'd half whip her life away.

The tea was conveyed to her daughter's own door,
All down by the oceanside;
But the bouncing girl poured out every pound
In the dark and boiling tide,
In the dark and boiling tide.

And then she called out to the island queen
O mother, dear mother, called she,
Your tea you may have when 'tis steeped enough
But never a tax from me,
But never a tax from me.

Sheet music cover for "The Progressive March." Printed by F. H. Gilson of Boston in 1880.

Lawrence Room, panelled with old English oak carving, Boston. From *Harper's Magazine*, May 1879.

The musical mind and taste of Boston followed the general history of music the world over. The period known as baroque came to an end with the death of Bach in 1750 and the commencement of the era of classicism with its perfection in forms of the sonata, symphony, concerto, and opera bouffe. But until 1840 there was not an organized musical movement in Boston. The reason lay largely in the kind of society Boston had created and perpetuated. It was a cold, unfeeling civilization, bred by commercial interests and isolation, a negative moderation, an excess of prudence, compromise, provincial good taste. The culture it reflected was based on the pursuit of the intellect. The lecture habit was the social habit of the city, until there appeared a new generation of young people who suddenly turned their backs on the format that had been their forefathers'. Their new feelings were expressed in the various institutions of art and music that began to appear.

Beethoven's *C-Minor Symphony* was played in the Odeon in 1840, a flowering of the Handel and Haydn Society that had put to rout the old psalms and glee tunes. The galleries became a rendezvous where art and love blossomed to the music of Mozart. Talk wandered into unexplored areas of spiritualism and mesmerism, and poetry was on every tongue. People commenced to hear music in the air and see beauty in the wild-flowers, the trailing arbutus, the night-blooming cereus. They believed the way to greatness lay in books, not battles; in art and music rather than bloody war. They wanted men to be true and wise, pure and aspiring.

In 1867 the New England Conservatory of Music was founded in Boston. Jordan Hall began to be filled with artists of note, and the study of music as a "culture" began in earnest. In 1881, Henry Lee Higginson founded the Boston Symphony Orchestra and was its director and sole financial backer until 1918. The first conductor was Sir George Henschel, who was as famous a singer as he was a conductor and composer. His wife, Lillian June (Bailey), was an American soprano who made her debut in Boston in 1876. The importance of the Boston Symphony to the city and its cultural life cannot be overestimated. In Boston the organization is referred to in a single word—symphony. Symphony is every Friday, twenty-six times a year, all winter. It is a social must for the women of the city. Saturday night is also symphony, when husband and wife appear at the concerts; but Friday afternoons, in the words of former Bostonian Lucius Beebe, "assume the aspect of holy days dedicated to the classics and a vast craning of necks to be certain that the Hallowells and the Forbeses are in their accustomed stalls."

The symphony is sponsored by "friends" or patrons, who contribute to the orchestra's annual deficit as well as regularly attending the concerts. Once a year the symphony program announces the complete list of friends, and publishes an honor roll of all who have attended the orchestra under each of its conductors from the day of its founding. Its outstanding regular conductors have been Arthur Nikish (1889–1893), Pierre Monteux (1919–1924), Serge Koussevitzky (1924–1949), Charles Münch (1949–1962), and Erich Leinsdorf (1962–   ). The influence of each of the men is reflected in the musical tastes of the generations of patrons. Nikish brought the music of Vienna and Wagner's Bayreuth to Symphony Hall (which was constructed in 1900); Monteux introduced Diaghilev's ballets with the music of Stravinsky, Ravel, and Debussy; Koussevitzky was the champion of new composers, such as Hindemith and Schönberg.

It was in 1936 that Koussevitzky and the Boston Symphony took over the Berkshire Festival—a summer musical divertissement held at Tangle-wood (once the summer home of Hawthorne, the scene of his *Tangle-wood Tales*), adjoining Stockbridge. The music shed, designed by Eliel Saarinen[2] was opened in 1938, and in 1940 a summer school, the Berk-shire Music Center, was started.

But all music that rings through Symphony Hall is not classical. The Boston "Pops" Concerts are performed there from the end of April through June. In July the members of the "Pops" and the Boston Sym-phony join in presenting free open-air concerts in the Hatch Memorial Shell on the Charles River.

Jazz has always found an audience in Boston, and such famous bands as Benny Goodman's, Woody Herman's, and Eddie Condon's have put on "out-of-sight" jazz concerts in Symphony Hall. One, a concert by Benny Goodman, was reviewed by H. T. Parker (H.T.P.), music critic for the *Transcript*—whose reviews were so erudite that it was rumored they were written in Latin, then translated into English for the Boston illiterate—observed that it might have been more proper if the sports editor had covered the event.

Recently, folk and rock groups have penetrated the once sacred musical haunts of Bach, Beethoven, Brahms, and Boston. In some instances the end result has been the manifestation of a new culture—the drug culture, with its contemporary code of ethics and social behavior.

Somehow, Boston has survived.

In the late nineteenth and early twentieth century grand opera was the time-consuming project of the American culture clique. Boston was no exception.

Two men shared the responsibility for the daring operatic venture in Boston in the beginning. One was Henry Russell, a bold impresario from London, who had piloted a troupe named after the Naples San Carlo Company through the United States for several seasons. His "angel" was Eben D. Jordan, Jr., Boston's department store prince, who guaran-teed a roof for Russell's coterie.[3]

The winter season of the San Carlo, made possible by Jordan's generos-ity, opened on December 9, 1907, to an unusual amount of fanfare. Two thousand Bostonians were in their seats when the curtain rose and more poured in; the standees could be counted in the hundreds. "All of Back Bay turned out!" was the delighted crow of Henry Russell. First night gowns, magnificent by all accounts, foreshadowed the elegance of the Boston Company's opening, which was to astonish even those who par-

ticipated in it. The Jordans entertained American opera's highest dignitary, Otto H. Kahn, tireless benefactor of the Metropolitan. In another box sat Boston's inescapable cynosure, Mrs. Jack Gardner.

The opera was *La Gioconda,* with Nordica in the title role; the conductor was Arnaldo Conti. When three weeks of the opera season had ended, opera lovers in Boston agreed with the *Post* that "Grand Opera Delights All." The cast was set for a permanent Boston Opera Company.

The Boston Common by Winslow Homer. From *Harper's Magazine,* May 22, 1858. Courtesy of The Metropolitan Museum of Art, Harris Brisbane Dick Fund, 1936.

With the architect Parkman B. Haven, Jordan set off for an extensive inspection of opera houses in Europe, determined to take advantage of the best and avoid mistakes if possible. At the time only half-a-dozen good houses existed in America: the Philadelphia Music Academy dating from 1857; the New Orleans French Opera House built in 1859 but demolished by fire in 1919; the Metropolitan in New York built in 1883; and the Chicago Auditorium, inaugurated in 1889. With the support of

Frederick S. Converse, one of Boston's most distinguished men of music, the project met with great popular appeal and the full amount for the undertaking was realized in less than six months.

The management stressed the educational value of opera, stating that native talent would be trained through an opera school in the New England Conservatory of Music. By the time the first opera would be performed in the new Boston Opera House, the home-grown chorus was in radiant song. One of Russell's plans was to eliminate the star system. He boldly proclaimed, "Every stockholder who signed the parchment buried in the Opera House cornerstone may also be said to have signed the death warrant of the star system in America." Although his plan was not successful, since stars are the essential ingredient of which grand opera is composed, Russell defended his effort in his memoirs. "The petty quarrels, the jealousies were unlimited," he wrote of the star system. "Singers like Eames, Sembrich, Calve, Nordica, Melba, and Geraldine Farrar were allowed to dominate any opera in which they appeared. Scenery was modified to suit their taste, lights arranged to suit their complexions, tenors chosen to suit their affections and conductors thrown out to gratify their tempers." Without the star system Russell maintained a very fine excellence of performance, but there is no doubt that he deprived Boston of the operatic talents of many stars, notably Farrar.

On November 30, 1908, at three P.M., a shivering crowd of two hundred "lovers of music, song-birds of the stage, and patrons of the art" (wrote the *Post*) gathered on a scaffolding near Huntington Avenue to watch and to sing the national anthem as a huge Deer Island granite slab, weighing more than a ton, was lowered into position. Then Eben Jordan wielded a silver trowel and smoothed the mortar into place.

Boston's greatest operatic day was November 8, 1909. Rains fell in almost ominous significance, making the pavements "not exactly such as suit embroidered slippers and pumps," observed the *Transcript*. Traffic was a problem; the Museum of Fine Arts opened by some studied calculation or miscalculation on the same night. Nevertheless, the dream had come true. Boston had a handsome building, noble in simplicity of line and material, which exuded a substantiality and pride that was becoming to its occupants—"the first Unitarian Opera House," it was dubbed by Arthur Whiting. But the building was perfect for Boston. The rococo and the baroques of grand opera, itself, was sufficient for Boston taste—too fancy a building would have been disturbing. Eben Jordan's speech at the end of the evening sounded the keynote of hope for opera in Boston permanently.

"I know by your applause you are satisfied. You must be satisfied with this theater, because it is a most beautiful theater, and I think future generations of Bostonians will be thankful they have the privilege of sitting in it."

Henry Russell went on to hope it would be "permanent—I might say an eternal—opera in the city of Boston."

Opera, more than any other social event—because it was considered "culture"—afforded Boston a reason for an orgy of dressing up. From the magnificence of dresses and the opulence of jewels, it appeared that the Boston dowager, who had acquired the reputation of being dowdy, had merely lacked the reason and opportunity to dress fashionably. And the critics, Philip Hale and H. T. Parker, harped away at the men for formal dress. The result was spectacular. The cost of opera gowns ranged from $250 to $1,000, and the gowns were ignored in the press if worn more than once—except in the case of Mrs. Jack who was of such social and opera importance that she was always reported, whether in "white satin and her fabulous pearls" or "black satin and her fabulous pearls."

The year was 1909, and until the end of 1910 grand opera had its peak of popularity in the United States. During the years up until America's entrance into World War I, the Boston Opera Company remained intact both at home and abroad during its traveling season; but in 1915 it filed voluntary bankruptcy proceedings in the United States District Court, stating its liabilities at $215,570, its assets at $78,000. The days were sad and disillusioning. The opera house seemed doomed to be the residence of occasional road shows. One attempt was made to revive grand opera in Boston late in 1915, but it failed. At the end of the fifth week of a previously announced seventh, the critic Philip Hale wrote: "Is it possible that opera in Boston is out of fashion?" The disheartening conclusion: "Yes!"

On a grim day in 1958, the Boston Opera House became a shambles in the dust. Boston's colorful operatic past succumbed with hardly a whimper, until a young woman named Sarah Caldwell resurrected from the ashes a new company called the Boston Opera. Miss Caldwell is an impresario of imagination and daring. She has conducted a number of operas. She has mixed with the staples of repertoire controversial fare, such as Alban Berg's *Lulu* and Luigi Nono's *L'Intolleranza*. She has presented a number of important singers, including Joan Sutherland, Beverly Sills, and Boris Christoff. Perhaps under her guidance the phoenix of Boston opera may rise again.

11
Battle Hymns and Hers

In the study of Boston we are conscious from the day of founding of the paradoxes that have ordained its history and the consummation of outside movements upon the lives of its citizens, which in turn affected the organism of the city proper. It has been said that modern civilization is composed of three elements—gunpowder, printing, and the Protestant religion. If this formula be exact, Boston is the finished product, since the end results of the three components are visible to the naked eye, protruding, as it were, from every venerable cornerstone.

The colonial period of Boston's history, spanning the time from its founding up to the outbreak of the American Revolution, covers one-half of the total history of the city. It has been referred to as the "neglected first half." Actually, this epoch constitutes the formative period, and it is only in the light of what was going on in these crucial one hundred and fifty years of colonial living that we can comprehend why the American Revolution occurred, originated in Boston, and was successful. In studying the colonial days we get some understanding of the city's revolutionary heritage and revolutionary origin.

A city is a very special kind of human association. It expects and exacts supreme loyalty from its population. The city's origin revolves around a common area of land where the inhabitants live permanently in the presence of one another. In the beginning, the populace should be banded together with a common interest. Boston, especially, fulfilled these qualifications. The Puritan settlers came with a vision of a land set aside by God for their occupation, a land entrusted to their care and development. It was to be inhabited by them, cultivated by them and their descendants. The first citizens, once they were located, had to increase their numbers by further immigration before the city could be expected to yield profit for the planters, merchants, and speculators who were typical empire builders.

The process of transplanting people throughout the seventeenth and eighteenth centuries is a sad story, entailing the sufferings of imported white servants and black slaves. Most of the white immigrants came from the British Isles and brought with them a common language, a common heritage, a common culture, and a common religion—Protestantism. Most of the black slaves came from sundry African tribes and were sold as field hands in the cotton and tobacco plantations in the South. The developing of the American nation by this means of population expansion eventually brought about a conflict of ideas and sentiments that were to create a serious breach and influence the city life of nineteenth-century Boston as well as all American cities.

At the outset, the use of gunpowder was required by the Puritans to gain rights over the Indians whose lands they had occupied. Since the settlers were outnumbered, the white man—regardless of his religious beliefs to the contrary—was obliged to use the gun to assert his claim to possession.

The French and Indian Wars were, in reality, colonial wars between Great Britain and France in their worldwide struggle for empire and were roughly joined to wars of the European coalitions. To the settlers

Paul Revere's view of Boston, showing landing of British troops, 1768. Courtesy of the Phelps Stokes Collection, The New York Public Library American Historical Prints Division, Astor, Lenox and Tilden Foundations.

An advertisement in the Boston *Gazette and Country Journal*, October 1750, offering a reward for the return of a runaway slave, Crispus Attucks, who was to be the first to fall in the Boston Massacre twenty years later. Courtesy of the Massachusetts Historical Society.

RAN-away from his Master *William Brown* of *Framingham*, on the 30th of *Sept.* last, a Molatto Fellow, about 27 Years of Age, named *Crispas*, 6 Feet twoInches high, short curl'd Hair, his Knees nearer together than common ; had on a light colour'd Bearskin Coat, plain brown Fustian Jacket, or brown all-Wool one, new Buckskin Breeches, blue YarnStockings, and a check'd woollen Shirt. Whoever shall take up said Run-away, and convey him to his abovesaid Master, shall have *ten Pounds*, old Tenor Reward, and all necessary Charges paid. And all Masters of Vessels and others, are hereby caution'd against concealing or carrying off said Servant on Penalty of the Law. *Boston*, *October* 2. 1750.

TO be Let, a convenient Dwelling-House suitable for a small Family, scituate in ... Street at the South-End. Inquire

of Boston and Massachusetts, the fighting meant not only raids by the French or the British but the horrors of Indian border warfare. It was sufficiently difficult for the early inhabitants to wrest a living out of the sterile earth without contending with the devastating raids of the hostile Indians. A part of the God-worshiping colonist's household equipment was his trusty musket, which was used not only to procure food but to protect his family. The constant alert brought the colonists in close harmony for self-protection, and a basis for their almost paranoid suspicion of strangers was created. Self-reliance and self-survival soon supplanted self-dedication to God. They defended their use of firearms by their identification of the Indians as heathen devils meant to be obliterated. The early friendships vanished, and an atmosphere of distrust descended upon the Boston community.

The wars ended in 1763, but they had wrought vast changes in the outlook of the people who had survived. The divergence from the mother, England, fundamentally based upon the ocean-wide distance, had become accented by differences between the European and American policies in the conflict. The preoccupation of England with the French threat had allowed the colonists freer range to develop their institutions, while at the same time the colonies had been dependent upon British arms and felt less dependent when the war ended. But the most important fact learned from the wars was that, contrary to our country's original spiritual concept, in reality it was based upon the shedding of blood.

Five years before Lexington, Concord, and Bunker Hill, the Revolution was begun in an incident known as the Boston Massacre. This almost mythological event represents the first tragic culmination of the British policy that provoked independence; it illustrates the physical sacrifice required to achieve independence; it establishes the concept of Boston as the "Cradle of Liberty." Its end result was to create the image of nobility of soul and loftiness of purpose that one is likely to associate with the early Boston fathers.

In reality, the presence of British soldiers in Boston during and after the French and Indian Wars was bound to create an explosion. The troops had been garrisoned in Boston since 1768, not for any military purpose but purely and simply as conservers of the peace. The real reason for their presence can be traced to the two prime sources of evil and corruption: money and power. The massacre did not take place like a classic tragedy. The forces that pointed the muskets on King Street on March 5, 1770, emerged out of the entire colonial experience. The troops had been harassed constantly by Boston mobs and finally, on that fatal night, they fired into the rioting crowd, which resulted in the deaths of three men. Crispus Attucks, a black man, was the first American to die for liberty, and although three men were killed, only the name of Crispus Attucks has survived.

The first great patriotic demonstration took place at the funeral of the dead men. The trial that followed might be called the birth of American justice, for John Adams undertook to defend the British killers, much to the damage of his own personal popularity; and he managed to win the acquittal of his clients despite a hostile jury. In short, the hour of revolution had not yet been born, but the seeds had been sown and the wild winds that were to blow from across the sea would turn the fire of the colonial muskets on the British soldiers at the Battle of Concord.

The scenario of American history has always pictured the hated Redcoats tramping through the peaceful town of Boston; the honest citizens quietly going about their evening business; a few schoolboys harmlessly taunting the soldiers; the troops forming a battle line, loading with military precision, fixing bayonets, aiming carefully, and on direct order, deliberately given, firing a deadly volley on the helpless civilians. This recorded historical fact is, in truth, closer to romanticized fiction, with the leading characters performing as the script director prescribed. A more realistic interpretation of the behavior in the city by the actors involved in the drama of revolution is that for years preceding the first shots, even before the Boston Massacre, violence had become so commonplace in the city and attempts to restrict it so absurdly futile that it

An account of the burial of the victims of the Boston Massacre, published in the Boston *Gazette and Country Journal.* Picture Collection, The Branch Libraries, The New York Public Library.

The 29th Regiment have already left us, and the 14th Regiment are following them, so that we expect the Town will soon be clear of all the Troops. The Wisdom and true Policy of his Majesty's Council and Col. Dalrymple the Commander appear in this Measure. Two Regiments in the midst of this populous City; and the Inhabitants justly incensed: Those of the neighbouring Towns actually under Arms upon the first Report of the Massacre, and the Signal only wanting to bring in a few Hours to the Gates of this City many Thousands of our brave Brethren in the Country, deeply affected with our Distresses, and to whom we are greatly obliged on this Occasion—No one knows where this would have ended, and what important Consequences even to the whole British Empire might have followed, which our Moderation and Loyalty upon so trying an Occasion, and our Faith in the Commander's Assurances have happily prevented.

Last Thursday, agreeable to a general Request of the Inhabitants, and by the Consent of Parents and Friends, were carried to their *Grave* in Succession, the Bodies of *Samuel Gray, Samuel Maverick, James Caldwell,* and *Crispus Attucks,* the unhappy Victims who fell in the bloody Massacre of the Monday Evening preceding!

On this Occasion most of the Shops in Town were shut, all the Bells were ordered to toll a solemn Peal, as were also those in the neighboring Towns of Charlestown Roxbury, &c. The Procession began to move between the Hours of 4 and 5 in the Afternoon; two of the unfortunate Sufferers, viz. Mess. *James Caldwell* and *Crispus Attucks,* who were Strangers, borne from Faneuil-Hall, attended by a numerous Train of Persons of all Ranks; and the other two, viz. Mr. *Samuel Gray,* from the House of Mr. Benjamin Gray, (his Brother) on the North-side the Exchange, and Mr. *Maverick,* from the House of his distressed Mother Mrs. *Mary Maverick,* in Union-Street, each followed by their respective Relations and Friends: The several Hearses forming a Junction in King-Street, the Theatre of that inhuman Tragedy! proceeded from thence thro' the Main-Street, lengthened by an immense Concourse of People, so numerous as to be obliged to follow in Ranks of six, and brought up by a long Train of Carriages belonging to the principal Gentry of the Town. The Bodies were deposited in one Vault in the middle Burying-ground: The aggravated Circumstances of their Death, the Distress and Sorrow visible in every Countenance, together with the peculiar Solemnity with which the whole Funeral was conducted, surpass Description.

was just a matter of time before further bloodshed would lead to actual warfare. That demagoguery (especially on the part of patriot Samuel Adams) played a leading role in the final break with England cannot be denied. The voice of Boston was loud in protest against the wrongs imposed by England before the Revolution occurred.

Today, the city cherishes the landmarks of historical violence. On State Street there is a bronze plaque that states: "The Boston Massacre Took Place Here." Actually, it occurred on the opposite corner of the street. The spot where indignant colonists led by Samuel Adams, Paul Revere, John Hancock, and James Otis tossed a cargo of tea into the Boston Harbor is marked for students of history to visit. Faneuil Hall, which was a meeting place for the Sons of Liberty and a theater for the British soldiers during the occupation, is a museum filled with paintings depicting battles from early times to the present day and is open to the public without an admission charge. The Bunker Hill Monument on Breed's Hill, the center of the Battle of Bunker Hill, is a 211-foot granite obelisk commemorating the event, and Soldier's Monument stands on Dorchester Heights.

The Old North Church at 189 Salem Street at the foot of Hull Street, the oldest church building in Boston, is the haunting ground of the Revolution. The steeple blown over by Hurricane Carol in 1954 was replaced in July 1955, for the second time in one hundred and fifty years. The window from which Paul Revere's signal lanterns burned was saved and built back into the steeple, along with other ancient woodwork. In the church's nave is the old organ, which was constructed in 1759 and from which the earliest peal of bells was heard in Boston. The bells have tolled for war and for peace, for the living and for the dead.

The Old State House at Washington, at the head of State Street, contains relics of the tea from the Boston Tea Party, and it was from the balcony facing State Street that the Declaration of Independence was read. There John Hancock was inaugurated as the first governor of Massachusetts in 1780, following the War of Independence. In the Granary Burying Ground, where visitors may make tombstone rubbings, with a free rubbing permit, the three signers of the Declaration of Independence lie buried—John Hancock, Samuel Adams, and Robert Treat Paine.

In the history of the American Revolution, Boston is a city of hallowed ground. However, after George Washington lifted the siege when he fortified the site of Soldier's Monument and drove the British from Boston

The Battle of Lexington, April 19, 1775, by Amos Doolittle. Courtesy of the Connecticut Historical Society. Photograph by E. Irving Blomstrann.

in March of 1776, the war moved in and around New York until it was culminated with the surrender of Cornwallis on October 19, 1781.

Actually, the Boston heroes of the Revolution were the prerevolutionary instigators, the orators, the pamphleteers, the learned statesmen. With the exception of Prescott, the hero of Bunker Hill, few military names survived. (Revere was court-martialed but exonerated.) It was the mind of the Boston revolutionist that created the incidents that perpetrated the military action, united the colonies into forming a new nation.

While Boston endured a period of poverty and apprehension during and following the Revolution, the shipping and merchant interests were growing to such a degree that the approaching War of 1812, "Mr. Madison's War" as it was referred to in Boston, was extremely unpopular in that city. The combat followed a period of stress growing out of the struggle between England and France in the Napoleonic Wars. During this era of strife abroad, Boston shippers took advantage of the hostilities in Europe to absorb the carrying trade between the French and Spanish Islands in the West Indies and in Europe. It was during this time that American shippers (mostly Bostonians) intervened in the slave trading that Britain had wrested away from France in the seventeenth and eighteenth centuries.

During the Napoleonic Wars the permanent servitude of the black slave replaced the indentured servitude of the white servant, who had endured a form of chattel slavery in the colonies. From the point of view of the planters and employers, indenture had many disadvantages, the most serious of which was its temporary nature, the relative scarcity of the supply of workers, the high cost, and the comparative ease with which the white servants could escape. This partially accounts for their replacement by black slaves on American tobacco, rice, indigo, sugar, and cotton plantations. To show how rapid and extensive this turnover was, in 1700 there were not more than 25,000 black slaves in America —they represented less than one-tenth of all the inhabitants in the mainland colonies. Ninety years later, the number had increased to 800,000 and they constituted one-fifth of the entire population.

Shipping and slave trading were highly profitable and Yankee shippers, by breaking the passage with a stopover in Boston or some other American port, evaded the British rule of 1756 that forbade, in time of war, neutral trade that was allowed in time of peace. The growing Yankee shipping displeased British merchants, and it also offered seamen opportunities to escape the hardships of British naval service. It was the *Chesapeake* affair in June 1807 that helped precipitate the War of 1812. Just outside American waters, the frigate was stopped by H.M.S. *Leopard,* which demanded the right to search her for British deserters. Captain James Barron refused, and the *Leopard* opened fire. Barron was unprepared for action and had to allow the impressment of four of his crew, two of whom were American born. The incident caused high indignation when the *Chesapeake* limped into port. (The *Chesapeake* was later captured in Boston Harbor during the war.)

The conservatives in Boston, led by Harrison Gray Otis, had opposed Jefferson's Embargo Act of 1807 and many other government measures before the war; and they continued opposition to the government after the fighting commenced. Though manufacturing and contraband trade brought wealth to Boston, the war became steadily more repugnant, due largely to the excessive expenses of the war. The federal loan of 1814 got little, if any, support in New England, guided in thought and action by Boston, the leading city. Talk of a separate peace between Great Britain was voiced in the Boston taverns, and just before the war's end Otis, George Cabot, and Theodore Dwight called representatives of Massachusetts, Connecticut, and Rhode Island to convene.

In this Hartford Convention the grievances of the war were reviewed; but the news of Andrew Jackson's victory at New Orleans and the Treaty of Ghent made any recommendations of the convention a dead issue. The importance of the convention was twofold: it continued the view of states' rights, which was to be the refuge of sectional groups, and it all but destroyed the Federalist party politically; it never regained its lost prestige. Alexander Hamilton's political policies had been superseded by those of Thomas Jefferson, and the results were felt politically in Boston for many generations to come.

When the War of 1812 ended, "the era of good feeling" began. The war had been good to Boston. It had largely destroyed the commerce of the smaller New England ports, and, strong enough to survive the crisis, Boston prospered with the ruin of so many rivals. It attracted more and more of the younger merchants of the rural areas who had taken advantage of the decline of shipping during the war years and the boycott of English goods, which followed the war, to build up a completely American manufacturing trade. Every little hamlet, township, and village on the outskirts of Boston that had water power became industrialized overnight. Boston became greedy and sought to absorb all of the outlying communities; but with their assets, Boston also acquired their liabilities.

In the meanwhile there was a "muttering abroad . . . and the muttering grew to a grumbling, and the grumbling grew into a mighty rumbling." (Robert Browning) The rumbling was the voice of anti-slavery. John Brown of Massachusetts became a symbol—but not for the people of Boston, nor was the rumbling the voice of Boston. John Brown was a martyr symbol for the simple, religious-minded people who opposed slavery. The rumbling was their cry of protest. Actually, in Boston most of the Establishment was linked to the South—the manufacturing of cotton goods and the textile industry. In many instances the ties also were matrimonial bonds of families of wealth married to other families of wealth.

But the rumbling would not go unheard. It grew and it grew like an organism, a specter that first talked then stalked across the ever-expanding new nation. As the young states sought admission to the Union, the question of slavery became more and more pertinent. The rumbling became political, and sectional partisanship commenced to evolve. The rumbling became an articulate sound, a formal speech, a "to be or not to be." In Boston, it was merely a matter of time before the headless monster acquired a head. The subject of slavery became a question that pierced the brains of Boston, planting the germ of war fever. Edward Everett, president of Harvard, reassured his Boston audiences—quite convincingly—that while visiting the plantations in Louisiana he had inspected the quarters of the slaves and had found them clean and comfortable with their beds covered with mosquito netting. To the owners of mills, who must have foreseen the cumbersome white slavery problems of the ever-growing Industrial Revolution, this bread-and-butter role of the slave was reassuring for a time, but not for long.

The words of William Ellery Channing introduced the fear of the disruption of the Union on the slavery question. Bostonians had not forgotten the Revolution or the near breach in the War of 1812; both were sufficiently awe-inspiring to sober their minds. Dr. Channing published a little treatise on slavery that made opposition to it a matter of self-respect. His pamphlet was embarrassing to the prosperous classes, who for a generation had nursed the idea that, having won their independence and acquired their wealth through diligence and Yankee shrewdness, they had conquered the world. But the educated mind of Boston could not ignore a calm intellectual essay that explained slavery in a philosophical light. It showed slavery and its disastrous effects, both on slave and master. It denounced this "peculiar institution" as a cancer eating away at the body politic.

Finally, the more the South pursued the rights of slavery, the more the North objected. In the beginning, the Boston merchants and lawyers, and even the organized church, aided by the press, were on the side of cotton and slavery interests; but as time wore on the movement of the Abolitionists found vocal support amongst the poets and the literary men who were in search of a cause—a just and logical focus for their talents and interests. What could have been a better sword of Damocles to hang over the heads of Boston households? Oratory, which had been the pride of ancestral Boston, but which had grown monotonous and drawling, was again inspired with tall tales—no less a person than

Violence in the Senate arose when Representative Brooks of South Carolina caned Massachusetts' antislavery Senator Sumner. Reprinted with permission from *The Saturday Evening Post* © 1958 The Curtis Publishing Company.

Jefferson's nephew was reputed to have chopped a slave to pieces with an ax. Their lurid descriptions of the beating, branding, and mutilating of slaves became commonplace. Proper Bostonians could not fail to listen to such men as Charles Sumner and Wendell Phillips; nor could they deny the power of such declamations. These were intellectual men, who were willing to fight for their beliefs. They were men of culture, men of worldly knowledge, and they easily roused indifferent minds and raised the flag of antislavery in Boston.

If the voices of the men of Boston were resonant, the writings of two women had extensive influence on the War of Rebellion (as it was officially titled by the Union). Harriet Beecher Stowe's *Uncle Tom's Cabin,* said Abraham Lincoln, was the cause of the Civil War. If it was not the ultimate cause it was one of the major causes—for it blocked the operation of the Fugitive Slave Law. Its publication was a major event; Heine, George Sand, and Macaulay reviewed it. Three Paris newspapers published the manuscript. To date, no other book, with the exception of the Bible, has appeared in so many versions.

Harriet Beecher Stowe was not residing in Boston when she wrote her epic piece, but she was considered a part of Boston because she had visited and lived there when her father, Lyman Beecher, was the minister of the Park Street Church. The seminary he founded in Cincinnati had been an abolitionist center. Mrs. Stowe felt that not she, but God, had written the tale while she lived at Bowdoin College, where her husband was an instructor. She wrote of the separation of husbands and wives, the scattering of mothers and children. Like Dickens, Cooper,

Scott, and Victor Hugo, she had the swing and rhythm of a great storyteller. Her characters were real, boldly conceived and presented; they became symbols of human conflict, and they have survived.

The immediate effect of Mrs. Stowe's book in Boston was electric, and the mind of the city, for the most part, became Abolitionist in its emotions. When war was officially declared, it was Julia Ward Howe —a banker's daughter from New York who had married Dr. Samuel Grisley Howe, had helped edit the abolitionist *Commonwealth,* and had watched the Union troops march into battle in 1861—who wrote "The Battle Hymn of the Republic," the official song of the Union force: "Mine eyes have seen the glory of the coming of the Lord . . ."

That the thoughts, words, and behavior of these writers and creators implemented the tragic course of events, no one could deny. The effect of this conflict upon Boston was intellectual, not physical, yet the remembrance of the Civil War is visible today in Augustus Saint-Gaudens's Shaw Monument, across the street from the State House. There is no biography of Robert Gould Shaw, and he has been little noted by historians. He was a minor figure; yet his life's sacrifice epitomizes, especially today, the truth that black men and white men can and must live together in equality in America if they are to survive. If the story of Robert Gould Shaw survives only in a bronze figure, to be seen by any passerby, and not as the dedication of the man, then such monuments are hypocritical—solid but meaningless. What is known of Shaw exists in the unpublished letters written to his parents and to his friends. Their content is more powerful than the Saint-Gaudens monument. In life and in death, Shaw is the personification of the Puritan mind, of which Boston can be proud.

Robert Gould Shaw was born in Boston in October 1837. His mother, Sarah Blake Sturgis, was the daughter of a successful and affluent Boston merchant, his father the son of a veritable merchant prince, whose money came from all of the worldly assets that had made the Hub the center of American industrial fortunes in the nineteenth century—overseas trade, banking and investments, railroads, real estate, and textiles. Francis George Shaw was wealth incarnate and he—in the Boston tradition—married riches, but both of these people took their social obligations very seriously. They felt committed to the principles of social morality that had been the concept of the original settlers. The responsibility of great wealth amassed by their ancestors did not fall lightly upon their shoulders. They were friends of George Ripley, the

William Lloyd Garrison, George Thompson, and Wendell Phillips discussing the question of forming a society for the abolition of slavery. Copied from the original picture taken in 1847.

founder of Brook Farm, and Robert was born near that project in living, to which his parents had generously contributed.

When the slavery issue became the dominant one in the country, the Shaws were leaders of Boston's progressive aristocracy, which was related by marriage and political association to all of New England's avant-garde—the influential New England intellectuals, Theodore Parker, Lydia Marie Childs, the Sedgewicks of Stockbridge, Charles Sumner, Edmund Quincy, Wendell Phillips, and English-born actress, Fanny Kemble—all of whom wrote, preached, and agitated against slavery. Young Shaw was educated abroad in Swiss and German schools before entering Harvard. By the time the war broke out, he had graduated from Harvard and entered into the family business. In contrast to most young men of his class, who chose to remain in civilian life by paying the wages of a mercenary, young Shaw enlisted and was sent to Washington to help defend that city. With a friend, he paid a call upon President Lincoln and wrote to his mother: "It is really too bad to call him one of the ugliest men in the country, for I have seldom seen a pleasanter or more kind-hearted looking one, and he certainly has a very striking face."

For the next two years, Shaw took part in the campaigns of Virginia and Maryland, became a battle-toughened veteran, and an advocate of the use of black troops. He was stationed at Harper's Ferry where John Brown had been hanged, and he spent his spare time reading about the case and trying to comprehend the full meaning of John Brown's life and sacrifice. "John Brown's body lies a-mouldering in his grave / His soul goes marching on." His soul—where was his soul? Shaw wrote to his father:

> Isn't it extraordinary that the Government won't make use of the instrument that would finish the war sooner than anything else—that is, the slaves? They would probably make a fine army after a little drill, and certainly could be kept under better discipline than our independent Yankees.

Shaw's thoughts were not unique for, with the Emancipation Proclamation, John Andrews, governor of Massachusetts, determined to establish

Julia Ward Howe, 1819–1910. From the painting by John Elliott. Courtesy of the Picture Collection, The Branch Libraries, The New York Public Library.

the first Negro regiment. For a leader, he chose young Shaw. It was not an easy decision for Shaw, who commanded loyal troops to whom he was tied by hours of long and honorable service. But he did accept the order and in February 1863, the 54th Massachusetts Infantry (black) was commissioned. On May 25 the regiment marched through Boston, amid an immense concourse of people singing Julia Ward Howe's "Battle Hymn," and embarked on a transport headed for Port Royal in South Carolina.

The locale was hardly a stone's throw from what had been the magnificent plantation of Pierce Butler and his wife, Fanny Kemble. As a little boy, Shaw had heard from Fanny's own lips the story of the hundreds of slaves, of her desire to procure their freedom and their rights to belong to the human race—but all of that was past history. When Shaw arrived, the plantation was in shambles. All that remained of Georgia's greatest plantation was a handful of decrepit slaves bemoaning the loss of their families and bewailing their misbegotten fate.

At the time, Shaw's greatest concern was the matter of his soldiers' pay. He was horrified to find that the government intended to pay his men $10 per month instead of the customary $13. He wrote in hot indignation that if his regiment was included in this outrageous discrimination it "should be mustered out of the service, as they were enlisted on the understanding they were to be on the same footing as other Massachusetts volunteers." It was Shaw's last correspondence. On July 18 the 54th moved to attack Fort Wagner, on Morris Island, commanding the entrance to Charleston Harbor. Shaw with his sword held high was the first to climb the ramparts—and the first to die. Stripping him of his uniform, the rebels buried his body in a common grave with a dozen or more of his black comrades.

When the Civil War came to a close and the actual fighting ceased, Boston was pivotal in the problems of Reconstruction, for it was Senator Charles Sumner who led the impeachment charges against President Andrew Johnson. Feelings ran high in Boston for punishment of the southerners who, according to Sumner, had virtually "committed suicide" with their act of secession. The two leading publications of the day were edited in Boston—*The Atlantic Monthly* and *Harper's Weekly*—and both had recorded the Civil War as no other war had ever been put down on paper. The photographs of Matthew Brady brought the visual agonies of the battlefield to the eyes of those who had not been spectators, and it was only a very short time following the war that the people of

Boston were, en masse, ready to concur with the words of the victorious but disillusioned Union general, William Tecumseh Sherman, when he said: "I am tired and sick of war. Its glory is all moonshine. It is only those who have neither fired a shot nor heard the shrieks and groans of the wounded who cry aloud for more blood, more vengeance, more desolation. War is Hell."

If war had not been the physical hell to Boston that it had to the ravaged southern city of Atlanta, it had been a mental and emotional hell. The survivors lived for a generation in a purgatory of mixed feelings and intellectual resolves—many of which got muddled and confused in the turmoil that followed when the tumult had died down. Many of the Boston Brahmins set up residence in Europe, where they wrote of people of the upper classes—genteel writing, as the works of Boston-educated Henry James, the master, have become known. The plight of the black man was lost in the maze of perplexities that were left in the war's wake. The subject of slavery had proven to be more complex than it had been explained by the Boston abolitionists; the integration of the black man into Boston white society did not happen with Mr. Lincoln's words of freedom. And, more serious still was the naked truth that the issue of state's rights had not been resolved by the horrible war that had rent the nation asunder. Great expansion westward saved the nation and the economy but left the people of Boston facing a civilization that Henry Adams deplored. Inward went the sentiments of the Boston aristocracy, and they withdrew, literally, mentally, and physically, leaving the control of the city to be assumed by the hated Irish.

The Boston Irish had fought in the Civil War in a strong battalion from Boston, and in fighting they had become cognizant of their rights and what results they could obtain by solid political force. In time, they ruled the twentieth-century Boston city, turning its identity from Republican to Democrat. As the problems of labor increased following the war and union strength became important, Boston became one of the leading cities in the organization of the now forceful Teamsters' Union (International Brotherhood of Teamsters, Chauffeurs, Warehousemen and Helpers of America), founded in 1903. In 1907 Daniel J. Tobin, an Irish immigrant and a Boston teamster, became president of the union and remained head until 1952. Tobin's policy of avoiding sympathetic action on behalf of other unions in distress and zealously guarding union funds helped the organization to grow. Tobin had not lived in the shadow of Boston's penurious merchant princes to no avail; he had learned his lesson well. By 1933 the union was unbreakable. Tobin managed to keep control of the most powerful union in America headquartered in Boston through the 1940s, despite the ever-growing union strength in the Middle West and the California coast.[1]

The forces of organized labor and the growing strength of the Irish and other immigrant groups in the political makeup of Boston were not the only post–Civil War movements. Philosophical and religious pacifism—almost as old as war itself—had been organized in the middle of the nineteenth century but had suffered a terrible setback with the Civil War. During the War with Mexico (1848–1860), which was precipitated by the annexation of Texas, drafting for the armed forces was most unpopular in Boston, and the war itself was remote. If the problem of slavery had not been involved in the statehood of Texas, there would have been little interest in American involvement. The expansion and rapid development of the western section of the United States was Jacksonian politics and was viewed with disfavor by most Bostonians. A generation following the Civil War's end, a generation after the causes and effects of the war had become subjects of doubt and questioning, the advocates of the policy of arbitration and mediation in disputes between nations found a sincere following in Boston.

The premise for the work of world peace proposals was the writing of a New York lawyer, David Dudley Field, whose *Proposals for an International Code* was the platform. The vocal advocates of Field's plans were the Boston "institutional" men who represented the powerful international and national moneyed interests of the city and its wealth. These Bostonians did not necessarily run the mills, the railroads, the banks, and the insurance companies; but they controlled the men who did. They were men like Endicott Peabody, Bishop William Lawrence, Major Henry Lee Higginson, and William Cardinal O'Connell. They stood in awe of no man and did not hesitate to issue orders for any mere mortal if they felt their behavior entitled a rebuke—personal or public. Major Higginson believed that "any well trained businessman is wiser than the Congress or the Chief Executive," and he especially believed this in relation to affairs of international significance. And war was such an affair.

The growing sentiment in Boston was antiwar, although many of the moneyed interests were involved with the ever-increasing nationalism that was apparent in certain circles in America with large vested benefits abroad. One of the wars in which America was to intervene was the

Spanish-American War in 1898, a conflict between Spain and the United States over Spanish policies in Cuba. The pro-rebel feelings were inflamed by the yellow press of William Randolph Hearst's New York *Journal* and Joseph Pulitzer's New York *World*. Heavy losses of American investment in Cuba caused by guerrilla warfare, the projected Isthmian canal, and a growing sense of U.S. power in the Western Hemisphere, plus the sinking of the U.S. battleship *Maine,* finally brought America to war with Spain. Inflamed by the press, troops enlisted, and some of the Boston population fought at San Juan Hill on foot with Leonard Wood and Theodore Roosevelt in the popular unit known as the Rough Riders. The war's end brought to the United States Puerto Rico and Guam; and the Philippines were surrendered for a payment of twenty million dollars. The United States emerged from the war as a power of consequence.

The war introduced an era that was characterized by Boston intellectuals and liberals as imperialistic. In addition to ties with Europe, America now was closely allied to the course of events in the Far East. The moneyed citizenry of Boston adhered to the gunboat diplomacy of President Teddy Roosevelt, who believed the way to deal with Latin America was to "speak softly and carry a big stick" and the dollar diplomacy of Taft, whose secretary of state, Philander C. Knox, had used U.S. troops to prop up Latin American dictators who were paid puppets of American big business. These philosophies were in direct conflict with the strong labor and feminist groups in Boston, and when Woodrow Wilson entered the White House with his avowed policy of trying to negotiate all international disputes by arbitration he had the support of the isolationist groups in Boston. Wilson curtly advised American business interests they could no longer expect U.S. military force to back up their investments. Harvard's ex-president, Charles Eliot, expressed the intellectual delight of Boston in his words: "America has now turned her back on the policy of Rome and Great Britain of protecting or avenging their wandering citizens by force of arms."

But Mr. Wilson's naïveté was not effective in coping with the revolutionary forces at work in Mexico. A statue of George Washington in Mexico City was toppled by mobs calling: "Death to the Gringos!" and Wilson was forced to send an expeditionary force under Brigadier General John J. Pershing into Mexico to capture Pancho Villa. The expedition was unsuccessful, costing one-and-a-half million dollars and only succeeded in intensifying Latin suspicions of Yankee imperialism. This "dirty little war" of Woodrow Wilson's (which was never an officially declared war)

Sheet music cover of famous World War I song, "Over There." Cover design by Norman Rockwell. Photograph by Charles Klamkin. From *Old Sheet Music: A Pictorial History* by Marian Klamkin (New York: Hawthorn, 1975).

was extremely unpopular in Boston. James Michael Curley, Boston's colorful political leader, denounced the war and openly criticized any Bostonian who volunteered to serve under Pershing. There were not many who did, and those who went to war upon returning home did not receive the traditional warrior's heroic reception but found themselves and their homes bombarded with stones, and epithets of disapproval were hurled at the returning veterans.

The increasing advancement of pan-Germanism on the Continent reached its climax when the Kaiser backed Austria-Hungary in outrageous demands upon Balkan Serbia and the First World War was launched—a conflict that was eventually to involve more than 93 percent of the world's population and more than eight million of sixty-five million armed men were to lose their lives, a larger number slain than in all the wars between 1793 and 1914 including the Napoleonic wars. In the beginning the feeling in Boston was pacifistic. To the civilized world, the German invasion of neutral Belgium in August of 1914 was a shocking blow to international law and the honor of national commitments, but the tone of the city was against entering into the war. As time moved on, the sentiments against the war were undecided until the reports of German atrocities in Belgium began to appear in the Boston press. The technique of propaganda that was most effective was the use of the famous Raemaaekers cartoons, which forcefully told the story of Belgium anguish. The cartoons, which appeared with strident patriotic appeals of such leading citizens as Henry Cabot Lodge, soon had their effect, and when America, in April 6, 1917, delared war against Germany, Boston became a patriotic city where the word "slacker" was used to designate any young man who did not volunteer to wear the khaki and join the army rushing to France singing "Over There" and lustily vowing to the memory of Lafayette, *"Nous sommes arrivés."* Recruiting tents blossomed on Lafayette Mall, "liberty bond" drives were started, and everyone who did not wear a button proving the purchase of a bond felt uncomfortable. Camp Devens at Ayer opened to train thousands of draftees. Bishop Lawrence worried about the preservation of "sound morals" at the camp, fearing that "the brewer and the prostitute" would become the "chauffeur, comrade and friend" of "our Sammies."

There was a harrowing intolerance of antiwar opinion that gripped the country and Boston. Pacifist Professor Clarence Skinner of Tufts College was shunned by colleagues, and Professor Emily Greene Balch of Wellesley was dropped because of her staunch peace opinions. Even Mrs. Jack got called "that hateful pro-German," and Karl Muck, then conductor of the Boston Symphony, was arrested as an enemy alien, accused of reporting troop movements through his contacts with the "white slave" business.

Bostonians who did not fight were busy with the Red Cross, the YMCA, YWCA, the National Catholic War Council, the Jewish Welfare Board, the Salvation Army, and other agencies that appeared to meet the war needs. Food and fuel shortages brought the war into everybody's home with wheatless, meatless, fat-saving and sugar-saving days. Coal was severely rationed, and Boston suffered through a merciless winter of 1918 when the final blow fell with the famed influenza epidemic during which Boston had ten times as many cases as New York.

However the war lifted Boston out of a temporary economic slump. A big army supply base was built at the cost of seventy-five million dollars. The city became the military and naval headquarters of New England and the principal war shipping port to Europe. The harbor was mined, and a wire net stretched across the channels to keep out German submarines.

On November 11, a whistle shriek was heard at 3:15 A.M. Church bells began to peal, and the Boston streets were crowded with joyful people. The Armistice had been signed and war had come to an end. In April 1919, the troops returned and Boston turned out en masse to welcome home the doughboys. The war to end war had itself ended. The doom of the glorious pan-Germanism was at hand.

Yet the Treaty of Versailles, which was meant to curb German warmaking, only served to present to the German people the harshest terms ever demanded of a defeated world power. In the fields of bitterness sown by the 1918 humiliation one Adolf Hitler reaped a harvest of nationalistic spirit that lent force to his National Socialist Party.

The coming of World War II, after the Munich Pact of 1938, did not surprise many Bostonians. The city's sympathies were largely with the Allies and against the Axis even before our involvement. "Bundles for Britain" was a popular pursuit among Boston women, and many of Boston's young men slipped away to the Canadian border and became members of the RCAF long before America entered the conflict officially with the Japanese attack on Pearl Harbor, December 7, 1941. Robert Frost, the New England poet, noted that it was the first war of radio, with that now popular household fixture "singing gay songs, big talk about our celebrating Christmas in Berlin and next Fourth of July in Tokyo." Boston people learned to press tin cans, use war-ration books, wear air-raid warden helmets, practice first aid, "knit for Britain," and report any suspicious acts. After February 1942, Boston lived in dimouts and blackouts. German submarines were sinking ships off the Atlantic coast, and Boston Harbor was filled with merchant ships that sailed out in convoy. War industries worked round the clock and, with most of the male populace drafted to fight, Boston women took their place in the factory ranks.

The war created in Boston many strange moral predicaments. While the burning of Jews in Auschwitz was taking place, a series of anti-Semitic uprisings occurred in Boston's Jewish community, where the Irish-Americans (influenced, no doubt, by the radio talks of Father Coughlin in Detroit) held the Jews responsible for the war. With a German Bund in operation in Boston and other cities in the United States, these occurrences—though unreported by the Boston press—were a section of the nasty film of war at home. The intellectual mind of Boston was concerned: with the firebombing of enemy cities, the inflexible demand for "unconditional surrender," the problems of a postwar world, and the consequences of dropping the atom bomb *twice.*

In Boston, where many of the first families had intermarried with European wealth, and in some instances, nobility, the stings and arrows of the outrageous fortunes of war did not fly without creating some intense schisms. In one prominent first family, the grandmother, in exile in neutral Switzerland, had through marriage a grandson in every army —Nazi Germany, Il Duce's Fascist Italy, Great Britain's RAF, and finally America's Army of Invasion. When Eisenhower landed on European shores, her blood kin were in open conflict on opposing sides. She alone was isolated and bewildered—remote in her Red Cross sanctuary in neutral Switzerland.

When President Truman took the United States into the Korean conflict in June, 1950, it was officially termed not a war but a police action. So indifferent was Boston to this war that the daily affairs of Bostonians went on as if nothing of martial action was occurring elsewhere in the world. Not until Congress reinstituted the draft and it began to affect young Bostonians was there any surface action—and that was antiwar. Young men in college composed a snap draft classification which would exempt most of them, and a break-in into the Dorchester selective service office destroyed more than five hundred registrants' cards. If there was overt action against the war, there was also indifference to the militant pacifists who attempted to denounce Americans who boasted of mass killings of Chinese in Korea. But the war was eventually stalemated, and written off. The effect upon Boston was largely seen in the future pattern of Boston's concern about war.

President Johnson's escalation of the Vietnam civil war into full-scale conflict greatly disturbed the intellectual mind of Boston. Boston became one of the active antiwar centers. Professors held teach-ins on the background of the conflict. Protest marchers paraded constantly, and the Common was overrun with resisters. More than one Boston campus was the scene of sit-ins against on-campus recruiting by Dow Chemical, CIA, or the armed services. The eloquent voices of John Kenneth Galbraith and David Riesman of Harvard, Noam Chomsky of MIT and Howard

Zinn of Boston University led the chorus of dissent. A draft resistance group was set up in Boston, and draft cards were burned in the Common and in some of the churches. Sanctuary spread to Harvard, Brandeis, Boston University, and MIT with students and faculty participating.

Although it seemed a contemporary action, actually the young Bostonians were acting out ancient Boston tradition. They were unconsciously, perhaps, obeying the first governor's admonition against "a standing authority of military men."

For three hundred and fifty years Bostonians have been involved in war, although only one was fought physically on their doorstep. Hundreds of Bostonians have been involved in the other wars, some fighting, some dying. The others merely gave thought to the wars, and in characteristic Bostonian fashion they refused to let another being do their thinking for them—even if that thought was embodied in the body of the elected president of the United States.

The wars, commencing with the War of 1812, altered the industrial pattern of the city of Boston, and the later wars saw an emergence of the new Boston, with its splurge into contemporary living. Boston was the only large city to lose population following World War II and during the postwar boom. In half a century it dropped from the fourth largest city in America to the thirteenth. For two decades there seemed to be an atmosphere of stagnation.

Then there appeared the space-based electronic industry; the multi-million-dollar National Aeronautics and Space Administration installations. A transformation took place and Boston, which had been a sort of Rip Van Winkle city, suddenly awoke. Human and natural resources were again summoned into action and a renaissance was under way—the shakles of the past were being discarded, a new revolution was abroad to awaken the old city.

With the technologists who had been summoned for the wars, there was, in Boston, a movement to utilize electronics constructively. "Towards a Planetary Civilization," the work of Emily Greene Balch, who led the Women's International League for Peace, was a premise for turning the word into the deed. The world recognized that a private citizen, who held no political office or public position, could be a leader in contributing to conditions for international peace. This woman, who had been ostracized in World War I, in 1946 received with Dr. John Mott the Nobel prize for peace, the world's highest acclaim for peace. Her life had not been in vain.

12

A Boston Crime Pie

Urban history is a vast, sprawling, and complex field of study. The historian is not unlike a detective seeking out a criminal about whom he knows nothing—except that a crime was committed. If one thinks of a city as a fixed place, with fixed people, everything fits into fixed areas; but a city is more fluid—people flow in and flow out. People live in cities because there are exits as well as entrances. When the population grows, the city grows out, enclosing the surrounding areas and enveloping its people. Cities like ideas have both an internal and external history, and cities are created by the people who inhabit them. These people, too, are subject to internal and external ideas.

Crime, as one of the existing factors in the city, is also a two-headed monster. Did the city create the criminal, or did the criminal select the city?[1] There is no simple answer. We only know that a certain degree of crime exists in any organized group of people. Certainly if there was ever a city designed from the date of origin to be free from the forces of crime, Boston was that city. But, from the very beginning, crime became a factor to contend with. The minor, petty crimes grew into the major crime of the Salem witches and their burners. In 1692 Ann Putnam, only twelve, led her little band of hellcats into swearing away the lives of nineteen persons who were hanged and one who was pressed to death, leaving an indelible stigma, which has hung over Boston and its suburbs ever since.

Numerically, as a city of crime, Boston is not outstanding. It has about fifty murders per year and the average percentage of petty larcenies and felonies identified with most metropolitan areas. There are people who say that there are aspects of Boston that remain essentially unchanged from the days of the Salem witch burning; a belief that only extreme rectitude and immediate recognition of sin can cope with the evil inherent in men. Boston cannot avoid its double legacy of Calvinist Puritanism, reflected in the Yankee Protestant population and the Jansenist repres-

"There is a flock of yellow birds around her head." Salem witch trials. From *Harper's Magazine*, December 1892.

sion, reflected in the Irish Catholic immigrant population. Certainly the crimes identified with Boston are unique. Are they the product of the city's environment, or are they the individual, flowing over in a seething cauldron of suppressed desires?

That the dark psychological effects of Puritan Boston still exist cannot be denied. Despite the progressive penal institutions in Massachusetts, despite the superb educational system, Boston is one of the few cities that permits physical punishment of children; over the "swinging" identity of present-day Boston hangs the shadow of Hawthorne's scarlet letter. In the annals of Boston crime, it is not only the crimes committed, but the enigmatic character of the crimes and the criminals that intrigue criminologist and historian alike.

"The morals of our people are much better; their manners are more polite and agreeable; they are purer English; our language is better; our persons are handsomer; our spirit is greater; our laws are wiser, our religion is superior; our education is better." (John Quincy Adams)

Adams is writing about Boston—his make-believe composite of Puritans, blue bloods, culture, first families, the broad *A* and the high hat, the city of legend. Yet, in reality Boston has no more culture, blue bloods, or first families than has New York, Chicago, Detroit, Denver, or Los Angeles. It is true that Boston is the oldest city in the country; history has rumbled down its streets and tied up at its wharves; but it is not perched so securely upon a pinnacle of virtue as John Quincy Adams contended. Boston has had its share of prudes, screwballs, zealots, bigots, and bums. It often displays a narrowness of mind, a tendency to lust in mob control. But there has never been, and probably never will be, in Boston any big-time crime comparable to that of New York, Chicago, or Detroit. It is not because of any puritanical justice awaiting the offender, but because Boston politics have never had any compatibility with gangland scavengers.

The Boston criminal is pretty small fry. He has, for the most part, been incapable of planning crime on a grandiose scale. Blood has been shed over trivial matters, but there has never been a St. Valentine's Day Massacre on the Boston police blotter. But there have been a few spectacular crimes that have achieved national and international recognition and have been the delight of authors of crime stories and professional criminologists. Two of the most famous—Pomeroy and Richeson—belong in a volume on criminal insanity.

Jesse Pomeroy spent fifty years in prison, forty-one of them in a solitary cell. He had abused and murdered twenty-seven children. He was thirteen years old at the time and certainly deserved the title of monster. When he was arrested in 1881 he cried, "I don't know why I did it. I couldn't help it!"

Pomeroy, in solitary confinement, made a sensational bid for freedom. He chipped away at one section of the granite walls of his cell with a crudely fashioned knife. His plan was literally brilliant—he reached a gas line, lit a match, and the explosion that followed blew up the entire wing. The three convicts in adjoining cells were burned to death, but Pomeroy emerged unscathed.

The Richeson case, in 1911, was started by the death of Avis Linnell, a young music student, from potassium cyanide poisoning. The postmortem discovery of her pregnancy was at first considered proof that she had committed suicide; but the evidence led to her former fiancé, the Reverend Clarence Virgil Thompson Richeson, who after preliminary denials, confessed to the crime and pleaded guilty. He had given the girl the poison, telling her it was an abortive. His insanity plea (which was undoubtedly authentic) and letters to the governor from thousands of women did not save him from the electric chair.

Two of the Boston murder cases are of interest historically. One concerned William McDonough who, in 1817, after killing his wife in a drunken frenzy, was the first person in the United States to plead insanity as a defense for murder. (He was hanged anyway.) The second, Luigi Storti, killed a man named Michele Callucci for betraying Storti's sister, and thereafter had the dubious honor of being the first man in Massachusetts to die in the electric chair.

To Boston goes the distinction of being the scene of America's classic murder—the killing of Dr. George Parkman by Professor John White Webster. The date was November 23, 1849. It was a warm day for Boston when Dr. Parkman left his home at 8 Walnut Street in Beacon Hill. Dr. Parkman was in a hurry—he was always in a hurry. His protruding chin jutted forth so distinctly that street urchins would whisper: "There goes Chin—Dr. Parkman," and giggle surreptitiously. Little did they know that this chin, which made the fitting of dentures an almost impossible task, would also make the remains of these dentures a positive identification after he walked off the face of the earth.

Dr. Parkman never practiced medicine; he merely enjoyed the pursuit of money. He was a New England miser without peer in the city of Boston. He enjoyed the lending (at high interest rates) and the collecting of money with a passion that made Shakespeare's Shylock appear a kindly banker unseeking of his pound of flesh. The sadistic pleasure that Dr. Parkman enjoyed while watching his victim squirm and writhe would ultimately cause his denouement, but that it would be brought about by a Harvard professor was beyond the comprehension or imagination of proper Bostonians. That Dr. Parkman himself was a proper Bostonian no one would deny. He was the very personification of "wholesale charity and retail penury," for he had given away large sums of money with wholesale generosity; yet with small sums of money on a retail basis, he was penny-punctilious.

The day of November 23, Dr. Parkman was after money. He visited the Merchant's Bank on State Street, then he dropped into a grocery store at the corner of Blossom and Vine and purchased a head of lettuce for his invalid sister. He left it in the store and said he would return for it on his way home. Wearing his familiar black coat and trousers, his purple silk vest, black stock, and high hat, he rushed north on Grove Street— never to be seen again. When the hour for dining arrived and there was no Dr. Parkman, the three ladies of the household became concerned, for Dr. Parkman was not a creature of changing habits. He was the personification of punctuality. As the evening passed and still no Dr. Parkman, his brother-in-law was contacted, as was his real estate agent, and it was decided to make his disappearance public. What had been his course of action throughout that unseasonably warm day? Whom had he visited?

Professor Webster! The very name threw Dr. Parkman into the doldrums. Professor Webster was a man who held a lectureship in a medical

Dr. John White Webster's pent-up fury made him a match for the taller Dr. Parkman. The murder blow was dealt with the piece of heavy kindling in Dr. Webster's left hand. From *A Pictorial History of American Crime, 1849–1929* by Allen Churchill. © 1964, Allen Churchill. Reproduced by permission of Holt, Rinehart, and Winston, Publishers.

college built on the land he—Dr. Parkman—had provided. The Parkman Chair of Anatomy in the college—occupied by Oliver Wendell Holmes—was named in Dr. Parkman's honor, as acknowledgment of the gift. What Dr. Parkman thought of Professor Webster he had told him to his face, and to be sure there was no misunderstanding he had written a very explicit, graphic note stating, "You are a defaulting, dishonorable debtor!" In Dr. Parkman's world, these words were harsher than words denoting mongrel maternity.

Dr. Parkman had reason to be indignant. Professor Webster had committed the heinous crime of quickly disposing of the fortune he had inherited from his father. He liked to live well and entertain his friends, and even in Cambridge, with a wife and three daughters it was not easy to live in the manner to which Professor Webster had become accustomed on the twelve hundred dollars a year the university paid him, with a slender addition from the sale of tickets for his lectures at the Medical College.

Seven years earlier, Dr. Parkman had lent Webster $400, taking a note secured by the mortgage of some personal property. In 1847, when the loan was not fully repaid, Dr. Parkman had been one of the group of men to lend the professor a larger sum, taking this time a note for $2,432, secured by a mortgage of all Professor Webster's property, including his household furniture and his cabinet of minerals. The following year, the professor, still financially embarrassed, went to Dr. Parkman's brother-in-law, Robert Gould Shaw, telling a pathetic tale of sheriffs and attachments, and prevailed upon that gentleman to purchase his cabinet of minerals; he negleceted to mention the fact that the collection was already in pawn to Dr. Parkman. Shaw talked about the transaction, and Dr. Parkman hit the ceiling, his long spindly legs elasticizing in the nervous spasm that went through his body when he heard of the fraud!

"Those minerals are not his to sell, I have a mortgage on them, and I can show you!"

From that moment on, Dr. Parkman set about in pursuit of the culprit. It has been reported that he used to come to Professor Webster's lectures and sit in the front row glaring at the confused professor, who was almost speechless as he stared at that prognathous jaw and those shining false teeth.

On the afternoon of November 23, Dr. Parkman headed for the Medical College for a confrontation with Professor Webster. The creditor and the debtor had made a previous arrangement to meet in the anatomical

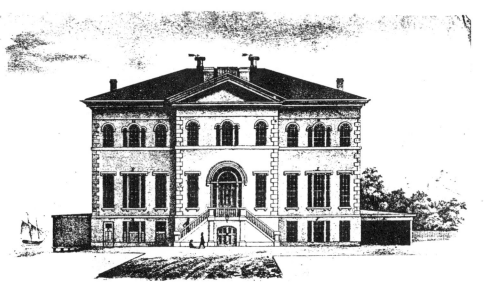

The ground floor of this chaste-looking building was the locale for the first American crime to attract national attention. The killing of Dr. Parkman has been called America's classic murder. From *A Pictorial History of American Crime, 1849–1929* by Allen Churchill. © 1964, Allen Churchill. Reproduced by permission of Holt, Rinehart, and Winston, Publishers.

building, amid those "pieces of sour mortality" as Charles Dickens later described the furnishings of the scene. Dr. Parkman entered the building Friday, six days before Thanksgiving, in broad daylight and then disappeared. When the starless night fell over the city, Dr. Parkman was lost in the Bible-black gloom.

The excitement which was caused by Dr. Parkman's disappearance emblazoned the festive holidays, making drab and uninteresting the customary glow of pumpkin, chrome yellow and crimson maple leaves, and pom-pom chrysanthemums heaped in a cornucopia in the turkey table's centerpiece. Tradition was bypassed as whispers and innuendoes were exchanged by strolling citizens in the Common. The Charles River was dredged, and empty buildings and cellars were searched.

Only Professor Webster offered some explanation. He told of their meeting and said he had paid Dr. Parkman the sum he owed him and the surprised man had departed, happily anticipating the oncoming holiday. Professor Webster offered the bewildered family his condolences, for his words seemed to intensify the belief that Dr. Parkman had been waylaid by a stranger and robbed, then murdered. But where were the lanky remains?

It was then that the janitor, a Mr. Littlefield, strode into the picture by deciding on Thanksgiving Day—instead of further celebrating—to thoroughly explore the Medical College. In Professor Webster's private vault, which Littlefield entered by breaking through the wall, he found the pelvis of a man and two parts of a leg. Very shortly thereafter three policemen apprehended Professor Webster and informed him he was in custody for the murder of Dr. Parkman.

"Have they found Dr. Parkman? Where did they find him? Did they find the whole of the body? How came they to suspect me? Oh! My children, what will they do? Oh, what will they think of me?"

He reached in his pocket and swallowed a pill that contained a heavy dose of strychnine; but it did not kill him. And the excitement in Boston became intense.

After a long trial Professor Webster finally confessed, telling a harrowing story of how he had been hounded by Dr. Parkman until in a moment of frenzy he accidentally hit him over the head and killed him. In his fright, he proceeded to dismember the body, and had it not been for the ubiquitous teeth, he might have been freed for lack of a corpse. But despite the popular sympathy for the professor, he was hanged on the last Friday in August 1850. To this day the question remains—was it a premeditated murder, or can it be considered manslaughter, done in a sudden passion and under provocation? Cries of "Puritan bigotry" and "Boston snobbishness" were hurled by those who felt Professor Webster innocent of premeditated murder. But the murder had made Boston conscious of the fact that a highly respected person may commit a crime of this nature; that he may solemnly lie in the name of God to escape punishment; and that a just conviction may be had upon circumstantial evidence.

"The eye of man hath not heard, the ear of man hath not seen, man's hand is not able to taste, his tongue to conceive, nor his heart to report what my dream was." (*A Midsummer Night's Dream,* Shakespeare)

On the glass-windowed front porch of a McKinley/Queen Anne house with a nonfunctional clapboarded turret on one side, Lisbeth of Maplecroft sat and might have murmured Shakespeare's words aloud as she looked over her spacious yard. In her mind's eye the little mill town of Fall River vanished in the purple twilight, and the yard became peopled with her father, Andrew Borden; her stepmother, Abby; her sister, Emma; and her faithful maid, Bridget Sullivan. But the dream enacted by Lizzie Borden had no awakening; it was a nightmare. Children sang, tauntingly,

Lizzie Borden took an ax
And gave her mother forty whacks;
When she saw what she had done
She gave her father forty-one!

Fall River is one of those towns neighboring Boston that become enveloped in the large metropolitan city. Fall River was a mill town, and the mills were the raison d'être for Lizzie Borden's little world. It also was a town linked to Boston by the Fall River Steamship Line, where it was an accepted custom for young men of social rank to work during the summer months on the boats that offered some training before shipping out to sea. So what happened in Fall River, happened also in Boston, and Lizzie Borden's performance had its most exacting audience in Boston when she was tried and acquitted for the murder of her parents.

The Lizzie Borden case is the crime supreme—the insoluble mystery, a mystery that hangs upon a missing weapon, a missing bloodstained dress, and a young lady's impeccable character. It is to American legend what Clytemnestra was to the Greeks. Lizzie is the eternal cause célèbre, the sane, civilized woman accused of a madman's crime—midmorning slaughter in a tiny house where she was not even alone with her victim parents (her maid was present). The driving motive behind this bloody and indiscreet violence is most commonly given as a cool desire to inherit the victims' considerable fortune.

The story has been told and retold until it is like "a tale told by an idiot, full of sound and fury, signifying nothing." It has been choreographed as a classic modern dance—*The Fall River Legend*—and it has been adapted to the stage as a vehicle for the delicate, ethereal Miss Lillian Gish who bore absolutely no resemblance to the florid, stocky Lizzie Borden. Lizzie has been defended and has offended, for she and the tragedy enacted on that sultry summer day are suspended in time and space and apparently will be with us forever.

Fall River owes its name and its existence to the Quequechan, a wild stream that rises in twin lakes on a high plateau at the city's eastern border and dashes, broken by waterfalls, through the city's heart. It had waterpower before the age of steam, and that brought the first mills there. Everyone in Fall River knows where "the hill" is and that it was not really a hill, but a steep drop from high land to the waterfront at the northern part of town. To live "up the hill" was Lizzie's ambition. And there was no reason except Andrew Borden's penury to prevent this move

Lizzie Borden at the time of the Borden murders. Courtesy of the Fall River Historical Society.

—for he belonged up on the hill. He was a Borden. The social structure of the town was such that, with an old Yankee name like Borden, a man who was a bank president, a director of mills, and worth three hundred thousand dollars plus real estate that pulled his assets up to half a million dollars, nothing but stinginess forced him to live where he did.

Andrew Borden was never known to give a penny to charity. He collected his rents in person, never trusting anyone, and the town reeked of stories of his over-prompt evictions. He was six foot two, and gaunt; his eyes were small, dull and black, his voice and skin were dry, and his lipless mouth turned down at the corner. But Lizzie loved him, and the killing of her father must have been a trauma from which she could never recover—that is, if she killed him. The killing of her stepmother, whom she loathed, and whom she thought was going to inherit her father's fortune, would not be too difficult a task.

Lizzie, by nature, was a spender, caring vastly for prestige and splendor. It is quite easy, today, to see how the legend grew of the miser's daughter hacking her way to wealth, and it is substantiated by the fact that she moved "up on the hill" as soon as she was freed and inherited her fortune. In fact, it was Lizzie Borden's style of life after the murders that ostracized her rather than the murders themselves.

Actually, Lizzie Borden became through the murders a martyr, a symbol of women's liberation before the word had ever been invented, because in her day the transference of money from the male to the female was a very complicated procedure. Women were almost chattel slaves, economically, and Lizzie drew great sympathy from other women who possibly had entertained the idea of murder but had never done the actual deed.

Victoria Lincoln, the writer who was brought up in Fall River in the shadow of Lizzie Borden's presence, has done considerable research and presents a rather convincing case that Lizzie suffered from temporal epilepsy and premenstrual tension.[2] Lincoln does not think that Lizzie killed her parents *because* she had an ambulatory seizure of temporal epilepsy. But all evidence indicates that she killed her stepmother during one.

Of Lizzie Borden's trial—in which she was acquitted—it has been said: "It was not the prisoner, but the Commonwealth, which did not have a fair trial." Lizzie was the heroine of the hour. Reporters crowded round her to shake her hand, and her ecstatic sympathizers filled the air, the telegraph wires, and the mails with their hallelujahs. The district attorney, his assistant, and a few discerning newspapermen turned away, disgusted with what they thought a miscarriage of justice, brought about by a biased court and a maudlin public sentiment. Lizzie was pictured by the press as an "injured innocent"; "a noble Christian woman" undergoing martyrdom. In actuality, her social position had assured her more than her share of consideration. With the acquittal, the case was closed, and the whole truth will never really be known. The last days of Lizzie Borden—now Lisbeth of Maplecroft—was something out of a Victorian novel; she kept hidden in her heart and mind, as she lay dying in her lonely house, the truth about a grim and terrible crime. With her, the truth perished. But Lizzie's ghost lives on.

Murder, they say, will out—and in Boston in the late summer of 1963 there began a series of murders of single women, most of whom were middle-aged, under circumstances as baffling as any in fiction. Each woman was strangled in her apartment. There were no signs of forcible entry. Around the necks of the victims were knotted nylon stockings or other articles of apparel. Each woman had been sexually molested or assaulted. No clues were found; nothing had been stolen; there was no discernible motive. The victims were modest, inconspicuous, almost anonymous women, leading blameless lives. Beyond the mystery of their deaths, there was something terribly sad and pathetic about these victims who apparently either knew or were unafraid of their murderer, let him into their apartments, and did not even put up a struggle before they were strangled to death. It was obvious that the murderer (or the murderers) must be insane.

Boston was a city near panic.

What happens to a city when it is besieged by terror—terror stemming from a violent sexual explosion that seems to be a part of contemporary life? How do people behave when all about them is the atmosphere of fear? What are their defenses? How can the rational mind contend with the irrational in an atmosphere of hysteria?

What was Boston like in the summer of 1963 when death began to stalk the streets and a concern with aspects of abnormal sexuality became commonplace discussion? Who were the guilty?

Boston was not a city that enjoyed the publicity attendant to crime. It turned down the tabloid exploitation and preferred to keep its crime closeted as a sordid behavior pattern peculiar to the Bowerylike south end—something that, like the poor, is always with us.

It is interesting that at the hour of the Boston stranglings, things were looking up for the city that had for more than a generation been slowly dying. There was a man in the White House who was a Boston Irish-Catholic, young, idealistic, ambitious, and wealthy enough to be beyond reproach. In addition, he had a beautiful, socially correct, photogenic wife. The world was anxious to welcome the new rulers of Camelot. In addition, the Speaker of the House of Representatives was a Bostonian, as was a ranking member of the Senate Foreign Relations Committee. Suddenly, enormous projects that would alter the face of one-fourth of the city commenced. Some billions of dollars were to be spent in construction that included the two-hundred-million-dollar Prudential Insurance Company complex, the similarly priced sixty-acre Government Center, the hundred-million-dollar waterfront development program, and some fourteen separate slum clearance programs. In downtown Boston, the tallest skyscraper outside New York City was being built.

And, for the first time two diverse elements in Boston—the old Protestant families, representing wealth, and the new Irish-Catholic families, representing political power—had joined hands in civic matrimony. Their new mayor was John F. Collins, a man of energy and ambition. His theme was a "new Boston"; it was at the very moment of the shaking off the lethargy of the past, relinquishing the old for the new, that the first strangling occurred.

If there was any outside force that could catapult a city these stranglings that occurred in Boston and the surrounding vicinity did the tumbling deed. They appeared to be the concoction of a mad playwright—a Marquis de Sade—come to descend upon Boston. Memories of the Salem witches were again revived, and once more Boston was haunted by the psychological conflicts of Puritan good and evil. The devil had again chosen to visit the earth! Except in the person of death incarnate, how could one explain why these particular women had been selected to die?

What brought them to Boston, at this time, to be the victims? The story grew. Murder succeeded murder, victim was added to victim, and the police of a great city seemed paralyzed. Here was being enacted one of the world's greatest multiple murders, one of the most exhaustive manhunts of all time, and finally what is unquestionably the most extraordinary and sustained self-revelation yet made by a criminal. Who? The Boston Strangler.

Every technique of detection was employed—natural and supernatural, computers, clairvoyants, "sensitives," men and women claiming ESP (extrasensory perception) powers, psychiatrists armed with hypnotic drugs, hallucinating agents, and truth serums, specialists in anthropology, graphology, forensic law, pornographic experts.

Boston was a city laid siege to by a killer whose insanity was equaled by his cunning, who apparently could materialize within locked apartments and not only kill but do terrible deeds to these women without leaving a clue! Not since Jack the Ripper had murdered and dismembered women in the streets of London three-quarters of a century before had any such thing been experienced.

The search would cut through social and political strata. It would involve the attorney general of Massachusetts, the FBI, police on all levels, the press crusading and demanding. It would affect the citizenry itself, setting wives against husbands, neighbor against neighbor, translating the sexual frustrations of men and women into acts astonishing and bizarre, bringing into the open an incredible cast of true life characters. Once again, as in the dark days of the Salem witches, a city would be laid bare, and its soul would be moldy, perhaps, like an old boarding house.

Who was the strangler?

He was a man named Albert de Salvo, a borderline psychopathic who, in jail, boasted of his sexual prowess and finally confided in a fellow prisoner—who was, himself, suspected of being the strangler—that this was his identity. No one believed him, but his convict friend related the story to his own attorney, F. Lee Bailey, and in due time the case was broken. But, as Bailey said, "Albert was on the left bank of a river and my job was to get him to the right bank without letting him down." Bailey's role was to see that de Salvo neither was set free nor sent to the electric chair. Bailey wanted him in a mental hospital where he could be studied—his voyeurism, his sexual frustrations, his inability to achieve climactic satisfaction—all of those sexual aberrations (or socially and religiously declared aberrations) that prompt the apparently senseless sex-rape murders which take place constantly.

What did the man de Salvo look like? In appearance, as in all of his life's dealings, he was rather commonplace. Besides having a Cyrano de Bergerac type of nose there was nothing unusual in the appearance of this short, well-built young man who neither smoked nor drank. But in the study of his life-style, sex reared its ugly head and created a monster. Masturbation was his specialty; his sexual needs might seem to be extreme, but when his wife indulged him in a form of sex love which was finally gratifying he abstained from imposing himself upon other women. His idea for his crimes was based upon a TV show in which Robert Cummings played a photographer in search of girl models—this was how the measuring man was born, and this was how he entered the apartments of single women.

De Salvo confessed, and by minor intimate details he revealed about the crimes—such as the fact that one of the girls was menstruating when she was strangled and where he had disposed of the sanitary napkin —he convinced F. Lee Bailey, his attorney, and most of his interrogators that he was, in truth, the strangler. But, he was never tried as such. He was committed to the Bridgewater State Hospital where, until he died, he wondered if the doctors "can cut out the corner of my brain that makes me do these things."

The three murders and the murderers mentioned here are all memorable. Their passion-evoking crimes instruct and horrify us, but they also remind us that they require understanding. Only one—that of Professor Webster—fits the commonly accepted definition of crime, since Webster is the only one who was tried and convicted of his crime and paid the court's sentence with his life. Lizzie was never convicted of killing her parents, nor was suspicion cast upon her maid—who was present in the house at the time of the murders. Albert de Salvo was institutionalized for life but never convicted by a jury of his peers of being guilty of the crimes of which he was accused.

Crimes are peculiar to the times, and their notoriety through the public press is the manner in which the public becomes acquainted with the sordid details. It is interesting that most crimes committed in Boston have not had wide coverage, but those that have, have managed to attract considerable interest. Their appeal was to the morbid curiosity of mankind, his indecipherable concern with the *art* of crime. The criminal becomes the extension of the individual's frustrations—he is the loudest, the gaudiest, the noisiest, the best remembered! But a roster of Boston murders, from the first recorded in 1644, the Franklin-Sewell case (Franklin killed his young apprentice and was sentenced to death despite the protests of 'prentice masters who lamented that the world had reached a stage where a man "couldn't correct" his own bound boy) to the latest homicide on record, makes the historian regard John Quincy Adams's appraisal of his fellow Bostonian a little dubiously. The sum total is that Boston is filled with the same types as any other city and eventually "murder will out"!

One of the crimes committed in Boston will never be forgotten, for it penetrated not only the city and the nation but eventually the highest court in the country. Playwrights, such as Maxwell Anderson in *Winterset,* have written about it, or used some part of it as part of the theme of their action. One of America's foremost painters, Ben Shahn, has depicted it on canvas, and many authors, notably Upton Sinclair in *Boston,* have used it as a thesis for papers on the sociological aspects of crime. Many people have questioned the justice in the sentence handed down. It will always be controversial.

It happened on April 15, 1920, in the humble Boston suburb of South Braintree, Massachusetts. At 3:00 P.M. that day a paymaster and his guard, carrying two tin boxes containing the sum of $15,765, the payroll of a small shoe factory, were robbed and killed. The crime was committed by men who made their getaway in an automobile. The details were not sensational to a country which had the exploits of Al Capone and his gang of hoodlums to concentrate upon. The affair was completely local and did not even get much space in the Boston papers.

Two weeks later two Italians of avowed radical sentiments were arrested, and a year later they were tried and found guilty. The coverage

Nicolo and Bartolomeo Vanzetti. International Newsreel Photograph, Boston, August 4, 1927.

was on the back pages of the newspapers in Boston. But the execution did not come off on schedule because three people had been working on the men's behalf—an Italian newspaperman, a Spanish carpenter, and a Jewish boy. Unpaid and racing against time, they wrote to all liberal and left-wing organizations in the world. Before the scheduled date of execution, demonstrations took place in Rome and Mexico, and two bombs went off in Paris at the home of American ambassador, Francis Hobart Herrick. Herrick looked into state department records about the two men whom he thought were the cause of the trouble. Their names were Nicola Sacco and Bartolomeo Vanzetti. They were a shoemaker and a fish peddler, respectively.

As time wore on, the names became household words in Boston. Appeal after appeal was denied, and the friends of the two convicted men became legion. But jurist Webster Thayer had vowed to punish the "anarchist bastards." For six years the cat-and-mouse game between the two prisoners and the courts was waged. Finally, it was decided that the case should be reviewed. The entire world was watching. No less a

Dr. Richard C. Cabot. Photograph by Frizell.

man than Felix Frankfurter declared the men had not had a fair trial. Dorothy Parker and Robert Benchley led pilgrimages from New York to Boston on behalf of the defendants. The press had almost unanimously reversed its position, and the conservative *Boston Herald* won a Pulitzer Prize for its editorial. Boston's social leaders, under the aegis of Bishop Lawrence and Dr. Richard C. Cabot, took it upon themselves to ask Governor Fuller to appoint a board to review the case. The committee was made up of Robert T. Grant, a blue-blooded judge of the probate court; Samuel W. Stratton, head of the Massachusetts Institute of Technology; and Harvard's president, Lawrence Lowell. Everyone seemed to have an opinion. The eyes of the world watched for the decision of the board. It was blunt; they saw no reason on the evidence submitted for a retrial or for clemency!

Execution was set for August 22, 1927. The hue and cry of the world was to no avail. The "dreamers of a brotherhood of man" were sent to the electric chair, and the case was closed; but the cold heart of Boston seemed frozen beyond human belief. "Is there no Christ above American courtrooms?" asked the foreign press when the Boston institutions had proven their power for the world to see. The men died as martyrs, although after their deaths there was some evidence to substantiate Sacco's involvement with the death of the guard. It is possible that, in the eyes of the world, the straight and narrow rule of the Boston Establishment was more on trial than were Sacco and Vanzetti.

It comes as something of a surprise, with overtones of irony, that the city which created some of the most authentic and capable business minds in the United States also was the scene of one of the greatest swindles.

Charles Ponzi was never anything more than a common swindler. Yet he perpetrated the simplest yet most gigantic financial hoax of the twentieth century. P. T. Barnum's famous quote, "There's a sucker born every minute," was the formula upon which Ponzi's criminal mind was fed. To put across his fantastic scheme, Ponzi banked upon the avariciousness of investors, the gullibility of the press, and the simplicity of Americans who believed that all things were possible in a free enterprise system. His system was childlike—the robbing of Peter to pay Paul—and it worked until the day Peter discovered his role as a patsy.

Ponzi emigrated to the United States from Italy in the 1890s. In his dream of becoming an American millionaire, he soon drifted into petty crime, but he managed to escape severe punishment for the act of forgery and the smuggling of aliens into the United States. In 1914, Ponzi moved to Boston where he married the daughter of a wholesale grocer. His get-rich-quick schemes fascinated the poor Italian population. When the Ponzi super-plan materialized in 1919, he had a captive audience. Working in an import-export firm, Ponzi noticed a packet of international postal union reply coupons. He learned that the coupons, purchased abroad and then sent to the United States—which was not suffering an economic depression—were redeemed for a considerably higher rate than when purchased in either Italy or Germany. When Ponzi stumbled upon this, he realized that he was in possession of a once-in-a-lifetime get-rich scheme. He quit his job and borrowed some money to send to relatives in Italy to purchase the postal coupons and mail them to him. He went to some Boston friends who gambled small amounts with him. In ninety days Ponzi had paid back $750 interest on initial investments totaling $1,250.

It seemed incredible. His investors were indeed impressed, and Ponzi, who made no attempt to explain his financial wizardry, merely suggested that they tell their friends to invest while they, too, reinvested. In a very short time, hundreds rushed to Ponzi to purchase postal coupons. When the numbers became thousands, Ponzi founded his Financial Exchange Company on School Street in the heart of Boston's financial district. So rapidly was the money coming in that the employees scooped up an estimated two hundred thousand dollars per day at the peak of his success.

Ponzi enjoyed the title the Great Ponzi, and was very upset one day when one of Boston's financial writers on a local newspaper questioned the validity—and the honesty—of him and his company. He sued the paper for half-a-million dollars in damages. The brazenness of this act quieted the inquisitive press, and Ponzi was able to reach the ultimate in luxury, apparent riches, and personal fame as the master of finance. One day he walked into the highly esteemed Hanover Trust Company, and with three million dollars he bought a controlling interest. When the *Boston Post,* very impressed, asked for an interview, Ponzi hired a public relations man, William McMasters. Instead of building up his man, McMasters became instantly suspicious and turned the problem over to the state investigators to examine Ponzi and his books. They were a maze of gibberish. Ponzi was a financial idiot; his co-workers were moronic drones who merely paid people who showed up at collection time and wanted money—at other times they took money from those only too eager to invest with Ponzi.

Ponzi had been proclaimed the greatest Italian of all despite his modest protests as he pointed out the fact that Columbus had discovered America and Marconi the wireless. "But you, mighty Ponzi," they acclaimed, "have discovered money!" Yet, when the bubble burst, there was no way to put Ponzi together again.

Finally, a few letters he had written to investors urging them to reinvest gave the federal government the opportunity to put Ponzi away on the charge of using the mails to defraud. It appeared to be the end. His fine wardrobe was gone, his mansion empty, and his wife, Rose, finished with him. He was banished to his native Italy. "I bear no grudges," he said, with Chaplinesque whimsy, "I hope the world will forgive me!"

His world of losing investors never did, but Benito Mussolini was fascinated with Ponzi's ability to con and gave him a high-ranking job in the financial section of his government. But he soon learned that Ponzi was unreliable as well as inept. Before charges could be brought against him, Ponzi skipped to South America with a large, unstated sum of Mussolini's treasury. He died in Rio de Janeiro in 1949. The Ponzi millions vanished in death—as did Ponzi.

In the beginning of the story of Boston and crime, there were no cops and robbers, no super criminals; there were, primarily, drunks. The punishment for drunkenness was swift and stern; fines, whipping and "billbowes"—shackles for the feet. In 1631, "watches" were ordered to be maintained in Boston every night from sunset. In 1636, in a February town meeting, Boston also made provisions for a "ward" to keep order in the daytime. In both units service was unpaid and was to be performed in turn by the citizens of the town.

At first, the duties of the watch and ward were not specified beyond the keeping of the peace. They were to serve under and assist the constable. His duties, detailed in a 1646 law, included serving warrants, organizing "hues and cries" after criminals, and arresting lawbreakers. The emphasis on the last was given to those "overtaken with drinke, swearing, breaking the Saboth, lying, vagrant persons," and Boston's special bête noire, the "night walkers." The constable's job was an unpopular one and soon involved the gathering of taxes, levying fines, assisting customs officials, keeping lists of lost goods and straying animals, summoning coroner's juries, and all sorts of miscellaneous jobs.

The first man hanged in Boston was William Schooler, who had arrived with a bad reputation from London. After agreeing to guide a young servant girl to a town beyond the Merrimac River, he abandoned her in the woods—or so he claimed. Six months later an Indian found her mutilated body. The crime was not fully proven against him, but he was, nevertheless, hanged. He was the first that Boston and the Commonwealth would treat as "worthy of murder."

The first prison was built in Boston in 1635. Located on the south side of Court Street, then called Prison Lane, it was a wooden building with barred windows. It was unheated in winter and was a place of "meagre Looks and ill smells." One jailkeeper reported he had sixteen people in prison, two of them women. Six were in for debt, three for theft, one for "buggary," one for adultery, and five for drinking. In the early Boston years particularly dangerous criminals were not kept in Boston jails but were sent on to the fort in Castle Island, which was a sort of local Alcatraz. Jailkeepers had many problems, such as persons being jailed for debt bringing their families in with them and damaging the building by "their Choping firewood on the Floors."

In 1712, there was instituted a system of paid watchmen. Watchhouses were built for them in different sections of the city—they were the predecessors of the precinct houses. The watchmen became notorious for sleeping on duty, a charge which they admitted, claiming that their low pay made it necessary for them to perform other jobs in order to support their families. "Moonlighting"—or, rather, "sunlighting"—would be the modern-day version.

Boston became a city in 1822, and the mayor and the board of aldermen administered the police and the first new police court on June 20. Police duties altered with the spectacular growth of the city, so that by 1838 a day police force, separate from the night, had to be organized. Behavior, fairly easy to regulate in a small community, became disruptive in a large city. Criminals were more mobile due to new transportation, and their crimes more sophisticated and better organized. But the plight of the arrested people did not go unheeded by one man, John Augustus, who at the age of fifty-seven began a career of working with people to rehabilitate them and became what is probably the first probation officer in America. He seemed a bit fanatic to some people, but actually his work was remarkable in the precedent he set. He did not go bail for just anyone; he selected his charges from those whom he felt would best respond to his treatment. His work is described in his own words: "The object of the law is to reform criminals, and to prevent crime, not to punish maliciously, or from a spirit of revenge."

The urbanization of the city called for the professionalization of the police. On May 26, 1854, the Boston Watch and Police became past history, and the Boston Police began. A force of 250 men under a chief of police was formed. They were paid two dollars a day each. The city was divided into divisions, and police stations were established with telegraphic communication linking them to the police headquarters at City Hall. Billy clubs and badges became symbols of police authority, but the question of uniforms was hotly debated until 1859. (Some people argued that uniforms would expose the identity of the police to the criminals, while others maintained that a citizen had the right to know how to identify a policeman when he needed one—they also contended that no policeman would frequent brothels and saloons if he were in uniform.)

It was obvious that the Boston police would get involved in the contest over slavery. Under the Fugitive Slave Law, it was mandatory that a runaway slave be apprehended by the police and returned to his master, but abolitionist thought was against such police action. On May 24, 1854, Anthony Burns had the distinction of being the last fugitive arrested before the Civil War. The trumped-up charge was larceny. The Antislavery Convention was meeting in Boston that same week, and feelings ran high. Upon learning of Burns's arrest, Theodore Parker published inflammatory pamphlets which read: "Shall Boston steal another man? See to it that no free citizen of Massachusetts is dragged into slavery!"

Later a mob incited by Parker, transcendentalist Bronson Alcott, and others led an attack on the courthouse where Burns was held and attempted to free him. They were unsuccessful, and eventually two thousand soldiers, preceded by two hundred Boston policemen, marched Burns through the streets of Boston to the ship that was to take him back to slavery. Burns himself observed that "was a lot of folks to see a colored man walk down the street." It cost the government a hundred thousand dollars to keep Burns a slave, and the money was wasted because Burns was purchased by the abolitionists and given his freedom. The legislature passed a law to fine police officers who cooperated in the capture of runaway slaves.

Up through the Civil War, the biggest crime problem of Boston was drunkenness. The reason seemed to be that liquor could be bought everywhere—hotels, groceries, barrooms, "jug-rooms"—more than three thousand places existed where Old Barleycorn held forth. There was an attempt to utilize the police force as a morality force and impose prohibition, but it was of no avail, largely because the force was controlled by politics. From 1853 to 1878 the chief of police was appointed by the mayor and aldermen, then the system was changed to a board of three police commissioners appointed by the mayor. But as the control of the city was wrested from the old Yankee inhabitants by the up-and-coming Irish, the visions of the dangers of a Democratic mayor and his aldermen having control of Boston's seven-hundred-man police force became nightmarish. The Republicans determined to do something, and in 1885 they passed a bill through the state legislature taking control of the department away from Boston and putting it under a three-man commission appointed by the governor, who usually was a Republican. State control of the Boston Police lasted from 1885 to 1962, when the power to appoint and remove the police commissioner was restored to the mayor of Boston.

Through the years, Boston police have had many functions. They once operated soup kitchens at the stationhouses where food was ladled out to the poor; they furnished lodgings for penniless vagrants; they covered strikes. The department continued to instigate improvements such as matrons at the stationhouses, park policemen to protect visitors to the parks, and ambulances with police surgeons to aid the sick or injured.

In 1906, the Boston Juvenile Court was founded for the development of better methods of dealing with juvenile delinquency, and under Frederick Cabot's leadership a clinic was established for "intensive study of baffling cases which fail to respond to the ordinary probation treatment."

In October 1969, Governor Francis Sargent appointed a new commissioner of the Department of Youth Services, Dr. Jerome Miller. Miller established an experimental program which was the first of its kind in the country. The intention is to abolish all juvenile institutions in the state. He announced to the press:

> The cost of jailing a juvenile for one year is $10,000 . . . enough to send him to Harvard University with a $100 a week allowance and a summer vacation in Europe. We made a basic decision that it would do no good to pump more money and more programs into the existing system because the system can chew up reforms faster than you can dream up new ones. It's a sick system that destroys the best efforts of everyone in it, and we decided to look for alternatives.

During Dr. Miller's first two years in office the population of the juvenile prisons was cut in half, from 1,200–1,500 to 650–750. By the autumn of 1972, the institutional population had been reduced to 80–100, about 6 percent of the numbers imprisoned when Dr. Miller took office three years earlier. The erstwhile prisoners were released to their own homes or placed in foster homes, prep schools that generally cater to upper- and middle-class youngsters, or residential centers where they are free to come and go. "We don't allow locks or handcuffs," said Dr. Miller. A youth placed in one of these programs is not reimprisoned if he commits another crime but is shifted to another program. Some of the older girls and boys are encouraged to find their own place to live and may be given a regular stipend from five dollars to ninety dollars a week for a short period to help them get started in their new life. Only those considered "seriously assaultive"—about 40 to 50—are housed in the one remaining "secure facility," and these are placed in the custody of a private ex-convict group. Another 50 to 60 youths are in a special psychiatric facility for those deemed disturbed.

The preliminary reports show there was no discernible increase in overall juvenile crime rates as a result of shutting down the prisons and, if anything, there has been a slight drop in arrests. Moreover, since the closing of the prisons there has been a "dramatic drop in the amount of violence among those committed to the department. The institutions generate violence. Taking the kids out had de-escalated the violence," says Dr. Miller.

Today, in Massachusetts, a genuine attempt is being made to deinstitutionalization, not merely a continuation of the culling process. It may eventually be one of man's noble experiments for the benefit of his fellow man.

It was Tuesday, September 9, 1919, when the famous Boston Police Strike took place. Following many weeks of unsuccessful negotiations to allow the policemen to have a union, which would guarantee better working conditions and higher wages, 1,117 of Boston's 1,544 policemen turned in their badges, leaving less than one-fourth of the city's force to protect Boston. Harvard sent 700 student volunteers, but it didn't take long for the forces of crime to realize that Boston was largely unprotected. A mob spirit, which at first was festive, started. In a very short time the mood changed from happy and carefree to ugly and brutal. Crap games were played in the Common, windows were smashed, looting began. In the business district men were backed up against the walls of the buildings and robbed of their wallets and watches while spectators looked on without intervening. The main rioting took place around Scolley Square, where professional criminals swarmed. Women were dragged into hallways and raped. The scene was chaotic madness and it did not end until the mayor called for the state guard and the then governor, Calvin Coolidge, sent in the troops to restore order to Boston. Public opinion was loud and outspoken against the striking police. President Wilson called the strike a crime; the local papers denounced the strikers, the *Transcript* proclaiming "All America Backs Boston."

The cleanup and reform following the strike brought about the modernization of the Boston Police Force. Women were added; ballistic and photographic sections were included in the detective services; and methods to improve the ever-increasing traffic problems were introduced. But crime in Boston still managed to make headlines every now and then, with such spectacular events as the Brinks robbery, the gangland murders, and the sensational "Boston Strangler."

However, for a complex metropolitan city with many diverse urban problems, the crust of the Boston crime pie lacks the hard and tough consistency of crime records of other large American cities. Crime in Boston is startling and lurid, not for the quantity but for the quality.

13

For Medicinal Purposes Only

In the earliest definition of a city, in the hieroglyphic, the ideogram meaning "city" consists of a cross enclosed in a circle. The cross represents the convergence of roads which bring in and redistribute men, merchandise, and ideas. The circle indicates a moat or a wall which need not be actually built so long as it is morally present to keep the citizens together, sheltered from the cold, wide world, conscious of belonging to a unique team, proud of their nonnomadic identity and aware of being germane to one another.

Alcaeus of Lesbos, the Greek poet and friend of Sappho, adds that a city is "not houses finely roofed or the stones of walls well-builded, nay, nor canals and dockyards make the city, but men able to use their opportunity."

So a city is not made of stones, but of people, as Walt Whitman said: "A great city is that which has the greatest men and women." And the greatness in man is in the final analysis his concern for his fellowman, in sickness and in health. A group of healthy men and women can be a band of happy, working humans, but the presence of sickness creates a fear, a withdrawal. Unlike animals who destroy their weak and sick, man, despite his usual inhumanity toward his fellowman, when he lives within the confines of a city, assumes the health care of his fellowman. In great cities one finds great hospitals and great doctors. Boston is no exception.

The evolution of the hospital and its place in the modern city is one of the most important concerns of any city historian, for it often reveals more of the men and women who make up the city than the narrative of merchants, transportation, housing, or even the arts, since man's health—his "second blessing"—is of prime concern, not only to the individual but to the community in toto.

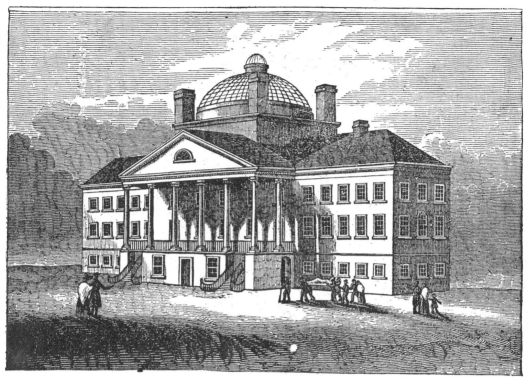

Massachusetts General Hospital, Boston, 1842. From *Sear's Wonders of the World*.

The hospital in its modern sense began in the late Roman times and coincided with the spread of Christianity across Europe. The word *hospital* is derived from the Latin *hospes,* meaning guest or host, and is the same root used for *hotel* or *hostel.* In point of fact, early hospitals were not much more than places like hotels where sick people could go to stay while ill, to be fed and taken care of until they recuperated or died. Hospitals were run by priests and nuns, and medicine was practiced by priests and monks in monasteries. It has been said that Christianity gave the sick man a place in society he had never before experienced, and when Christianity became the official religion of the Roman Empire, sick people became a national responsibility. However, this was not a good situation; the medieval hospitals for the most part were famous for their cruel and inhumane rather than their cheerful and humane treatment. Most of the institutions were essentially custodial, keeping troublesome and diseased persons out of touch with the rest of the people in a community. Most people developed the idea of avoiding hospitals and felt that commitment to one by a physician was certain death. George Orwell observed:

> If you look at almost any literature before the latter part of the nineteenth century, you find that a hospital is popularly regarded as much the same thing as a prison, and an old fashioned, dungeon-like prison at that. A hospital is a place of filth, torture, and death, a sort of ante-chamber to the tomb. No one who is not more or less destitute would have thought of going to such a place for treatment.

Under such a blight it is quite understandable why the early colonists were not overly concerned with the building of a hospital. The Founding Fathers of Boston were, generally speaking, very well educated, and the first medical article written and published in the new world came from Massachusetts. It was the work of Thomas Thatcher, the first minister of the Old South Church, entitled "A Brief Rule to Guide the Common People of New England how to order themselves in the Small-Pocks or MeaSels."

In addition, Boston in 1646 contributed the first epidemic of syphilis in the New World.

It was Cotton Mather who persuaded Zabdiel Boylston to inoculate for smallpox (when the inoculation was by human pox) and supported the inoculation for the residents of Boston even when his own life was threatened. Despite the concern of the early settlers for the health and welfare of the people of Boston, there was no hospital for nearly two hundred years after their arrival. During the two centuries Boston had been growing rapidly—from 4,500 in 1680 to 11,000 in 1720 to 32,896 in 1810. Two professors at the newly formed Harvard Medical School needed a hospital for clinical teaching, and the almshouse (which was where the sick were isolated) was inadequate. It was also pointed out that New York and Philadelphia had already erected a hospital for the training of young doctors. The appeal was successful, and the hospital was under way in 1816. The state granted a charter to incorporate the Massachusetts General Hospital, gave some real estate along the Charles River, contributed granite, and supplied convict labor to build it.

The building was designed by Charles Bulfinch, who was himself the son of a local physician. With its dome, the building was an architectural marvel of its day and was considered the most beautiful structure in Boston for many years afterwards.

The first patient was admitted September 3, 1821. But the hospital was not instantly popular with the citizens of Boston. The reasons for reluctance to use the hospital were many, but the most outstanding was the people of Boston's experience with the military hospitals of the Revolution, which according to Benjamin Rush (Philadelphia's famous physician) "robbed the United States of more citizens than the sword."

The concept of cleanliness as a preventative for infection was unknown. There was little systematic attempt to keep the hospital clean. Physicians went directly from the autopsy room to the bedside without washing their hands, and surgeons operated in whatever old street clothes were considered too shabby for social wear. It is none other than Oliver Wendell Holmes whose medical thesis was "the disease known as Puerperal Fever is so far contagious as to be frequently carried from patient to patient by physicians and nurses." He is credited with saving the lives of many young mothers who formerly died of childbirth fever. To Holmes goes the credit for rubber gloves, use of antiseptics in operating rooms, masks on the faces of physicians and nurses.

In 1821, the stethoscope was a newfangled French gadget—a hollow tube, designed to break in two pieces so it could be carried inside a physician's top hat—and as such it was the second reason why a hospital dependent upon the importance of diagnostic instruments was still evolving in popular acceptance. In addition, the syringe for injection was a novelty; the clinical thermometer would not be introduced for another half-century, and the X-ray for further diagnosis was almost a century away.

A third reason was the limited use of drugs. In 1821 the average list of drugs carried by a physician consisted of such substances as live worms, oil of ants, snakeskins, strychnine, bile, and human perspiration.[1]

In addition to the lack of modern drug knowledge and therapy—which belongs to Sir Alexander Fleming and the development of the sulfa drugs—in the Boston of 1821, the most popular "home" physicians were homeopathic doctors. (Homeopathy was a method of treating disease by giving to a healthy person, in minute doses, drugs which would produce in that person symptoms of the disease itself.) Again, our hero, Oliver Wendell Holmes, opposed his fellow doctors and delivered a lecture denouncing the practice of homeopathy. In his famous lecture Dr. Holmes also attacked the doctor issuing to his patient "placebos" compiled of ineffective drugs, derived from formulas of old wives' tales. "Homeopathy and its Kindred Delusions,"[2] was delivered to the Boston Society for the Diffusion of Useful Knowledge in 1842, but it was many years before the last of the homeopathic doctors ceased to practice in Boston.

In 1821 there was also a fourth deterrent to the use of the hospital—that is, the lack of anesthesia. As a consequence there were few operations. In addition, the postoperative infection was nearly 100 percent. Surgical mortality was 80 percent, and the mortality for the early years was a minimum of 10 percent.

Again, in the large hospital as an important unit of a city's life culture, we see the influence of outside forces. The hospital grew with the city's growth, which was evidenced when the Irish immigration flooded the city and the ills of this mass invasion were beyond individual doctor's ability to cope. In time, the hospital, like the city, has undergone an astonishing growth in size and complexity since its founding. Whether such a growth is of value is one of the many pro and con arguments relative to urban life.

The size of a hospital—like the size of a city—has its advantages and disadvantages. In the large hospital one has a sense of the impersonal relationship of man to man. The building is awesome, cold, and even burdensome in the amount of travel involved within the hospital walls. Certainly, the intimate atmosphere of some of the smaller hospitals found in Boston would appear to be more supportive and offer an atmosphere more conducive to recovery and more amenable for an intimate patient-doctor relationship. But in the complex life design of the "new" Boston, one must recognize the assets of a large hospital such as Massachusetts General. One, a large patient population offers a wider research on disease, and two, the highly technical procedures requiring trained personnel and expensive machinery can be supported financially by a large institution and carried out with a high degree of expertise. It is in such large institutions that patients who require open-heart surgery or complicated radio-therapy, for example, can find both the equipment and the trained staff capable of operating such equipment.

Boston is a city with many arteries, and as such it is a city which requires a large hospital to fulfill the medical needs of its citizens. The city that was a township on a sea-washed peninsula has long since disappeared, as has the port town of 1775 and the burgeoning merchant city of the nineteenth century. What has emerged is a pragmatic growth that has created the commercial, industrial, and suburban metropolis of the present-day Boston. To care for the ills that flesh is heir to and the accidents which one incurs in the complex modern city of Boston today, one must have the most advanced medical technology available. The type of medical assistance needed is exemplified in Logan International Airport—which, incidentally, is the only airport so close to a major city—the eighth busiest in the world. In addition to the steady stream of incoming and outgoing passengers there are more than five thousand employees. The problem of providing medical care is a major one. The population of this one unit of urban life is too large to be ignored, but too small to support a full time resident physician. The airport, while only a couple of miles away from Massachusetts General Hospital, is isolated, due to the rush-hour traffic congestions of the city, thus making a journey from the airport to the hospital impractical in an emergency. To solve this problem Logan Airport has established the Tele-Diagnosis, a system by which patients are interviewed and examined by television.[3]

The equipment is too enigmatic for the average patient to understand, but, while the system is still experimental, the results have been quite satisfactory. The patient is interviewed via television, and there is an adjoining computer which takes the patient's history and sends it on to the physician. Obviously, there is something bizarre about the procedure and the first reaction is the sensation that one is truly living a science-fiction existence; but, amazingly, the patients do not seem startled after the first immediate reaction but quite calmly adjust to the undertaking.

The hospital of today is radically different from the hospital of fifty years ago. Modern technology has updated today's hospital and Boston, with the presence of the Massachusetts Institute of Technology in connection with the Harvard School of Medicine, probably offers the most advanced medical technology available. From automated diagnosis to automated therapy is a role in modern medicine which has already commenced its inception at Massachusetts General Hospital. The future of the medical health of an urban community is being tested daily in Boston and the odds are that the day of the researcher-clinician is at hand. Yet it was one of Harvard's great men of medicine, Oliver Wendell Holmes, who, in 1867, said he did not desire a researcher-clinician for a doctor. "I want the whole man for my doctor, not a half one." Certainly, the arguments against such a medical care future are based upon the anonymity of the patient—that hospitals such as Massachusetts General Hospital are more interested in the disease than in the patient.

The health of a city is pertinent to the population and the same city which a century ago advocated increased population and which reached out and embraced all outlying communities, today is anxious to decrease population. In the past few years the legalizing of abortion has become a prime population factor. In a heavily Roman Catholic city such as Boston, the Right to Life Committee has been the voice of antiabortion sentiment. In Boston City Hospital, which is one of the few places in Boston where those who could not afford to pay could terminate unwanted pregnancies, an event took place recently which is more dramatic than accurate.

> The jury for the Commonwealth of Massachusetts on their oath present that Kenneth Edelin . . . did assault and beat a certain person, to wit, a male child described to the said jurors as baby boy (blank) and by such assault and beating did kill the said person.

On these charges, Kenneth Edelin, thirty-five, the first black resident in obstetrics and gynecology at Boston City Hospital, was indicted. No one seriously believed that the physician beat the baby to death. Nor did anyone take literally the charges that four of Edelin's colleagues exhumed human bodies to get tissues for a series of studies conducted at that hospital. Yet in a brace of cases that could have far-reaching implications for research as well as women's rights, all were indicted. Edelin, who performed a demonstrably legal abortion, was accused and convicted of manslaughter; his fellow physicians are charged with violating an 1814 law against grave-robbing.

Ever since the Supreme Court struck down restrictive state abortion laws in 1973, antiabortionists have been seeking ways to attack the decision. In Boston, they found their opportunity. Three Boston City Hospital researchers—Drs. Agneta Philipson, L. D. Sabath, and David Charles—described in the *New England Journal of Medicine* their experiments to determine how effectively two antibiotics designed to treat congenital syphilis passed through the placenta from mother to fetus. To get their results they had administered the drugs to women who had come to the hospital for abortions and then had measured the levels of the medicine in the aborted fetuses. The article aroused the Boston-based Right to Life Committee, which protested to both the hospital and the Boston City Council. Sensitive to political pressures, the council scheduled hearings on the research. The result of the antiabortion sentiment was so strong that the council called for a criminal investigation.

The district attorney's office conducted an eight month study of abortions at the hospital and then charged the researchers and Dr. Leonard Bernman, a pathologist who supplied them with fetal tissues, with the unauthorized use of a body. The investigators also came upon the records of Edelin, one of only two doctors at Boston City Hospital willing to perform abortions. In October, 1973, Edelin used a saline injection to abort a woman believed to be about twenty weeks pregnant. When the procedure failed to end the pregnancy, he performed a hysterotomy, a form of caesarian section, delivering a fetus that pathologists estimated to be between twenty-two and twenty-four weeks old. Despite Edelin's insistence that the fetus was dead upon delivery, the district attorney charged the doctor with manslaughter.

The indictments shocked the doctors. "I just can't believe that I've been arrested, fingerprinted and mug shot for trying to find a way to prevent congenital syphilis," said Dr. Sabath.

In March, 1975, Dr. Edelin's trial came to a close with the alarming pronouncement by the all-white, largely Roman Catholic jury of "guilty of manslaughter." The trial itself had been conducted amid severe racial tension triggered by Boston's violent school-busing system controversy. It soon became enmeshed in complicated and contradictory testimony. Edelin's defense, which had commissioned a poll showing general acceptance of abortion among Boston residents, argued that the procedure was a legal one, and that the fetus involved had never shown signs of independent life. The prosecution charged that the fetus was, in effect, born at the moment Edelin severed its connection with its mother's uterus, and that the doctor had not taken sufficient steps to sustain its life.

In his charge to the jurors, Judge James P. McGuire reminded them of the conflicting testimony and warned them they could not find Edelin guilty of manslaughter unless they believed that the fetus was indeed a person. After seven hours of deliberation, the jury did just that—to the amazement of most physicians and lay persons alike. The maximum sentence for manslaughter in Massachusetts is twenty years, but McGuire put Edelin on one year's probation, and stayed execution of the sentence pending the final determination of the doctor's appeal. Dr. Edelin's colleagues on the hospital's executive staff returned the doctor to his official position.

Edelin's appeal will be based upon the introducing of the photo of the dead fetus into evidence—which clearly had an emotional impact upon the jury—and the even more important fact that the crime with which Edelin was charged had not been previously defined. At the time the abortion was performed, Massachusetts had no abortion law on the books; thus the effect of what the jury did was to make new law. Legal experts seem agreed on this point. Harvard Law professor Alan M.

Dershowitz has predicted a swift reversal on appeal simply because "there's no state statute connected with it."

But the case as decided by the jury has increased a new doctor's dilemma. The jury's decision of manslaughter highlights a paradox that has long been troubling doctors and hospital administrators on both sides of the abortion issue. It is simply stated. Even as abortion has in recent years come increasingly to be regarded as both the woman's right and an acceptable medical and social practice, research has made it possible to save prematurely born infants at even earlier stages. That is what makes abortions in the second trimester of pregnancy—between the twelfth and twenty-seventh weeks—a matter of such complex concern. The problem remains unanswered as to what stage late abortion may be performed without violating medical, moral, and social ethics. As a result of Dr. Edelin's personal persecution, the problem seems to have become increasingly complex.

The impact of the Edelin decision will be enormous. Scientists routinely use fetal tissue in essential studies of diseases ranging from chicken pox to cancer. Some—especially in Massachusetts—are now reluctant to do any further work with fetal tissue. In addition, the Edelin case increased support for bills before the Massachusetts legislature that would require physicians to try to extend the lives of even unviable fetuses and forbid experiments like the ones for which the other doctors were indicted. The case, as usual, has worked hardships on the poor. Boston City Hospital has now forbidden abortions except in medical and psychiatric emergencies.

So, in Boston, the concern for community health moves in two of its biggest hospitals—forward and backward, depending upon whose eye is on the stethoscope.

Once can never accuse Boston of being a city lacking in imagination, and in class. "Did you ever take enough of anything stimulating so that you felt yourself just going off, letting go of the present and grasping for a moment a real conception of the universe?" One would think those words might have come from one of the two professors, Timothy Leary or Richard Alpert, who first experimented with hallucinogenic drugs —notably LSD. But the words were those of William James and were uttered in 1895. "The only differences in the world are differences between degrees of difference and no difference at all," he further commented upon taking some mescal sent to him by a medical friend promising him splendid visions of color. The incident is quoted here to indicate the interest span of the Boston intellectual and to point out the fact that the city has always presented the two faces of the coin—the probing, scientifically curious and the bigoted, prejudiced noncurious. The community in which the hospital stands, and the doctors who practice there, in the final analysis, constitute the physical and mental health of that city.

It was in 1845 in Boston that a practicing dentist, William Thomas Green Morton, sponsored a demonstration of the use of laughing gas, which his partner Horace Wells had discovered. While this demonstration was unsuccessful, it brought together Morton and Charles Thomas Jackson, who developed the anesthetic properties of ether. In 1846, Morton demonstrated its use in an operation performed by J. C. Warren in Massachusetts General Hospital.[4]

Although the discovery of the anesthesia brought about great progress in the advancement of surgery by relieving people of excruciating pain, the discovery brought about the mental collapse of Jackson. He had to concede the actual discovery to C. W. Long, who had operated using ether before the event in Boston, but had not published his account.

In addition to the many fine hospitals which have been built in Boston since the beginning of the twentieth century—namely, the Peter Bent Brigham, the Beth Israel (in Roxbury), the Floating Hospital, Children's and Infants, the Lahey Clinic, and Boston University Hospital, which in 1911 transformed from homeopathy to allopathy—Boston has given America two of her most prominent physicians, Harvey Williams Cushing and Paul Dudley White.

Harvey Cushing is noted not only for his great contributions to brain surgery, but also as a teacher and author, winning in 1925 the Pulitzer Prize for his life of Sir William Osler. He was the first to describe Cushing's disease (a disorder attributed to hyperactivity of the cortex of the adrenal glands). Paul Dudley White—whose name became famous during his treatment of Dwight Eisenhower—was one of the great heart specialists. He began his medical career interning at Massachusetts General Hospital in pediatrics and, through the technological developments of MIT, his concern for the nation's number one killer, heart disease, attracted his medical interest. His life work was involved in cardiovascular research, cardiovascular training, and cardiovascular teaching, both medical and lay. His special interest outside his medical practice was his public health service appointment as executive director of the National Ad-

Dorothea Lynde Dix.
Engraving by R. G. Tietge.

visory Heart Council of the National Heart Institute. His involvement with world peace through the influence of international medicine is as important as his medical researches and discoveries.

Like so many people prominent in the field of medicine in America, both of these men owed much of their skill to their experiences as young medical officers during World War I. The pursuit of the study of medicine advanced further from that date to this than in the hundreds of years preceding. Medicine became not only a means of saving life but also a social force in the form of preventive medicine, where the emphasis is more on the prevention of disease than the cure. Mental health as well as physical has become the concern of the modern city fathers, and today's doctor is embroiled with the teacher, the social worker, the minister, the criminologist as well as the citizen-patient. To keep the citizen of Boston healthy is as important as to cure man of a death dealing illness.

In 1802, in Hampden, Maine, Dorothea Lynde Dix was born. She later moved to Massachusetts and resided in Boston where her concern for the sick—especially the insane—was to have a profound influence on American medicine. She taught school in Boston and in her spare time became interested in the welfare of prisoners. In 1841 Dorothea Dix visited a jail in East Cambridge, and after making a tour of similar institutions she wrote her famous memorial to the state legislature in which she protested the conditions she found and the indiscriminate mixing of criminals and the insane. Her crusade ended in the founding of state hospitals for the insane in Massachusetts and in many other states. During the Civil War, she was superintendent of the women war nurses and in this capacity became America's own Florence Nightingale.

To cope with the problems of civic health there is the Board of Health department, which came into being when the first settlers realized that in order to create a larger Boston—to build a real city—they had to resolve the basic problem of the disposal of waste. In filth was the germ of disease and litter is part and parcel of communal life.

When the Indians lived in the area of Boston, the litter of their existence was left behind them to become historical relics of value. The natural waste in heaps of oysters and clam shells naturally disintegrated and caused no problem, because the Indians continually moved on to newer regions. When the Europeans of the early seventeenth century arrived, problems were created. In the English custom they dumped their rubbish and waste indiscriminately into the streets. Natural decay and winds took care of some, and scavenging hogs devoured the rest. Rubbish left on the shore proved an early danger. Garbage buried in holes was a source of offending odors until, in 1652, the selectmen voted to fine anybody who threw "any intralls of beast or fowles, or stinkeing thing," on the streets or the Common.

Privies were, of course, necessary things and were called necessary houses, or houses of office. Naturally, necessary odors accompanied these necessary houses so that by 1701 the privy builders were required to build privies forty feet away from streets, shops, or wells, unless they be vaulted six foot deep "and sufficiently enclosed."

It was some local mind that conceived the idea of linking house drains together in what is recognized as a sewer which carried the waste down to the shore and vented it into the sea. By 1763, the selectmen had issued permits for over 650 sections of sewer to be laid and by the middle of the century Boston had the best drainage system in the world—all built by private initiative. But the sewers got clogged from not being cleaned out, and when the yellow fever epidemic hit in 1798, action to clean out the sewers filled with human excrement became imperative. The Board of Health was established that year, but it was not until 1868 that a positive effort was made to eliminate the unsanitary conditions in Boston. Expanding suburbs aggravated the waste problem, since everyone was dumping their waste into the rivers flowing to Boston.

It was decided there should be two drainage systems, each with a main and a branch intercepting sewers. One was the Northerly System, the other the Southerly. Completed in 1855, the Boston Main Drainage System was the first construction of its kind in the United States, and the basic design is still used as the metropolitan sewerage system of Boston today. Forty-two towns are served by this sewerage system. There are some 225 miles of metropolitan sewers which connect with over 3,700 miles of town and city sewers with many more than 315,000 house connections. The sewerage division of the Metropolitan District Commission operates twelve pumping stations, two treatment plants, and three headworks. The men of the division maintain metropolitan sewers and their general plants, while the cities and towns care for their local lines. Well over five hundred men are daily involved in keeping the Metropolitan District Commission veins flowing and the metropolitan area of Greater Boston cleansed.

Drinking water has been a concern for the good health of Bostonians since their arrival. In the early days, springs and wells were sufficient, providing they were of good quality and regularity. It was the lack of good fresh water that prompted the first settlers to desert Charlestown for the Shawmut peninsula. The most famous early spring was the Governor's Spring, so called because it was near Winthrop's house on the northeast corner of Milk Street. The early wells were built so no waste water would flow over into the streets and protected so children could not fall into the well. For the benefit of the poor people, the town erected the town pump, sunk at the head of the present State Street, then the marketplace. By the end of the seventeenth century Boston was well equipped with springs, wells, pumps, and watering places, but as early as 1727 the inhabitants began worrying about the quality of the water they consumed. "Noxious water" was to be avoided. In 1795 the Aqueduct Corporation was formed with permission to bring water from the Town of Roxbury to the Town of Boston. The Corporation continued for more than half a century when it was decided that Boston needed its own water system, publicly owned and operated. The site selected for the source was Long Pond, renamed Lake Cochituate.

On October 25, 1848, water from this source was introduced to Boston with great ceremony. Guns saluted the sunrise, church bells pealed, and the children of Boston sang aloud an ode written by James Russell Lowell to commemorate the occasion:

I come from far o'er hill and mead,
And here, Cochituate's envoy, wait
To be your blithesome Ganeymead,
And brim your cups with nectar true
Than never will make slaves of you.

By 1851, every part of the city of Boston was supplied with good water. The system continued to grow until there was formed the Metropolitan Water District to keep the quantity and the quality of the water consumed by Bostonians both excellent and ample in supply. Today more than 250 million gallons of water provide the cities and towns adjoining Boston and it is estimated all's well—at least until the year 2000.

From the beginning Boston has had to contend with the dangers of fire leading to accidents and death. Today in Massachusetts General Hospital major disasters in which many lives are at stake are called Operation Cocoanut Grove, in memory of the tragedy of 1942. Ironically, the techniques of treating burns were developed in the aftermath of this fire, and many important stricter laws were passed throughout the country to avert similar tragedies.

The early fires caused Boston to be called the "dreadful city of fire." The first fire was that of Thomas Sharp's thatched house which burned down March 26, 1631. The fire was caused by a defective wooden chimney, and at once the town passed a law prohibiting wooden chimneys in thatched houses. After this the first "Great Fire" came on April 14, 1653. It destroyed eight houses and killed three children, the first recorded deaths by fire. Immediately after the fire the town called a meeting and ordered the people to have long ladders and a "twelve foot pole with a good large swab at the end of it" to dampen sparks that might land on the roof. Robert Keayne bequeathed money to construct a reservoir for water to be used in "danger of fire," and Joseph Jenks designed a vehicle "to convey water in case of fire."

The early fires were attributed to arson—of which one Afro-American servant girl, Maria, was accused and "burnt to Ashes in the fier"—and to the "profaning" of the Sabbath, the Lord's Day. The accidents caused by the early fires were unattended except by friends or relatives, and finally a volunteer fire department was organized. In 1798, the Massachusetts Mutual Fire Insurance Company was founded by Paul Revere and other Bostonians to establish funds to help those made destitute by fire, and to develop better ways of fighting and preventing fires. But it was not until after the great fire of 1872—a seventy-five million dollar loss that left two churches (one was Trinity) in ruins, killed at least fourteen people, and burnt out 1,000 firms. The catastrophe brought about a complete reorganization of the fire department. It was reconstructed on a professional basis, and stringent building laws were passed.

Fire is and has always been a hazard for any large metropolitan area, regardless of laws, attempts to prevent them, and modern methods of fighting them. Human life, where fire is concerned, is always in danger —usually, today, from smoke inhalation. Fortunately, the hospitals in Boston are now scientifically prepared to lower the mortalities of any future disasters.

The other source of injury and death in the city is the complicated traffic on the city's main thoroughfares and highways. Like all other major metropolises, good rapid transportation in and out of the core of the city is essential to its economic viability. Large public reliance upon automobile transportation has created many problems for Boston. Too many cars come into Boston. Highways need too much space—there is too little room for parking areas or garages. Speed and carelessness cause deaths and accidents daily in and around Boston. Pollution from exhaust contributes to the smog that hangs over the city and affects the health of the people of Boston. Emphysema is a familiar disease in Boston, as it is in other cities.

All of these problems are only gradually being solved as they are studied by the best brains available at MIT and other universities. Perhaps the day when such city problems will be resolved is not too far away, but to many of the people of Boston as in the other large cities, the grass is certainly greener in the hinterland.

For the most part, Boston, as a city, has an exceptional health record. It has not been victimized, uncontrollably, by plagues, and its citizenry has an exceptionally low mortality rate. Bostonians suffered from dyspepsia during the affluent years and tuberculosis during the Victorian era when that disease was almost symbolic of the fragility of women. Problems in alcoholism, sexual frustration, and mental ill health are of universal coincidence rather than Boston specificity. There appears to exist a spirit of survival peculiar to the city and its citizens from the day of founding. They are aware that the Town of Boston has a history.

Great Boston Fire, 1872. Destruction of newspaper office, Franklin and Hawley streets. From *The Romance of Firefighting* by Robert S. Holzman (New York: Harper & Row, Publishers, 1956).

It is not an accident, not a windmill, or a railroad station, or crossroads tavern, or an army barracks grown up by time and luck to a place of wealth; but a seat of humanity, of men of principle, obeying a sentiment and marching loyally whither that should lead them; so that the annals are great historical lines, inextricably national; part of the history of political liberty. (Emerson)

Boston is the city of the historian, whatever be the point of view.

14
Ramp's End

It has been said that in the seventeenth century a dissociation of sensibility set in; in the twentieth, perhaps, we have gone round and round the clock, completing the charm. We approach the "big city" Boston by air and look down and see the site which made that location so perfect a settling spot for those original founders. Through a glazed amber fog we first view again that unreal city. Suddenly the eastern sun flashes a brilliant light upon that eternally deep and restless ocean which first separated Old England from New. We see with birdlike eyes, while in flight, the white breakers, striking with their mighty force the craggy rocks of the mainland, the stretches of sandy beaches dotted with humans that appear as little black ants, the harbor islands, and the reefs where the whitecaps romp and play and occasionally are mistaken for the billowing sails of a schooner setting out to sea.

Inland, the earth is green with reedy marshes and inlets which rise to a sort of highlands that curve and embrace Boston and the satellite towns —a natural wall with which to encompass a little universe. We see the Charles and Mystic rivers meet, and we observe the advantages Boston offered to those first visitors in the early seventeenth century—a sheltered harbor, deep enough for seagoing vessels; two navigable rivers, a country-side designed for farming and grazing, ample timber for building and firewood, and fresh water in the little ponds and streams.

On land we are conscious of the transportation routes which helped create the city of today. The bridges of the Revolutionary War which linked the peninsula to the mainland are there—Charles River Bridge, 1785; West Boston Bridge, 1793; South Boston Bridge, 1805; and Craigie's or Canal Bridge, 1809. All of them made it possible for people to live on the outskirts of Boston and still walk into town.

Then came the stagecoaches, which enabled people to travel to Salem, Providence, and even New York. But for the real interlacing of Boston and

The first aerial photograph take in the United States in 1860, by J. W. Black. Boston Harbor is pictured from a captive balloon at 1,200 feet. Oliver Wendell Holmes said of the photograph, "As a first attempt, it is, on the whole, a remarkable success." From the collection of General Aniline and Film Corp. (GAF). Courtesy of George Gilbert.

Worcester Railroad Station, Boston, c. 1850. From *Yankee Life* by Barrows Mussey (New York: Knopf, 1947).

her adjoining towns, the steam railroads were necessary. The first of these were the Boston and Lowell, 1830; the Boston and Providence, 1831; and the Boston and Worcester, 1831. By 1846 Boston had seven distinct railroad stations serving the commuting lines, making it possible at an early stage of the city's development for the well-to-do citizens to work in Boston and reside in the lush, pleasant countryside. By 1845, Boston had acquired street railways, and by 1887 there were 470.2 miles of streetcar lines. Scolley Square, Haymarket, and Bowdoin Square all were centers for these street rail lines, which then were drawn by horses, but which were electrified in 1899 and became known as trolleys. The result was the dissipation of country life. These adjoining communities were unplanned suburbs which focused on the center city.

Meanwhile, transportation continued to expand and improve and a subway was built under Tremont Street and opened for service in 1898. It was not only the first subway built in America but the second in the world to be constructed just below the surface of the street and not in a deep tunnel. Opposition to the underground subway was largely for reasons of public health, and elevated structures were installed in East Boston, Cambridge, Dorchester, and other areas. Today, Boston has a rapid transit system which is run by the Massachusetts Bay Transportation Authority and is supported by assessments against some seventy-nine cities and towns in the larger metropolitan areas on the premise that the citizens of all these communities are benefited by the system. Like all such systems in all big cities the system has its problems, but during the gasoline

A Busy Boston Street at High Noon by W. L. Taylor. From *The Ladies' Home Journal,*
July 1901.

The descent to the Subway, Public Gardens, Boston. From *Harper's Magazine,* November 1899.

shortage it was one of the first that lowered rates to encourage usage. The result was significant in a period of duress.

The other two transportation problems of the city today are handled by the Massachusetts Port Authority, which is responsible for Logan Airport in East Boston, the Mystic River or Tobin Bridge from Charlestown to Chelsea and most of the docks and wharves along the waterfront. The other is the Massachusetts Turnpike Authority, which manages the turnpike from Boston to the New York state line as well as the Callahan and Sumner toll tunnels from Boston underneath the harbor to East Boston.

We stand on the Boston Street where the past and present meet and there comes to mind the words of William Blake:

> I wander through each charter'd street
> Near where the charter'd Thames doth flow
> And mark in every face I meet,
> Marks of weakness, marks of woe.

Here is a city that is the embodiment of the idea of a city as a social order. The city must have moral and intellectual dignity, but it cannot be summed up merely as a symbolic form of human life. Social order involves the practical as well as the historical life of this city of Boston and its relation to the countryside out of which the city grew. All of these links of transportation are the practical means by which the city expanded. In the lives and works of the men and women who have dwelt here, we are conscious of the moral, intellectual, and artistic identity of the city. Walking through the streets surrounded by the ghosts of the past and overawed with the incredible spectacles of the present, our mind searches the mind of the American intellectual in regard to the city per se. In the beginning, the favorable attitude of man toward the city was argued by the original civic booster, Benjamin Franklin:

> Even in this new, and as yet uninformed American world, a Boston, a New York, a Philadelphia add lustre and dignity to the colonies to which they belong, and are advancing with rapidity toward perfection in arts and sciences, commerce, and mechanics.

We wonder—is it not possible that intellectuals see cities in different lights at different times? Or is the American city confused because right from its beginning it developed a suburban atmosphere where people dwelt in homes with gardens, in contrast to the urban tradition of Europe where people dwelt in their own apartments? Beacon Hill, once an area of splendid homes with gardens, has now been converted into small apartments within the former residences. And when will these be replaced with the more practical high-rise, the elaborate condominium with the shopping center, the city within the city?[1] Then the Boston lady can surely say: "Why should I travel? I am already here."

Can we walk the streets of Boston today and not hear the words of John Adams, "It has ever been my hobby-horse to see rising in America an empire of liberty, and a prospect of two or three hundreds of millions of freemen, without one noble or one king among them"? Was he expecting America to be urban, or was he visualizing an agrarian population— he also wrote:

> In the present state of society and manners in America, with a people living by agriculture, in no small numbers, sprinkled over large tracts of land they are not subject to those panics and transports, those contagions of madness and folly which are seen in cities where large numbers live in small places in daily fear of perishing for want.

Here Adams expressed one of the basic fears held by intellectuals in their opposition to the city—political fear. In the founding days Boston was largely controlled by gentlemen. The fear was concerned with a propertyless element, the volatile city mob, the agitators who incited the mob. It was this philosophy that caused Adams to defend Captain Prescott against the mob in the Boston Massacre. In time, Boston witnessed the growth of slums and the violence of mobs beyond John Adams's worst fears. And yet, in the recent period of mob uprising, cities like Los Angeles and Detroit suffered mob and racial disturbances while Boston remained reasonably calm, if one considers that mob behavior was more peculiar to Boston than any other American city.

We do not have to travel very far from Boston to see the new "unurban" way of doing things. On route 128, the circular highway that surrounds Greater Boston, we encounter an area studded with electronic factories. These factories represent the last word in modern technology. They produce electronic equipment, micro-ball bearings and precision instruments. They represent the number one industry of Boston, today—and tomorrow.

Characteristic parkway scene near Boston in the year 1902, showing horse-drawn buggies, sulkies, carryalls, and racing rigs. After snowfall, horsedrawn sleighs appeared in similar or even greater numbers. There were then less than a half-dozen automobiles in the United States. Photograph from the Metropolitan District Commission.

They represent the economic city.

The first city was agrarian primarily for reasons of necessity and survival; this area where the farm has been replaced by the factories for producing the implements of a technological society we must assume is technological for reasons of necessity and survival. We are suddenly aware that Boston, which was born a theocracy, developed into a democracy, and is today the city of technocracy. Can a city be that adaptable to the changing mind of man, or will man destroy the past and create the environment his needs demand? How much of Plato's philosophy of reason exists in the minds of the men and women who plan the cities?

We stare at the monstrously ridiculous buildings with windows of plywood and shake our heads in disbelief.

We walk the crowded midday streets. We pause in front of Filene's and see a Boston lady—today still wearing her hat—and walking a Boston bullterrier on a leash, an almost obsolete breed, wearing his steel spike-studded collar and looking absurdly vicious, as if in caricature of his cousin the English bull. We remember the white gloves that could be purchased, slightly soiled, in Filene's basement for less than a dollar—

Aerial view of Boston showing the construction of the Prudential Tower. From *Fortune*, January 1964. Courtesy of the Time-Life Picture Agency.

marked down and grabbed up because they could be cheaply cleaned and appear as good as new, or almost as good as new, or even better, because in Boston who, but a noveau, would have to buy white gloves? "We" already had them!

But fashions in shopping change with the times, and we bypass Jordan-Marsh and R. H. Stearnes (where once the clerks boasted knowing the size of every lady customer's glove and shoe) and peer into the boutiques, bargain basements, second-hand shops and salons in the Back Bay in the potpourri to be found amid the nineteenth-century American architecture. We browse among the antiques on Charles Street, and momentarily we forget where we are. We've seen this lore before. Where was it? New York, New Orleans, San Francisco—like their owners the heirlooms moved westward, too.

In recognition of our modern day, we take a look at the gay subculture. Gay people tend to congregate in big cities—and Boston is no exception. However, there are few popular bars for a city of Boston's size. For Lesbians, Boston has two popular spots—the Saints, and Jacques; for the male counterpart, the Sporters (which was formerly the West End Tennis Club), the 1270 (a dance bar), and the Cabaret, which has a related bar in San Francisco.

Most of the colleges and universities have active homophile leagues. The Charles Street Meeting House sponsors a gay coffeehouse and weekly gay dances. The late Prescott Townsend, of a prominent Boston family, was one of the earliest organizers of a socially recognized gay society. Currently, a self-proclaimed Lesbian, Elaine Noble, successfully entered state politics and Barney Frank, the state representative from the Back Bay and Beacon Hill areas, has been one of the leading proponents of the gay rights bill. It is interesting that a city with a background of closets filled with skeletons—many of them, viewed by today's sociological observations, obviously "gay lords and ladies"—has been one of the first to open the doors and invite the inhabitants to come off their hangers!

We recall the spectator sports we relished and ask where are they today? Baseball, the Boston Red Sox in Fenway Park; football, the New England Patriots at Schaeffer Stadium in Foxboro; hockey, the Boston Bruins and the New England Whalers; and basketball, the Boston Celtics in Boston Garden. Horse racing? Where else but at Suffolk Downs Racetrack in East Boston.

We recall our youth, when in Boston at Christmas thousands of lights sparkled to commemorate the birth of Christ, and happily learn that the custom has survived. The tradition started in 1893 when young Alfred

The *Mayflower* in Cape Cod Harbor.

Shurtleff placed a burning candle in the fourth window of the Shurtleff home at 9 West Cedar Street. By 1908 the custom had spread, and Beacon Hill is said to have been the first locality in the United States to celebrate Christmas by illuminating windows on Christmas Eve. Mr. and Mrs. Ralph Adams Cram started carol singing by gathering groups of children at their home for practice on Christmas Eve. Soon there were experienced bands of carolers marching and singing "Adeste Fidelis" and other familar Christmas songs. By 1930, Christmas Eve on Beacon Hill had reached its zenith. "On the ground floor curtains in all the houses were drawn aside and each window was decorated with special care. A Madonna, perhaps a bas relief, or a decorative fruit arrangement was illuminated by a handsome pair of candlesticks. . . . The large, square Sears house was a special attraction, with its display of one hundred and ten candles in its fifteen windows, including the lookout on top of the house. . . . Singing bands wandered about in a haphazard manner and the crowds were anxious not to miss a window or a chorus." Today, visitors swarm the city from the nearby communities to celebrate the present in the light of the past.

In a nostalgic mood we tour the cape to the very tip, where the first Pilgrims landed in 1620. With the changing lights falling on the Cape Cod cottages, silvered by the salty sea, we fall into the still remaining static way of life while we ferry from Wood's Hole to Nantucket, where we romped and played, sang and danced, swam and sailed when our hearts were young and gay. Our mind is with that Puritan father, Thomas Macy, who in 1659 settled Nantucket, when he was fined for giving shelter to four Quakers during a storm. His words are on the wind, "I'll take up my abode among savages where religious zeal has not yet discovered crime in hospitality." With thirty pounds and two beaver hats, he purchased the island. Up the cobblestoned main street we plod, standing before the whaling museum, filled with logbooks, scrimshaw and ship models—relics of a long gone day when the tiny island was the leading whaling port in the new world. In our mood of remembrance of things past, we recall the day a whale came ashore and lay dead in front of the big old house in South Duxbury. We see again the group of hooded monks staring at the gargantuan mammal, muttering prayers, and we hear the voices of the whaling men whistling through their thin, pipe-filled lips. "Know that whale . . . harpooned her myself . . . a year ago, off the coast of Nova Scotia. . . ." She was one of a herd, a cow without her bull to lead her. In time, she was demolished and became whalebone, oil, and blubber. The remains of her carcass were used as fertilizer to make the garden flowers bloom with greater radiance, the privet hedge thicken, and the grass more verdant.

On the mainland once again we cruise the countryside until we reach the dead-end ramp. Is this significant?

Fare forward, traveler! To where, the end of the world? Will it come abruptly to a halt, leaving man with no alternative except a turnabout?

We must go home again! We put our foot upon that self-same rock that first the Pilgrim fathers touched and cast our eyes toward Boston, a city fading in the falling night. The sea is the same sea that rolled against that shore, the land is the same land where those first Pilgrims trod—but the story of man is constantly evolving, and the history of the city he creates evolves with him. It appears to be changing, but is it? All is made of man's passion, and that has altered little since his creation.

We put our foot on the blue clay upon which Boston is built and look at Bulfinch's dome—the architect's symbol of the city and the state political. Today, two hundred years since that musket shot rang forth from Concord, the politic state of Massachusetts is governed by a white Republican, represented in the Senate by a black Republican, and has for a congressman (who is also the minority leader of the House of Representatives), an Irishman. It is fitting that it should be thus, for

The Pilgrims: "A Lusty***
Rambunctious***Rarely
Humble Crew." A woodcut by
Charles Child. From *The New
York Times,* August 5, 1945.

this state has from its founding been a maverick state, and in our lifetime it and the city of Boston have put the first Irish Roman Catholic president in the White House, and have the distinction of being the only areas not to vote for Richard Nixon.

In the years since we left Boston we have visited every major city in the United States and have resided in some; but upon returning we have become conscious of the fact that Boston is a special city. Through the eyes of Boston we see the history of our country—its weaknesses and its strengths; its ugliness and its beauty; its shabbiness and its grandeur. As a people we are proud at some moments; at others we are bowed with shame. We are human, and we are wedded to this nation—for better, or for worse.

As John Quincy Adams said, "Think of your forefathers! Think of your posterity!"

In Boston, we think. Right or wrong—we think.

Notes

CHAPTER 1

1. The most socially desirable woman's club in Boston, designed along the lines of a men's club, is named for Mary Chilton. No member of the press is admitted, and society editors are not allowed to mention its activities. Membership is restricted to about one-tenth of Boston's female population.

2. The *Arbella* was named for Lady Arbella, wife of Isaac Johnson of Boston, England. The couple were passengers on the ship. The group landed in Salem, but because of scarcity of food it was decided to break up the colonists into small units. Governor Winthrop and his group settled in Charlestown, where the lack of good water caused difficulties. Across the river the Reverend William Blaxton (or Blackstone) lived alone in his cottage on the highest hill. We read:

> Mr. Blackstone dwelling at the Other Side of Charles River alone, to a place by the Indians called Shawmutt, where he had only a Cottage at or not far off the place called Blackstone Point. He Came and Acquainted the Governor of an Excellent Spring there, withal Inviting Him and Soliciting Him Thither. Whereupon after the death of Mr. Johnson, and Divers Others the Governor, with Mr. Wilson and the Greatest Part of the Church, Removed Thither Where also, the Frame of the Governors House was carried, when People began to build their Houses against Winter and this Place was called Boston. The date for the naming was September 17, 1630. (*John Josselyn*)

3. The first Faneuil Hall, completed in 1742, burned down in 1761. It was rebuilt in 1763. That structure, enlarged by Charles Bulfinch in 1805, is embraced in the present building. Before and after the Revolution many patriotic meetings were held in Faneuil Hall, and because of these meetings it became known as the "Cradle of Liberty."

CHAPTER 2

1. This verse has been controversial since its origin, the question being whether the "Lowells talk to the Cabots and Cabots speak only to God" would be more proper. We leave the choice to the reader.

CHAPTER 4

1. One of the early lady muckrakers, Anne Newport Royall, writing a book to be called *The Black Book,* sought an interview with President John Quincy Adams. She stormed the White House in an effort to discover the president's sentiments on the Bank of the United States. Adams refused to see the half-mad lady in her tattered shawl and her green umbrella, which she waved with unprecedented vigor. Indeflectible as an angry bee, Mrs. Royall learned that the president's routine included his morning swim in the nude. One morning while her prey was in the water, Mrs. Royall made her way to the riverbank and planted herself upon his clothes.

As the president swam in the water, Mrs. Royall demanded her interview. Wearily, fully aware of his predicament, the president capitulated and answered her questions about the bank. As Anne Royall was an ardent Jacksonian who wanted the bank's charter revoked, her questions were doubly annoying to the president trapped in his birthday suit. Nevertheless, he answered—and thereby conducted the first executive press conference in American history. When he finished Mrs. Royall triumphantly hobbled away, and John Quincy Adams was free to wade out of the water and assume the dignity proper attire commands. Later, when someone asked Adams what he made of Mrs. Royall, he ruefully replied: "Sir, she is like a virago errant in enchanted armor."

CHAPTER 5

1. Music and words copyright © by John A. Scott, 1963. All rights reserved

2. That oatmeal is a proper Bostonian custom is illustrated by an anecdote told in the Lowell family:

> The Lowells have seated themselves, as is customary at 7:30 in the morning, for breakfast in their Chestnut Hill home. Mrs. Lowell is seated at one end of the table, her husband, the judge, at the other. The maid comes into the room and whispers in Mrs. Lowell's ear. The judge is paying no attention, for he is absorbed in his morning paper. What the maid says to Mrs. Lowell is unnerving; she tells her mistress that the cook has burned the oatmeal and there is no more in the pantry. For Mrs. Lowell this is no minor domestic tragedy; her husband has eaten oatmeal for his breakfast every single morning of his life. Timorously she approaches her husband with her announcement: "John, there isn't going to be any oatmeal this morning."
>
> Not knowing what to expect, she waits for her husband's reaction. He lowers his newspaper, peers at his wife, and replies: "Frankly, my dear, I never did care for it."

CHAPTER 6

1. "It was an unhappy thing that in later years a Kind of Drink called Rum has been common among us," wrote Increase Mather in 1686.

2. The proper Boston Sunday breakfast, with its many courses, was the forerunner of the fashionable brunch of the 1960s, where the hour of serving was lunchtime, the menu resembling the elaborate breakfasts of the nineteenth century.

CHAPTER 7

1. Headmaster Arthur Irving Fiske, a frail, scholarly classicist, was hailed in his day as the greatest teacher of Greek in New England.

CHAPTER 8

1. That they had other than food for thought is evidenced in a menu from a breakfast given by the members of the Saturday Club in honor of Dr. Oliver Wendell Holmes in 1879:

Little Neck Clams

Grilled Trout   Cucumbers, Sautéed

Omelette with Mushrooms in Cream   Grilled Plover

Filet Mignon   Asparagus with Hollandaise Sauce

Potatoes

Tomato and Lettuce Salad

Ice Cream   Strawberries   Cake   Coffee

The members present were Henry Wadsworth Longfellow, Ralph Waldo Emerson, Nathaniel Hawthorne, James Russell Lowell, Louis Agassiz, Richard Henry Dana, Jr., Francis Parkman, John Greenleaf Whittier, William Dean Howells, Henry Adams, and Henry James.

With the exception of Howells, Whittier, and James, all were Bostonians. At the time, Howells was editor of *The Atlantic Monthly*, the magazine which claimed James Russell Lowell as its first editor. James was residing in Boston, developing, no doubt, material for his later novel, *The Bostonians*.

2. It was the pleasure of this writer to be seated with Myron Brinig, author of *Singerman* and *The Sisters*, and with Edith Wharton's Boston nephew, who answered Mr. Brinig's inquiry as to his "Aunt Edith" with a nonchalant, "Oh, yes, Aunt Edith . . . well, she wasn't really a Wharton . . . she was merely a Jones from Manhattan." And Mr. Brinig aghast at such audacity rose from the table in the Ritz and said, "Mr. Wharton, your family name may only be remembered because your uncle had the good fortune to marry a Miss Jones from Manhattan!"

3. Actually Mt. Vernon Street was given greater preeminence than Beacon Street in the minds of the Boston literati. Not only did Louisa May Alcott and Oliver Wendell Holmes reside there but numerous fictional Bostonians as well.

CHAPTER 9

1. "Where are your poor?" asked Lafayette upon visiting Boston after the Revolu-

tion. However, although the slum was a thing of the future, there was at that time one region in Boston, on the Cambridge side of Beacon Hill, that is said to have been extremely squalid and vicious. It was filled with crowded tumbledown tenements where crime ran riot. This region greatly exercised the Boston humanitarians, notably the father of Lowell, the poet, and Charles Eliot Norton, president of Harvard.

CHAPTER 10

1. The Washington mansion of Bostonian Henry Adams was Richardson's work.

2. Saarinen's son, Eero, built the circular brick chapel at the Massachusetts Institute of Technology and also the auditorium, notable for its thin-shelled concrete dome.

3. The first Eben Jordan, founder of Jordan-Marsh, came along just a few years too late to establish a "first family"; that charmed circle was beginning to square away just as Jordan was emerging as a personage in the retail world. However, Jordan's money was accumulated through qualities a proper Bostonian holds in high respect—hard and honest toil, salted by rectitude and peppered by a dash of the shrewd trading so dear to the Yankee. What did distinguish the Jordans was their love of spending their money—not foolishly, or with vulgar display, but in public benefactions—mostly in the cause of musical culture.

CHAPTER 11

1. It was another Irish Bostonian who brought about the end of Boston power. In 1958, Robert Kennedy became the chief counsel on the Senate Labor Rackets Management Committee and gained his reputation by exposing the corruption of the Teamsters' Union.

CHAPTER 12

1. "Cities, like Cain, may not hope to shield their crime by legislation, excusing themselves from being their 'brother's keeper' thereby, nor hold any guiltless who disregard for gain, the health, comfort, or virtue of a single citizen." A. Bronson Alcott, *Journals*, July 31, 1870.

2. Premenstrual tension has been held accountable for a large percentage of female crimes, especially crimes of passion. In Lizzie's day such an affliction was unheard of, but the actions of Lizzie would indicate that she suffered from such emotional disturbances just before her menstrual period. She was menstruating following the murders, and it is assumed by many that she killed during a "blackout" peculiar to the syndrome.

CHAPTER 13

1. If this startles the reader, it should be recognized that as late as 1910 some doctors considered strychnine to be good for the treatment of pneumonia.

2. In the lecture Dr. Holmes attacked the Perkins theory of "Metallic Tractors"— yet, in the past few years the wearing of copper bracelets by sufferers of arthritis has been resumed. Medically, the wearing of the bracelets is another placebo— ornamental, but of questionable therapeutic value.

3. It is believed that the Logan Tele-Diagnosis is the first to have been installed in this country.

4. The anniversary of the event is celebrated annually in the famous dome of the Massachusetts General Hospital.

CHAPTER 14

1. To repair Boston's neglected downtown retail center, the city plans a $220 million project called Lafayette Place, designed to make downtown shopping attractive once again. The strategy is to make it easy for shoppers to get around the twelve-acre project. There will be a 1,500-car parking garage for suburbanites, and for city dwellers a direct underground link to the existing subway system. Once at Lafayette Place, shoppers will be able to move from store to store at three levels: in a subterranean concourse, on ground level, and by way of flying bridges on the second floor. Instead of recreating the usual shopping center—a fortress for retailing, with all attention focused inward—there will be continuity with the surrounding area. The architectural firm of I. M. Pei and Partners, with Cossutta and Ponte, have designed malls and glassed-in galleries, which will have the same twists and unexpected shop-filled alleyways as old Boston's streets.

Chronology

1620   Mary Chilton stepped from *Mayflower,* first person to set foot upon Plymouth Rock.
1621   Governor Bradford proclaimed first Thanksgiving.
1630   Puritans sailed from England aboard the *Arbella,* landing in Boston Bay.
1630   John Winthrop of Massachusetts Bay Company established main colony.
1630   Boston named by court order on September 17.
1631   Governor Winthrop recorded meteorological findings of Boston.
1631   Watches ordered for Boston at night.
1631   Letter of Governor Thomas Dudley to Bridget, Countess of Lincoln, described settling of English immigrants.
1634   Anne Hutchinson emmigrated to Boston.
1635   Boston Public Latin School opened.
1635   First prison erected in Boston.
1635   Colonists experienced first hurricane.
1636   Harvard College founded in Cambridge, Massachusetts.
1636   Henry Adams departed for New England, settled in Quincy, Massachusetts.
1636   "Wards" organized for day protection.
1637   Anne Hutchinson banished for "traducing the ministers," later joined Roger Williams in founding Rhode Island.
1637   Samuel Appleton settled in New Ipswich.
1640   The *Bay Psalm Book* published in Boston.
1643   New England confederation formed.
1645   Pilgrims sought help from Governor Winthrop and his Bostonian Puritans against invading French.
1649   Governor Winthrop buried in King's Chapel Burying Ground.
1650   Anne Bradstreet's poems published.
1653   April 14, first Great Fire.
1659   Thomas Macy settled Nantucket.
1660   Old Granary Burying Ground laid out.
1660   Charles II proclaimed king of England. Restoration period began.
1662   Michael Wigglesworth's *Day of Doom* published.
1664   Increase Mather assumed pulpit of Old North Church.
1664   Freemanship no longer restricted to church members.
1676   King Philip (Indian warrior and son of Massasoit) executed.

1686   Sir Edmound Andros arrived in Boston; first fully commissioned governor of New England.

1688   Mrs. Glover executed in Boston as a witch.

1689   King's Chapel established.

1691   Boston absorbed Plymouth under Massachusetts Bay Colony charter.

1702   Cotton Mather wrote his thesis.

1704   *News-Letter*, first Boston newspaper, appeared.

1708   Thomas Brattle brought first organ to Boston for King's Chapel.

1713   Old State House built.

1716   Boston Light, oldest lighthouse in United States, erected in Boston Harbor.

1717   First tomb built in Copp's Hill, Boston's second burial ground.

1723   Thomas Tippin and Thomas Bennett, master builders, built Old North Church after manner of Sir Christopher Wren, with steeple 190 feet high.

1730   John Smibert's art exhibit held in Boston.

1736   Jonathan Edwards wrote *The Life and Death of Abigail Hutchinson*.

1742   The first Faneuil Hall completed and donated to Boston by Peter Faneuil.

1740   The Great Awakening.

1744   Abigail Adams (*née* Smith) born.

1748   Old State House (originally erected in 1713) rebuilt following destruction by fire.

1754–1763   French and Indian War.

1759   Longfellow House, formerly Craigie House, 105 Brattle Street, Cambridge, Massachusetts, built by tory Major John Vassall.

1759   General James Wolfe died at Quebec.

1760   George III became king of England.

1763   First Boston sewer laid.

1763   Treaty of Paris ended French and Indian War.

1765   The Stamp Act imposed.

1765   Sons of Liberty formed.

1767   The Townshend Acts adopted.

1768   John Hancock's ship *Liberty* seized by the British.

1770   March 5, the Boston Massacre.

1773   December 16, the Boston Tea Party.

1774   The First Continental Congress organized.

1775   The Intolerable Acts passed.

1775   Midnight ride of Paul Revere.

1775   April 19, Battles of Lexington and Concord began the Revolution.

1775   June 17, Battle of Bunker Hill.

1775–1776   Boston under seige.

1775   George Washington appointed commander-in-chief of Continental Armed Forces.

1776   Thomas Paine published "Common Sense."

1776   Boston evacuated by British.

1776   July 4, John Hancock and other revolutionary leaders signed Declaration of Independence, drafted by Thomas Jefferson.

1779   Washington Allston born.
1780   John Hancock elected first governor of Massachusetts following the Revolution.
1781   Cornwallis surrendered.
1785   The Charles River Bridge built.
1785   Trinitarian doctrine removed from the liturgy in King's Chapel.
1786   Shays' Rebellion.
1789   George Washington unanimously elected first president of the United States, inaugurated April 30.
1789   Protestant Episcopal Church adopted constitution and revised edition of *Book of Common Prayer.*
1791   Porcellian Club founded at Harvard.
1791   Massachusetts Historical Society founded.
1793   West Boston Bridge erected.
1794   Julien opened his Restorator in Boston, became known as the Prince of Soups.
1796   John Adams succeeded George Washington as president.
1797   Frigate *Constitution* launched.
1798   Yellow fever epidemic.
1798   Massachusetts Mutual Fire Insurance Company founded by Paul Revere.
1799   Charles Bulfinch designed the State House.
1799   Bronson Alcott born.
1800   The United States Navy Yard established on Moulton's Point.
1803   Ralph Waldo Emerson born.
1804   Elizabeth Peabody born.
1805   South Boston Bridge built.
1806   African Methodist Church dedicated.
1807   Jefferson's Embargo Act passed.
1807   Henry Wadsworth Longfellow born.
1809   Craigie's (or Canal) Bridge erected.
1810   Park Street Church dedicated.
1810   Margaret Fuller born.
1810   Father Jean Louis Lefebvre de Cheverus ordained bishop of the diocese of Boston.
1812   "Mr. Madison's War" declared—War of 1812.
1812   Francis C. Lowell and Nathaniel Appleton built first cotton textile mill.
1813   The *Chesapeake* captured.
1814   Treaty of Ghent signed.
1815   George Ticknor and Edward Everett attended University of Gottingen.
1816   Massachusetts General Hospital was under way.
1817   Henry David Thoreau born.
1817   William McDonough was first American to plead insanity in defense of murdering his wife.
1819   James Russell Lowell born.
1822   Boston incorporated as a city.
1825   Boston to Lowell railroad proposed.
1825   First Presbyterian Church founded in Boston.

1825   John Quincy Adams elected president.
1825   American Unitarian Association formed.
1826   Horsepower line from Quincy to Boston built.
1826   July 4, John Adams and Thomas Jefferson died.
1826   Union Oyster House founded at 41 Union Street.
1829   Samuel Francis Smith wrote "My Country 'tis of Thee."
1830   Horace Mann established public school system.
1834   The Ursuline convent in Charlestown burned.
1835   Abolitionist William Lloyd Garrison suffered violence at the hands of Boston mob.
1839   Boston University founded.
1840   Richard Henry Dana wrote *Two Years Before the Mast.*
1840   Isabella Stewart Gardner born.
1840   The *Dial* published.
1841   Dorothea Lynde Dix visited jail and wrote famous memorial protesting conditions.
1841   George and Sophia Ripley founded Brook Farm.
1842   Charles Dickens visited Boston.
1842   Oliver Wendell Holmes, M.D., delivered paper on "Homeopathy and Its Kindred Dulusions."
1843   William Hickling Prescott wrote *History of the Conquest of Mexico.*
1843   Congregation Ohabei Shalom founded.
1845   The potato famine ravaged Ireland.
1845   The Boston Assembly balls organized.
1845   Thomas Fitzgerald left Ireland for Boston.
1845   *Narrative of the Life of Frederick Douglass* published.
1846   Louis Agassiz came to Boston; assumed professorship of geology and zoology at Harvard in 1848.
1846   Laughing gas demonstrated at Massachusetts General Hospital.
1848   John Patrick Kennedy left Ireland for Boston.
1848   October 25, Boston water flowed from Lake Cochituate.
1846–1848   War with Mexico.
1849   Dr. George Parkman killed by Professor John White Webster.
1850   Fugitive slave laws passed.
1850   *The Scarlet Letter* by Nathaniel Hawthorne published.
1850   Daniel Chester French born.
1851   Donald McKay's China clipper, the *Flying Cloud,* made record run from Boston to San Francisco.
1852   Harriet Beecher Stowe's *Uncle Tom's Cabin* published.
1852   Tufts College chartered by Universalists.
1852   First Boston Public Library founded.
1854   Temple Israel formed.
1854   Thoreau's *Walden, or Life in the Woods* published.
1854   Boston Police Department formed.
1855   Boston Main Drainage System installed.
1855   Harvey Parker opened his restaurant, served meals a la carte.
1861–1865   War Between the States, the Civil War.
1861   Julia Ward Howe composed and published "The Battle Hymn of the Republic."

1861 Elizabeth Peabody founded first kindergarten in the United States.
1861 Charles Francis Adams appointed ambassador to England.
1863 Boston College founded.
1863 Hancock House demolished for nonpayment of taxes.
1863 Lincoln issued Emancipation Proclamation.
1863 John F. Fitzgerald (Honey Fitz) born.
1863 Lincoln declared Thanksgiving a national holiday.
1863 Robert Gould Shaw, leader of 54th Massachusetts Infantry (all black), killed in battle at Charleston, South Carolina.
1865 Massachusetts Institute of Technology opened.
1867 New England Conservatory of Music founded.
1869 Phillips Brooks became minister of Trinity Church.
1869 Charles W. Eliot elected president of Harvard.
1870 Wellesley College for Women chartered; opened 1875.
1872 Trinity Church destroyed by fire.
1872 Henry Hobson Richardson rebuilt Trinity Church—completed 1877.
1874 Amy Lowell born.
1875 *Science and Health* completed by Mary Baker Eddy.
1876 Alexander Graham Bell invents telephone in Boston.
1879 Church of Christ, Scientist, chartered in Boston by Mary Baker Eddy.
1879–1903 Elizabeth Cabot Cary Agassiz served as first president of Radcliffe College.
1881 Henry Lee Higginson founded Boston Symphony Orchestra.
1881 Jesse Pomeroy jailed for murdering twenty-seven children.
1885 Hugh O'Brien elected first Irish mayor of Boston.
1886 Joseph Patrick Kennedy born.
1888 John Singer Sargent's portrait of "Mrs. Jack" exhibited at St. Botolph's Club.
1889–1893 Arthur Nikisch conducted Boston Symphony Orchestra.
1890 Rose Fitzgerald Kennedy born.
1892 Lizzie Borden accused of killing parents with ax.
1896 Fannie Farmer's *The Boston Cooking School Cook Book* published by Little, Brown & Co.
1898 Tremont Street subway, first underground subway in America, completed.
1898 Spanish–American War.
1900 Symphony Hall constructed.
1905–1906 George Santayana published *The Life of Reason*.
1906 H. G. Wells visited Boston.
1906 Boston Juvenile Court formed.
1907 Daniel Tobin became president of Teamsters' Union.
1907 William O'Connell becomes archbishop.
1909 Boston Opera House opened.
1911 William O'Connell became cardinal.
1911 Reverend Clarence Richeson murdered Avis Linnell.
1914–1918 World War I.
1914 James Michael Curley became mayor of Boston.
1917 April 6, America declared war on Germany.

1918   Boston influenza epidemic.
1918   November 11, Armistice.
1919–1924   Pierre Monteux conducted Boston Symphony.
1919   Boston Police Strike.
1919   The Ponzi superplan materialized.
1920   Sacco and Vanzetti reputedly robbed shoe factory in South Braintree, killed the paymaster and guard.
1924   Isabella Stewart Gardner died. Deeded Fenway Court to Boston as public museum to be maintained without charge.
1925   Harvey Cushing, M.D., won Pulitzer Prize.
1924–1949   Serge Koussevitzky conducted Boston Symphony.
1938   Eliel Saarinen designed Music Shed at Berkshire.
1941   Pearl Harbor—World War II.
1942   Cocoanut Grove fire.
1946   Emily Greene Balch and Dr. John Mott received Nobel Peace Prize.
1947   Logan International Airport opened.
1949–1962   Charles Münch conducted Boston Symphony.
1950–1953   The Korean War.
1952   Henry Cabot Lodge defeated by John F. Kennedy.
1954   Tower of the Old North Church toppled by Hurricane Carol.
1958   Boston Opera House demolished.
1961   John F. Kennedy elected thirty-fifth president of the United States. Youngest man and first Roman Catholic to hold this office.
1962   Erich Leinsdorf became conductor of Boston Symphony.
1963   The Boston Strangler terrorized city.
1963   President John F. Kennedy assassinated.
1965   Boston was scene of protests when President Johnson escalated Vietnam war.
1966   Sarah Caldwell resurrected a new Boston Opera.
1969   Governor Francis Sargent appointed Dr. Jerome Miller head of Department of Youth Services.
1970   Richard Cardinal Cushing died.
1974–1975   Boston school busing created riots.
1975   Kenneth Edelin, M.D., found guilty of manslaughter and placed on probation.
1975   Elaine Noble, self-acclaimed Lesbian, elected to public office.

Bibliography

To compile a bibliography for this book on Boston, which encompasses such a vast span of time and a conglomeration of so many personalities, is a formidable task. A complete bibliography would have to include practically every publication I have read during my lifetime, in addition to numerous personal interviews and visits to museums and libraries both here and abroad. From my early childhood readings of Louisa May Alcott's *Little Women* and Harriet Beecher Stowe's *Uncle Tom's Cabin* to my more mature studies of the writings of Ralph Waldo Emerson, Henry David Thoreau, Amos Bronson Alcott, Margaret Fuller, Theodore Parker and many others, which formed the cornerstone of my interest in Boston and Bostonians, the city and its people have never ceased to intrigue me. In the writing of this book the conflict between affection and intellect, which has been a Boston prerogative since the founding of the original Puritan colony, surfaced into a solid form. With my loyalist maternal heritage, I sought the writings of some of those who represented the other side of the Revolution, as well as delving into the acts of those Bostonians who had vast interests in the cotton industry of the South and shunned the abolitionists in their Boston society.

Today's Boston is essentially different. It cannot be understood except in context with the more comprehensive communities of which it is a part. The process of change has made this study exciting and challenging, and its passing characters tragic, humorous, compassionate, violent, obstinate, and, at times, unbelievable.

To list all bibliographical and biographical sources would be impossible, but the most recently researched and reviewed material appears below.

BOOKS

Adams, Abigail. *Letters, 1850–1860.* Edited by Charles Francis Adams. Boston: Houghton Mifflin, 1913.

Adams, Brooks. *Emancipation of Massachusetts.* Boston: Macmillan, 1919.

Adams, Charles Francis. *An Autobiography.* Boston: Houghton Mifflin, 1919.

Adams, Henry. *The Education of Henry Adams.* Boston and New York: Houghton Mifflin, 1938.

Adams, James Truslow. *The Adams Family.* Boston: Little, Brown, 1930.

Adams, John. *Familiar Letters of John Adams and his Wife Abigail Adams.* New York: Hurd and Houghton, 1876.

317

————. *Life and Works, 1850–1856,* edited by Charles Francis Adams. Boston: Houghton Mifflin, 1913.

Adams, John Quincy. *Memoirs, 1850–1856.* Edited by Charles Francis Adams. Boston: Houghton Mifflin, edition, n.d.

Addison, Albert Christopher. *Boston History.* Boston: L. C. Page, 1912.

Agar, Herbert. *The Formative Years.* Boston: Houghton Mifflin, 1947.

Alcott, Louisa May. *Little Women.* New York: Grosset & Dunlap, 1947.

Aldridge, Alfred O. *A Man of Reason.* Philadelphia: Cresset Press, 1959.

Allen, Frederick Lewis. *The Lords of Creation.* New York and London: Harper, 1955.

————. *Only Yesterday.* New York and London: Harper, 1931.

Allison, John M. *Adams and Jefferson, Story of a Friendship.* Norman: Univ. of Oklahoma Press, 1966.

Amory, Cleveland. *The Proper Bostonians.* New York: Dutton, 1947.

Andrews, Charles M. *The Colonial Period in American History.* London: Oxford Univ. Press, 1938.

————. *The Boston Merchants.* New Haven: Yale Univ. Press, 1917.

Anthony, Katherine. *Margaret Fuller, A Psychological Biography.* New York: Harcourt, Brace and Howe, 1920.

Appleton, William. *Selections from the Diaries of William Appleton.* Boston: privately printed, Susan M. Loring, 1922.

Ashburn, Frank. *Peabody of Groton.* New York: Coward, McCann, 1944.

Bailey, Thomas A. *Wilson and the Great Betrayal.* New York: Macmillan, 1945.

Bailyn, Bernard. *Ideological Origins of the American Revolution.* Cambridge, Mass.: Harvard Univ. Press, 1967.

Baxter, W. T. *The House of Hancock.* Cambridge, Mass.: Harvard Univ. Press, 1945.

Beard, Charles A. *An Economic Interpretation of the Constitution of the United States.* New York: Macmillan, 1913.

Beebe, Lucius. *Boston and the Boston Legend.* New York: Appleton-Century, 1935.

Bemis, Samuel F. *John Quincy Adams and the Foundations of American Policy.* New York: Knopf, 1949.

Bowers, Claude G. *Jefferson and Hamilton.* Boston: Houghton Mifflin, 1925.

Brodie, Fawn M. *Thomas Jefferson, An Intimate History.* New York: Norton, 1974.

Brooks, Van Wyck. *The Flowering of New England.* New York: Dutton, 1936.

Beacon Street, Its Ancient Pastures and Early Mansions. Boston: Houghton Mifflin, 1925.

Cappon, Lester J., ed. *The Adams–Jefferson Letters: The Complete Correspondence betwen Thomas Jefferson and Abigail and John Adams.* 2 vols. Chapel Hill: University of North Carolina Press, 1959.

Cabot, Elizabeth. *Letters of Elizabeth Cabot.* Boston: privately printed, 1905.

Carter, Morris. *Isabella Stewart Gardner and Fenway Court.* Boston: Houghton Mifflin, 1925.

Cary, Thomas G. *Memoirs of T. H. Perkins.* Boston: Little, Brown, 1856.

Cash, W. J. *The Mind of the South.* New York: Knopf, 1945.

Coolidge, T. Jefferson. *The Autobiography of T. Jefferson Collidge.* Boston: Houghton Mifflin, 1923.

Crawford, Mary Caroline. *Famous Families of Massachusetts*. Boston: Little, Brown, 1930.

————. *Romantic Days in Old Boston*. Boston: Little, Brown, 1922.

————. *St. Botolph's Town*, Boston: L. C. Page, 1908.

Crichton, Michael. *Five Patients*. New York: Knopf, 1973.

Cullen, James Bernard. *The Story of the Irish in Boston*. Boston: James B. Cullen & Co., 1889.

Cutler, John Henry. *"Honey Fitz," Three Steps to the White House*. Indianapolis and New York: Bobbs-Merrill, 1962.

Dana, Richard Henry. *Two Years Before the Mast*. New York and Boston: Houghton Mifflin, 1911.

Dempewolff, Richard. *Famous Old New England Murders*. Brattleboro, Vt.: Stephen Daye Press, 1942.

Dineen, J. F. *The Kennedy Family*. Boston and Toronto: Little, Brown, 1959.

Drake, Samuel. *The Histories and the Antiquities of the City of Boston*. Boston: Luther Stevens, 1854.

Early, Eleanor. *And This Is Boston*. Boston: Houghton Mifflin, 1938.

Eaton, C. *Boston Opera*. New York: Appleton-Century-Crofts, 1965.

Eddy, Mary Baker. *Science and Health*. Boston: Privately printed by W. F. Brown & Co., 1895.

Emerson, Ralph Waldo. *Essays*. Boston: Houghton Mifflin, 1803.

Farmer, Fanny. *The Boston Cooking School Cook Book*. Boston: Little, Brown, 1896.

Forbes, Allan, and Greene, J. W. *The Rich Men of Massachusetts*. Boston: Fetridge & Co., 1851.

Forbes, Esther. *Paul Revere and the World He Lived In*. Boston: Houghton Mifflin, 1942.

Frank, Gerold. *The Boston Strangler*. New York: New American Library, 1966.

Franklin, Benjamin. *Writings*. Edited by Albert Smythe. Vols. 1–7. New York: Macmillan, 1906–1907.

Frothingham, O. B. *Boston Unitarianism*. New York: Putnam, 1890.

Gilman, Arthur. *The Story of Boston*. New York: Putnam, 1889.

Greenslet, Ferris. *The Lowells and Their Seven Worlds*. Boston: Houghton Mifflin, 1946.

Hall, Florence Howe. *Social Customs*. Boston: Estes and Lauriat, 1887.

Handlin, Oscar. *Boston's Immigrants 1790–1880*. New York: Atheneum, 1959.

Hawthorne, Nathaniel. *Collected Works*. Reading, Pa.: Spencer Press, 1937.

Higginson, Mary Thacher. *Thomas Wentworth Higginson*. Boston: Houghton Mifflin, 1914.

Hofstadter, Richard. *American Political Tradition*. New York: Knopf, 1948.

Howe, Julia Ward. "Social Boston Past and Present." *Harper's Bazaar,* 1909.

Howe, M. A. DeWolfe. *The Boston Symphony Orchestra*. Boston: Houghton Mifflin, 1931.

————. *Boston, the Place and the People*. New York: Macmillan, 1903.

————. *Holmes of the Breakfast Table*. New York: Oxford Univ. Press, 1939.

————. *Later Years of the Saturday Club*. Boston: Houghton Mifflin, 1921.

————. *A Venture in Remembrance*. Boston: Little, Brown, 1941.

Hughes, Sarah Forbes. *Letters and Recollections of John Murray Forbes*. Boston: Houghton Mifflin, 1899.

Kemble, Frances Anne. *Further Records.* New York: Holt, 1891.

Krutch, Joseph Wood. *Henry David Thoreau.* New York: William Sloane Assoc., 1948.

Lodge, Henry Cabot. *Early Memories.* New York: Scribner's, 1913.

Lowell, A. Lawrence. *What a University President Has Learned.* New York: Macmillan, 1938.

Lundberg, Ferdinand. *America's 60 Families.* New York: Vanguard, 1937.

Malone, Dumas. *Jefferson, the Virginian.* Boston: Little, Brown, 1948.

Manchester, William. *Death of a President.* New York: Harper & Row, 1967.

Marquand, John P. *The Late George Apley.* New York: Washington Square Press, 1944.

Marshall, John. *The Life of Washington.* The Santa Monica Library, 1926 edition.

Mashachusetts' Archives, Vol. 1350. *Witchcraft 1656 to 1750.*

Masters, Edgar Lee. *Lincoln the Man.* New York: Dodd, Mead, 1931.

Mather, Cotton. *The Ecclesiastical Trial: History of New England.* New York: American Press, 1970.

Mather, Increase. *Cases of Conscience Concerning Evil Spirits Personating Men.* New York: Oxford Univ. Press, 1971.

Makris, John N., ed. *The Boston Murders.* New York: Duell, Sloane & Pearce, 1948.

Mason, Alpheus Thomas. *Brandeis.* New York: Viking, 1946.

Mayo, Bernard. *Myths and Men.* New York: Harper & Row, 1959.

Meade, Robert D. *Patrick Henry—Practical Revolutionary.* Philadelphia: Lippincott, 1969.

Miller, Perry. *The American Transcendentalists, Their Prose and Poetry.* New York: Doubleday Anchor Books, 1957.

Moley, Raymond. *After Seven Years.* New York: Harper & Bros., 1939.

Morgan, Edmunds. *The Puritan Family.* New York: Harper & Row, 1966.

Morison, Samuel. *A Maritime History of Massachusetts.* Boston: Houghton Mifflin, 1961.

———. *Builders of the Bay Colony.* Boston: Houghton Mifflin, 1964.

———. *Life and Letters of Harrison Gray Otis.* Boston: Houghton Mifflin, 1913.

———. *History of the Plymouth Plantation.* New York: Knopf, 1952.

———. *Three Centuries of Harvard.* Cambridge, Mass.: Harvard Univ. Press, 1936.

Murdock, Kenneth B. *Increase Mather: Foremost American Puritan.* New York: Macmillan, 1926.

Nash, J. Robert. *Bloodletters and Badmen.* New York: M. Evans & Co., 1973.

Paine, Thomas. *Common Sense.* New York: Liberal Arts Press, 1963.

Pearson, Edmund. *Studies in Murder.* New York: Macmillan, 1926.

Quincy, Edmund. *Life of Josiah Quincy of Massachusetts.* Boston: Ticknor and Fields, 1867.

Robbins, Chandler. *Memoirs of Hon. William Appleton.* Boston: John Wilson and Son, 1863.

Rossiter, William S. *Days and Ways in Old Boston.* Boston: R. H. Stearns, 1915.

Sandburg, Carl. *Abraham Lincoln.* New York: Harcourt, 1926.

Santayana, George. *The Last Puritan.* New York: Scribner's, 1936.

Schlesinger, Arthur, Jr. *The Politics of the Upheaval.* Boston: Houghton Mifflin, 1960.
———. *The Coming of the New Deal.* Boston: Houghton Mifflin, 1950.
Snow, Edward Rowe. *The Romance of Boston Bay.* Boston: Yankee Pub. Co., 1944.
Spring, James W. *Boston and the Parker House.* Boston: J. R. Whipple, 1927.
Stearns, Frank Preston. *Cambridge Studies.* New York: Lippincott, 1905.
Steffens, Lincoln. *Autobiography.* New York: Harcourt, 1931.
Tharp, Louise Hall. *The Peabody Sisters of Salem.* Boston: Little, Brown, 1950.
Thoreau, Henry David. *Essay on the Duty of Civil Disobedience.* New York: Lancer Books, 1968.
Thwing, Anne Haven. *The Crooked and Narrow Streets of Boston.* Boston: Marshall-Jones Co., 1920.
Ticknor, Caroline. *Dr. Holmes, Boston.* Boston: Houghton Mifflin, 1915.
Tocqueville, Alexis de. *Democracy in America.* New York: Knopf, 1945.
Wagenknecht, Edward. *Mrs. Longfellow, Selected Letters and Journals of Fanny Appleton Longfellow.* New York: Longmans Green, 1936.
Washburn, Frederick A. *The Massachusetts General Hospital.* Boston: Houghton Mifflin, 1939.
Wecter, Dixon. *The Saga of American Society.* New York: Scribner's, 1937.
Woodham-Smith, Cecil. *The Great Hunger: Ireland 1845–1849.* New York and Evanston: Harper, 1963.
Ziff, Larzer. *The American 1890's.* New York: Viking, 1966.
Zobel, Heller B. *The Boston Massacre.* New York: W. W. Norton, 1970.

PERIODICALS AND NEWSPAPERS

American Heritage
The Atlantic Monthly
Boston Evening Herald
Boston Evening Transcript
Boston Globe
Boston Post
The Christian Science Monitor
Fortune
Harper's Monthly

Human Sexuality
Leslie's Illustrated
Los Angeles Times
Mankind
Munsey's Magazine
Newsweek
The New York Times
Time and *Life*
World Medical News

PAMPHLETS

U.S. Works Progress Administration. *Urban Housing, Summary of Real Property Inventories Conducted as Works Progress,* Washington, D.C., 1938.
Pritchett, Herman C. *The Tennessee Valley Authority, a Study in Public Administration,* Chapel Hill, N.C., 1943.
Spielvogel, Samuel. *A Selected Bibliography in City and Regional Planning,* Washington, D.C., 1951.
Van Tyne, Claude. *Loyalists in the American Revolution,* New York, 1902.
Smith, Paul H. *Loyalists and Red Coats,* Chapel Hill, N.C., 1964.

MANUSCRIPT COLLECTIONS

American Antiquarian Society, Worcester, Massachusetts
The Boston Athenaeum
The Boston Public Library
The Library of Congress
The Massachusetts Historical Society
The Massachusetts Institute of Technology
Harvard University, Cambridge, Massachusetts
The New York Public Library
Santa Monica Public Library
Los Angeles Public Library (main branch)
Huntington Library, Pasadena, California
University of California Library at Los Angeles

Index